Connected

■ SMART STRATEGIES SERIES ■

Connected

A Global Approach to Managing Complexity

Willy A. Sussland

Business Press
Thomson Learning™

Australia • Canada • Denmark • Japan • Mexico • New Zealand • Philippines
Puerto Rico • Singapore • South Africa • Spain • United Kingdom • United States

Connected

Copyright © 2000 Willy A. Sussland

Business Press is a division of Thomson Learning. The Thomson Learning logo is a registered trademark used herein under license.

For more information, contact Business Press, Berkshire House, 168–173 High Holborn, London, WC1V 7AA or visit us on the world wide web at: http://www.itbp.com

All rights reserved by Thomson Learning 2000. The text of this publication, or any part thereof, may not be reproduced or transmitted in any form or by any means, electronic or mechanical, including photocopying, recording, storage in an information retrieval system, or otherwise, without prior permission of the publisher.

Whilst the Publisher has taken all reasonable care in the preparation of this book the Publisher makes no representation, express or implied, with regard to the accuracy of the information contained in this book and cannot accept any legal responsibility or liability for any errors or omissions from the book or the consequences thereof.

Products and services that are referred to in this book may be either trademarks and/or registered trademarks of their respective owners. The Publisher/s and Author/s make no claim to these trademarks.

British Library Cataloguing-in-Publication Data
A catalogue record for this book is available from the British Library

First edition published 2000 Thomson Learning

ISBN 1-86152-505-2

Typeset by LaserScript, Mitcham, Surrey
Printed in the UK by TJ International, Padstow, Cornwall

Contents

List of figures vii
Acknowledgements viii
Foreword ix
Preface xi
Introduction xiii

CHAPTER ONE
Managing in a globalizing environment 1

CHAPTER TWO
The Process of Management 26

CHAPTER THREE
The Policy Fundamentals 54

CHAPTER FOUR
The Policy Dynamics 77

CHAPTER FIVE
The performers 111

CHAPTER SIX
The processes 133

CHAPTER SEVEN
The product 158

CHAPTER EIGHT
The key partner: the customer 179

CHAPTER NINE
The Policy Assessment and Audit 207

CHAPTER TEN
The conclusions 222

Bibliography 226
Index 229

List of figures

1.1	The 'glob-local' organization	9
2.1	The Process of Management	28
2.2	Doing the right thing right	35
2.3	The behavioral modes	38
2.4	Vision and confidence	39
2.5	The Deming Wheel	43
2.6	Connecting the 5 <P> of performance	45
2.7	The 5 <P> of performance top-down and bottom-up	46
3.1	The Policy Fundamentals	58
3.2	The strategic thrust, the market lifecycle, and the macro- and mega-trends	63
4.1	The Policy Dynamics and the model of the 'Two Rings'	84
4.2	The policy deployment process	97
4.3	The policy deployment	98
5.1	The five performers	113
5.2	The timing of time	115
5.3	The process of human capital	124
5.4	The five enablers of organizational capital	128
6.1	The five macro-processes	136
6.2	The chain of processes	139
6.3	The ten elements of a process	141
9.1	The assessment model	214
9.2	The business cycle	218

Acknowledgments

The Process of Management, the mind-maps and the management principles presented here are the result of over a decade of research and consulting practice. I wish to thank Mr Franz Nawratil, Chairman and CEO of Hewlett-Packard Europe, Middle East and Africa, and Mr Fernand Ducheyne, Quality Director of Hewlett-Packard Europe, who have provided information on the management systems of this world-class enterprise.

Many executives and academics have contributed their thoughts and experience. I will just mention here Mr Georges Darrer, Director of Logistics and Procurement of Du Pont Europe, Mr Murray Duffin, Corporate Vice President of ST Microelectronics, the 1997 winner of the European Quality Award, and Mr François Escher Director of Strategy and Special Projects Motorola Components Europe. Last but not least, I am greatly indebted to our son Anton Walter who has reviewed my drafts and contributed valuable comments.

All authors say it – and I can attest that it is true – without the solid support of my family this would have been an insurmountable task. Hearty thanks to my wife Mimi and to Anton Walter who join me in dedicating this effort to our beloved Pierre Otto.

Foreword

The world has never been so tightly interconnected as it is today. These connections have been realized at almost no cost to the customer and at a reasonable cost to the supplier. Even small artisanal companies have access to a vast global market where they can sell their products while also comparing the quality of services offered by their suppliers.

Connectivity enables competitiveness. The customer becomes better informed and thus develops higher expectations towards the quality of the products and services being offered. Poor quality or incompetence is soon exposed. Connectivity encourages benchmarking, and highlights the global differences in the value of individual segments of production or consumption. The gap between rich and poor companies, regions, and nations is growing faster than ever.

Connectivity also helps to educate people. A typical household in the USA is already spending 45 minutes a day on the computer, surfing the web, dialoging, comparing, asking, sharing objective and subjective information, and consequently developing greater analytical capacity.

More education inevitably leads to more power. The consumer of today is more powerful than ever but consequently probably more volatile. Suppliers have to adapt their business practices to meet the ever increasing demands, and retain the confidence of, their clients. However, there can be no confidence without transparency and therefore the way organizations are conceived and managed also has to be adapted. New forms of management emerge from connectivity; with greater flexibility and sensitivity to the needs of customers.

Originally people created organizations designed to serve themselves, but instead ended up serving the organizations, which became rigid, linear, and hierarchically split into specialized functions. Connectivity enables management to dislodge the inertia of organizations so that they may once again become more reactive. As a result, integrated supply-chain management is now at the center of business transformation. The frontiers of the extended enterprise change rapidly requiring a strong logistics organization based upon Total Quality Management.

In *Connected*, Willy Sussland takes us into this fascinating world, providing useful hints, methodologies and tools that will be of great benefit to managers who possess this new found spirit.

Professor Dr Francis-Luc Perret
Director of the International Institute for the Management of Logistics
The Swiss Federal Institute of Technology, Lausanne

Preface

Best management practices are methods that can increase the efficiency of a particular activity, but, to increase the effectiveness of the whole enterprise *shared management practices* are needed because they help establish a common basis for mental, behavioral, and action processes.

Shared management practices ensure that all the nodes of the organization are interdependently connected and that they are capable of interacting dynamically within a shifting business environment. As markets and the organizations that serve them have become increasingly complex, it has become increasingly important to provide a compatible way of working that facilitates communications, commitment, cooperation, and collective creativity.

Shared management practices require a comprehensive and integrative framework. The best-in-class have developed their own system of shared management practices, but even some of the most prestigious names struggle with a patchwork of methods and measures of performance.

In order to help management introduce and support the appropriate shared management practices, the author presents the *Process of Management*, an interactive and integrative framework of management, which ensures transparency and understanding from mission statement to measures of performance.

Connected provides a comprehensive itinerary that managers can follow to introduce shared management practices or they can use it to improve the management system already in place.

Willy A. Sussland, Ph.D., is an independent consultant specializing in organizational effectiveness and revitalization. A lecturer of post-graduate courses on general management, he has published *The Manager, Quality, and ISO Standards* and regularly contributes essays and articles. Dr Sussland has also been on the consulting staff of Arthur D. Little and has held ascending management positions with Corning International.

Introduction

Connected

The human brain is capable of extraordinary creativity. Some 10^{24} neurons instantly connect to other neurons to obtain a given result. Then, they swiftly switch to make different or complementary connections.

Of course things are not always easy. Sometimes a delicate balance has to be found between the two lobes of the brain, the left one essentially rational, and the right one predominantly creative and emotional. Sometimes completely new patterns have to be traced to deal with unprecedented situations. The human brain can cope with this sort of challenge. Wouldn't it be nice if the enterprise could operate in such a way? The nodes of the organization would connect to form appropriate networks capable of responding effectively to new impulses coming from inside or outside the enterprise.

The brain is pre-programmed by instincts and is conditioned by training. The organization can be pre-programmed by corporate directives and guidelines. However, it also needs to be conditioned by shared management practices to ensure that all the nodes of the organization are interdependently connected and capable of interacting dynamically with a shifting business environment.

Shared management practices, with the appropriate leadership, help establish a common basis for mental, behavioral, and action processes. Thus, endowed with a compatible way of working, the organization is 'connected'. As a result, communications, commitment, and cooperation are facilitated, and collective creativity is fostered. As both the markets and the enterprises that serve them have become increasingly complex, it has become increasingly important that the organization be 'connected'.

Connected is a highly desirable state. It is how the whole organization should feel, how it should operate in the internal and external environments: *connected and focused on* shared strategic ambitions in order to sustain superior performance; *connected and fluid*, as self-managed units assemble and reassemble in networks while remaining connected; *connected and fast* as the self-managed units can take the initiative to trigger the appropriate actions.

It is a new ball game

As illustrated by the advent of the Internet, globalization has created a new environment, a complex web of interactions and interdependencies. It is a new ball game and a chaotic one because we do not quite understand how it works. The complexity of the business environment exacerbates some of the dilemmas confronting management. On one hand, the scope of the market, its size and its shifting complexity call for centralized strategic coordination. On the other hand, the prominent role of human competencies and the necessary speed of reactions require empowered decentralization, allowing self-managed units to move freely but purposefully within a fluid organization.

Responding to the challenges of today's business environment may possibly call for new approaches, new managers, and new methods of management.

Those who do not apply new remedies must expect new evils

Heeding Francis Bacon's aforementioned advice, dynamic enterprises have launched into a frantic search for best management practices. Academics and consultants have eagerly responded to this need; new management tools and techniques have sprouted and a trail of fads and fashions has followed. However, by and large, the results have been disappointing. The situation can be explained by the following reasons.

First, the traditional approach of analyzing a problem by breaking it down into its components overlooks the interdependencies between the components and precludes a global approach. Secondly, pressed for quick results, managers focus on the areas for which they are accountable and have little concern for the big picture. Finally, the search for a better mousetrap has resulted in a distracting turnover of new management theories and consultants. Finding more sophisticated ways to do the same thing, if anything, has continued to accentuate specialization and organizational fragmentation.

Best management practices are methods that can increase the efficiency of a particular activity, but it takes *shared management practices* to increase the effectiveness of the whole enterprise. Sharing will allow the appropriate best management practices to be brought together into an integrated methodology of management whose company-wide scope and systemic or *global* approach enables the focused, fluid, and fast networks to achieve superior performances.

The methodology, the methods, and the tools

The 'quality management systems', such as ISO 9001:2000, *kaizen*, Total Quality Management (TQM) etc., provide an array of different methods and tools. However, they do not show how to integrate all the various tools and techniques into a methodology. 'TQM', stated Sarv Singh Soin, Operations Manager Hewlett-Packard Asia Pacific, at the time of the publication of his second book, 'is more explicit on the destination than on how to get there'.

The best-in-class, like Hewlett-Packard, have developed their own model of shared management practices, which integrates the main principles and practices of TQM. Nonetheless, a majority of enterprises, including some of the most prestigious names, continues to struggle with a patchwork of tools and techniques.

In order to help management to introduce the appropriate shared management practices or to improve the management system in place, we have developed and now present in this book the Process of Management. The four main aspects of the Process of Management are as follows.

- The Process of Management or POM provides the framework for *shared management practices*. It shows a clear, coherent, and comprehensive pathway from the mission to strategies, from strategies to actions, and from actions to performance assessment.

- The Process of Management features four sub-processes that are interactive and interconnected. The first two sub-processes of the POM focus on *doing the right thing*, the third on *doing the thing right*. The last sub-process assesses the performance of the operations and audits the 'business value' to make sure the enterprise is *doing the right thing right*.

- The Process of Management structures the major managerial tasks as well as the formal interactions between the management layers. Transparency over the whole process and a fabric of feedback loops ensure that all the life-forces of the enterprise are organically and *purposefully connected*.

- The Process of Management is complemented by a set of five simple principles that guide the approach to managing the business enablers in day-to-day operations. Together they influence the managerial approach and the collective behavior.

Reader's map

In Chapter One we discuss some of the characteristics of the business environment and their impact on management of the 'glob-local' organization.

Chapter Two presents the four sub-processes of the Process of Management, which may be summarized as:

- the *Policy Fundamentals* which set corporate guidelines for direction and behavior;

- the *Policy Dynamics* which coordinate the activities of senior and operative management as they evolve separate strategies for *business breakthrough* and for *continuous business improvement*, and then deploy them through empowered action plans;

- the *Policy Implementation and Review* which ensure effective day-to-day management of the five business enablers: the action plans, the strategic resources, the processes, the products, and the partners (customers and suppliers) – their interdependencies are emphasized and set the basis for cross-functional cooperation;

- the *Policy Assessment and Audit* which feature operative management's assessment of the effectiveness of day-to-day management, and senior management's valuation of the strategic resources that constitute the *business value* of the enterprise. In addition to tangible assets the strategic resources include intangible assets such as 'intellectual capital' and 'marketing capital'.

Chapters Three and Four present, respectively, the Policy Fundamentals and the Policy Dynamics. Chapters Five to Eight present mind-maps that we consider important to the establishing of shared management practices in the Policy Implementation and Review. Chapter Nine discusses Policy Assessment and Audit and Chapter Ten presents our conclusions.

These ten chapters cover a very large field. In order to remain as concise as possible, we focus on the mind-maps that implement concepts, and on their integration in the framework that buttresses shared management practices. For specific tools and techniques we refer to the literature listed in the bibliography.

CHAPTER ONE

Managing in a globalizing environment

The Plan

Globalization, the dominant factor of our economy, is contributing to the ever-increasing complexity of our business environment. We need to understand what is changing, and how it affects organizational effectiveness. This will lead us to discuss how management has met these challenges, and some of the problems it has encountered. We will then show why a systemic or 'global' approach is necessary in order to manage effectively in a globalizing environment.

The Mind-Maps

- The salient elements of globalization.
- The 'glob-local' organization.
- The methodology, the methods, and the tools.

1.1 The global economy vs. the economy of proximity

Let us start with the meaning of 'globalization' because, as an old Chinese proverb suggests, 'wisdom starts by understanding the meaning of words'. Etymology could lead us to treat 'global' and 'worldwide' as synonymous. This can be misleading. Commodity markets have operated worldwide for decades, while global corporations do not necessarily operate worldwide.

The Gillette Company, for example, has operated internationally since the turn of this century, but it is only since the 1980s that it has been managed as a global player.

Another interpretation of the word, as in a 'global approach', refers to taking a systemic view of interdependent parts of the whole system. We believe that the latter is applicable to the business environment whereby 'global', a designation for a relatively new phenomenon, transcends geographic criteria. It is the characteristics of globalization rather than the territorial dimension that makes a difference.

Globalization already covers the most dynamic part of the economy. However, next to the global economy, there is – and there will continue to be – an economy of proximity, which includes government, public services, local services, and local craft. According to Helmut Maucher, chairman of the Nestlé Group, 'Not all parts of the economic life will globalize. The offer will, but not necessarily consumption.' Professor Matthias Finger of IDHEAP adds 'Everything that is mobile globalizes; everything that is not localizes and socializes' [1].

Comparing the two types of economy may shed some light on the differences between the two environments, and their implications for management.

In the economy of proximity, enterprises are sheltered from outside competition by local regulations. There are established rules of the game, and the business environment evolves relatively slowly. Opportunities tend to stabilize at a level which is reasonably comfortable for the established players, and incremental improvements of organizational efficiencies allow them to stay in business. As a result, the interdependencies of the forces at play are relatively straightforward and stable, and management can deal with what we call *stable complexity*.

As illustrated by the advent of the Internet, globalization has created a space, maybe not an entirely new space, but certainly a different space. This environment is different because the many forces at play converge and merge. They form an intertwined web of interactions and interdependencies that hovers over the globe. Within this socioeconomic–geopolitical fabric, the patterns consisting of a myriad of connections are subject to sudden shifts. As a result, we are confronted with shifting complexity or what Senge calls *dynamic complexity* [2].

As holds true for the Internet, globalization appears unruly and chaotic because no private or public body has total control over this environment. As a result, what has been called 'the global village' is characterized by what Gleick calls an *order without predictability* [3].

The Internet will partly coexist with and partly challenge traditional forms of communication. Likewise, globalization will partly coexist with and partly challenge the economy of proximity. However, directly or indirectly, the global economy continues to expand its influence on the local economy. First, globalization of one sector tends to spill over to the sectors of its major suppliers. Therefore, if local enterprises do not reach out to the global market, the global market will come to them and upset the apple cart. Secondly, local players are not exempt from comparisons with the performance achieved by the global players. For example the public sector – while anchored in the economy of proximity – is now increasingly pressured to perform more like the global players. This led Osborne and Gaebler [4] to speak of 'reinventing government'. As a result, at this time it is difficult to say where the local economy stops and the global one starts. For all practical purposes we can say that globalization comes as close as the nearest supermarket.

As it sets today's management standards, we can focus our discussion on the globalizing environment and its many challenges. Peter Drucker warned us back in 1968 that we were entering the *Age of Discontinuity* [5] and in 1980 he predicted that we were going to be *Managing in Turbulent Times*, a fact that nobody would dispute today [6].

Since then, globalization has amplified the virulence and the magnitude of discontinuities and of the resulting turbulence to the point that macroeconomic and microeconomic gyrations make our environment particularly unstable. If American historian Alfred North Whitehead was right when he observed that 'on the whole, great Ages have been unstable Ages', then ours must then be one of the all-time greatest! And indeed our age is a great one both in terms of opportunities and in terms of problems.

Technology speeds an unprecedented amount of data, sounds, and images through a worldwide telecommunications web. It also provides for highly interactive connections among a variety of players or groups that plug-and-play at will. The low costs made possible by technology such as the Internet attract new players, activate new needs, and therefore create opportunities and threats of an unprecedented magnitude. As a result the rules of the game are changing in sectors as diverse as book sales, auctions, and private banking.

The interaction between rampaging technology and powerful global competition constantly stirs up the market. With all the changes that are going on, new needs or different needs are constantly created, combined, or recombined. This results in unprecedented opportunities in terms of *economies of scale, economies of scope, economies of space, economies of time, and economies of systems*. The latter, a recent addition to management's arsenal, results from the application of information technology and from aligning the management systems so that the various business units can interact efficiently with one another and with their business partners. Economies of systems are achieved by optimizing how the parts of the business system fit and perform together. In other words, by implementing a global approach substantial savings in terms of money and time can be achieved. Without economies of systems the economies of scale, scope, space, or time cannot be optimized.

Globalization is like a flood, it submerges the whole landscape, but everything that can float will rise with the water level. While floods come and go, globalization is here to stay. It behoves us to understand what it requires in terms of management and organizational effectiveness.

1.2 Managing in a globalizing environment

Traditionally management's mission was to direct and to control all activities. It established roles, responsibilities, and allocated resources to centrally imposed structures and systems. The controls were designed to keep the organization operating in a stable way, following the practices that had proven efficient in the past. The desire to keep things under control engenders a reverence for tools and techniques.

This approach to management works well in the case of the economy of proximity, but not in the frame of a globalizing economy because 'the future is not what it used to be'. The complexity and unpredictability that characterize our global and chaotic business environment elude comprehension and therefore control.

Of course, some controls are ineluctable. However, any prearranged order can rapidly become obsolete and counterproductive. Stability may be a natural craving, but is it desirable? Stability is the opposite of growth, control the antonym of creativity. Why should we shun chaos; is it inherently bad?

It should be noted that *order as well as chaos are inherently unstable states*. The reality often migrates from one state to the other. A good example is the process of creativity. This process starts with a given order, this order is upset with ideas and situations that create confusion and chaos, from which a new order – hopefully a better order – will evolve. What matters is the conclusion of that loop. Value-adding creativity goes from order to chaos and to a new order. Value-draining confusion goes from chaos to a tentative order and back to chaos.

Both chaos and order are parts of the business ecosystem that encompasses the internal as well as the external environment of the enterprise. Since we cannot change the business environment, the internal environment has to be modeled in symbiosis with the external environment. Therefore, we have to learn to live with the revolving loop of order and chaos. Better yet, we should profit from surfing the shifts in the business environment. Change creates opportunities!

Adapting or anticipating the erratic movements of the market, the organization must be mutable and nimble, allowing business units to combine and recombine in focused, fluid, and fast networks. By so doing they will be moving from the order that was to the chaos that is, and will find a new order to deal effectively with the new situation.

Confronted with an environment that is global and chaotic and with new organizational structures, management has resorted to the research that has been done on the theory of chaos since the 1980s. Scientists have looked to Nature for answers. They have found that in the universe and on Earth, Nature provides simple principles, and allows structures to self-organize. Eventually, order emerges out of chaos and the ecosystem finds a new and viable balance. These insights have been transposed to human organizations by authors like Margaret Wheatly [7] who submit that if corporate management provides simple principles, that they call 'self-referentials', then the 'self-organized structures' will smoothly migrate from order to chaos, from chaos to order.

We find these theories thought provoking. However, self-regulatory mechanisms may not work as well in human organizations as they do in Nature. Neither do we have the wisdom or the millenary experience of Nature. Therefore we must construct a framework that synergistically integrates systems, structures, style, and strategies so that people can understand how the various parts fit together in order to work in synchronization with the rest of the organization.

Actually, we do not need to gaze at the universe to find examples of managing order amid chaos. On our routes, vehicles are free to choose their path and, as long as certain ground rules and practices are respected, the traffic remains fluid. Self-regulatory mechanisms set in when things start to get out of hand. For example drivers choose alternative routes or schedules so as to avoid traffic jams. However, if these mechanisms are not operating properly, facilitators may have to step in. In the case of traffic they are called policemen.

Our 'Information Age' provides the means for the traffic center to remain connected in real time with all the drivers of a given traffic system, and to implement regulatory mechanisms such as modifying the program of the traffic lights and displaying information on panels.

In order to apply the somewhat lofty theories of chaos to the more mundane reality of business, we should gain a better understanding of the organizational requirements of the globalizing environment. Taking a cue from Davis and Meyer's *Blur* [8], we can characterize the salient elements of globalization as follows.

1. Technology and de-regulation have created a market in real time of *unprecedented size and scope*. Mega-competition, mega-mergers, and mega-risks are some of the logical outcomes.
2. Everything is becoming increasingly interconnected, interactive, and interdependent. As a result, the business environment has become increasingly *complex*.
3. As new ground is broken and the rules of the game change, the patterns of complexity also change. This results in sudden shifts in the business environment that confront management with problems of a new dimension, the *unpredictability of dynamic complexity*.
4. *Intangible assets* have become the major contributors to the value added by the enterprise. They drive tangible assets. They are the enabler of, and are enabled by dynamic complexity. The management of these assets requires special attention. It must be realized that the approach to managing tangible assets may not be adequate for managing intangible assets. The latter do not show up in traditional accounting, their performances are hard to evaluate, cause and effect relationships are blurred.
5. Technology and aggressive competition drive the *wheel of time* that spins faster and faster. The windows of opportunity are getting shorter and shorter while the time cycle to prepare for market-entry is getting longer and longer.

These characteristics, while part of the same phenomena, lead to apparently contradictory organizational models. Some elements favor a centralized management that oversees the big picture and steers global activities. Other elements advocate a decentralized management, which distributes empowerment to the local operations as far as possible down the hierarchy and as close as possible to where the action takes place.

Let us start with the elements that call for global steering and centralized controls.

1. *The size and the scope of the market* require a large, long-term commitment of resources, which only top management can make.
2. *The growing complexity* of the external environment requires a systemic or holistic view to optimize the approach to interdependent factors.
3. *Shifts* – whether caused or endured – require long-range strategies, which corporate management should take on a global basis.

Likewise, the responses to global competitors should be addressed on a global basis.
4   As Peter Senge [2] pointed out, the forces at play in an environment of *dynamic complexity* produce a tangle of reinforcing loops, balancing loops, and delays that are increasingly difficult to grasp, let alone to anticipate. These loops and delays cover up the intricate patterns of connections and interdependencies, and accentuate the unpredictability we referred to earlier. A systemic view is necessary to make sense out of this maze. Corporate management at the core of the organization should be well placed to take such a broad and all encompassing view.
5   *The internal environment* is increasingly complex, a medley of different business units, different specialties and of different local cultures. Strategic alliances and mega-mergers are in the hands of a few corporate managers who negotiate the deal and who are responsible for the integration of the merged businesses.

Furthermore, when continuous business improvement no longer suffices, it is often corporate management that decides the *business breakthrough projects* that will get top priority and override local management's agenda.

However, other elements militate in favor of distributed empowerment.

1   *Some of the stakeholders* may operate on a global basis, while others operate on a local basis. For key customers and some of the critical suppliers – as already pointed out – local factors remain critical.
2   *The complexity of the external environment* is clearly beyond the grasp of the few people who sit at the top of the organizational pyramid. Global projects and global strategies must translate into detailed and dedicated strategies that are understood, accepted and committed to by the local business units.
3   *The complexity of the internal environment* is accentuated by the diversity of the business and by the resulting specialization. Cross-functional cooperation is necessary to optimize the performance of the different business units. Corporate management cannot act as a switchboard that makes all the necessary connections. The units must be able to establish their own pathways to make connections.
4   *The intangible assets* that drive progress and prosperity need freedom in which to blossom, and a fluid and occasionally virtual environment to move in. Centralized controls can restrain connectivity by substituting procedures and approvals for initiative and self-management.

5   *The escalating spiral of speed* limits the time available from strategy to strike. Therefore empowerment has to be distributed as far down as possible in the organization, as close as possible to where the action takes place. Individuals and groups must be alert and ready to take the initiative.

A high-impact televised advertisement by Andersen Consulting suggests 'companies cannot perform unless they perform together'. This raises the question of how corporate togetherness can best be achieved. Should management think globally and manage globally? In this case it would run the global organization with centralized directives and controls. Alternatively, should management think locally and act locally? It would then set up a decentralized organization with distributed local autonomy. Most probably neither of the above approaches can provide an optimal solution. At one extreme, central controls repress local initiative and local responsiveness. At the opposite extreme, lacking coordination and consistency of purpose thwarts effectiveness. Thus, management has to arbitrate an organic combination of these two approaches. This is the solution ABB and other multinationals have adopted. Under the motto 'think globally and act locally' they have set up what we call a *'glob-local' organization*.

1.3 The 'glob-local' organization

The 'glob-local' organization features various strategic business units (SBU) that follow the directives and the guidelines of the corporate management. Within each SBU there is a constellation of self-managed units that follow the strategies of their senior management.

The corporate guidelines are comparable to Wheatley's 'self-referential', and the self-managed units relate to the 'self-organizing structures'. However, as we have already pointed out, human organizations need an infrastructure that enables the *connectivity* (i) between the corporate core and the different SBU; (ii) at the SBU level between its senior management and the two to three levels of operative management; and (iii) between the various self-managed business units and their business environment. That infrastructure is provided by *shared management practices.*

Shared management practices include all those management principles, business policies, management practices, and even procedures that must be shared throughout the organization in order to ensure a common way of working. Shared management practices must be comprehensive to cover the key managerial activities; they must be cohesive to get everybody to pull in the same direction; they must be interconnected.

In order to facilitate the implementation of shared management practices, Du Pont and other multinational corporations have instituted an intermediary management level, which we call Tutorial and Shared Services management or T&S. Following their example, we have developed a sketch of the 'glob-local' organization, which as shown in Figure 1.1, looks like the three levels of a fountain. We will now discuss in turn these three management layers and their functions.

1.3.1 Corporate management

Corporate management, a small team of executives with their staff, is on the top level of our organizational construction. They receive input bottom-up from the organization as well as from outside sources. In turn they establish and pass down corporate guidelines and directives concerning strategic goals and desired behavior. These guidelines and

FIGURE 1.1 The 'glob-local' organization

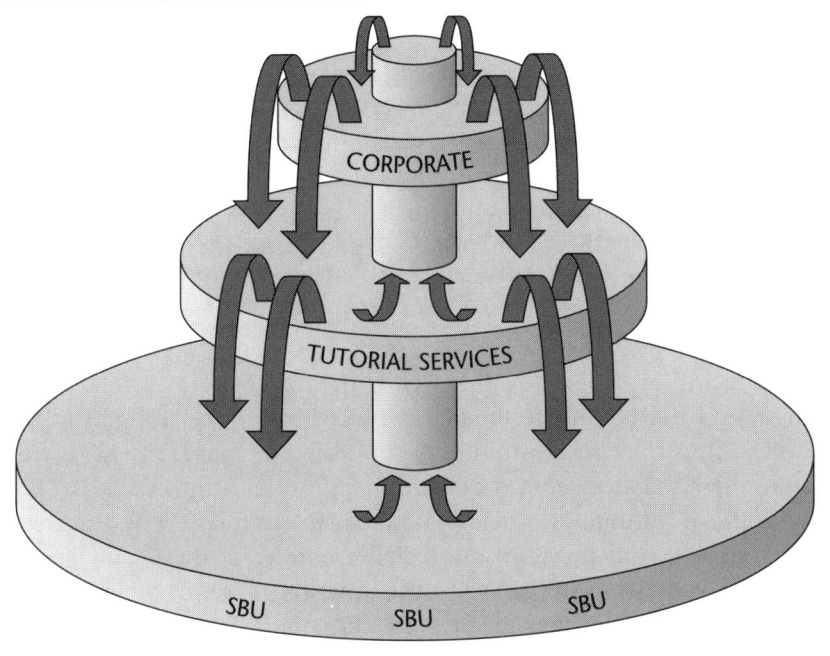

directives are the foundation of shared management practices. We refer to them as *Policy Fundamentals* and discuss them in Chapter Three.

People need to know where the enterprise is going and where other players are going. They also need to believe that things will work out all right. These two basic psychological/professional needs must be completely fulfilled. If the Policy Fundamentals do not completely fill these needs, each individual and each group will fill the unsatisfied needs with their own ideas, interpretations, and imagination. This will result in confusion, misunderstanding and mistrust that will block organizational effectiveness. Thus, the Policy Fundamentals should act like a magnet aligning all the electrons in the same direction.

1.3.2 Tutorial and shared services management (T&S)

Shared management practices are a comprehensive framework for the management of mental, behavioral, and action processes. They must be understood, accepted, and effectively implemented throughout the organization to ensure connectivity.

The first difficulty is to keep the shared practices supportive of the business units rather than prescriptive and limiting. The second difficulty is to keep them systemic, stimulating, and simple. The third difficulty is that the appropriate shared practices must be developed, coached, reviewed, and improved upon.

It is the role of corporate management and of the senior management of the SBU to endow the organization with the appropriate shared management practices. T&S acts as an internal consultant and assists corporate and SBU management as called for in the development, coaching, review, and improvement of these practices. T&S must help management maintain a *cultural force-field* so that the shared management practices are felt to be really supportive rather than a figment of managerial imagination.

The difficulty of establishing an effective frame of guidelines and directives and of supporting them with the appropriate cultural force-field should not be underestimated. Unless they are meaningful to the people, unless they are continuously supported by management, shared management practices will stick on a wall but not in people's minds. Next to the official cultural force-field that management talks about, there will be an insidious but powerful unofficial cultural force-field, and people will apply what Scott-Morgan calls 'the unwritten rules of the game' [9].

The tutorship of management practices and the responsibility for shared services enable T&S to act as a *collector and distributor of knowledge*.

It should contribute to maintaining a leading edge on all the critical competencies either through continuous development of in-house resources or by ensuring good cooperation with outside sources. T&S should also provide a bridge for knowledge and competencies to pass between the various SBU. T&S may also provide feedback from the SBU to corporate management. However, we do not see tutorial and services management as an alternative to direct communication between the SBU and corporate management, but rather as a complement.

1.3.3 The self-managed units of the SBU

The self-managed units are business units that have been empowered by the SBU's senior or operative management to pursue autonomously the strategic objectives they have been given with the resources that have been allocated.

As long as the self-managed units remain dynamically connected with one another and effectively supported by SBU senior management and by T&S, they generate self-motivation and, with it, a critical mass of creative energy. SBU senior management does not have to meddle in day-to-day operations and can concentrate on preparing for the future.

Being given autonomy, the self-managed units can become dynamic, in other words they can structure and restructure themselves, responding quickly to internal or external impulses. However, that is not good enough. These self-managed units should be able to connect effectively with the other nodes of the organization, and to connect as appropriate to stakeholders outside the organization.

The *ability* of organizational nodes to self-organize depends at least as much on the corporate directives and guidelines and on the management practices as on the capabilities of individuals and groups as it does on shared management practices. Guided by business concepts that are understood, accepted, and committed to throughout the enterprise, the self-managed units will evolve their own *guidelines and directives for self-management*. Shared management practices will ensure that these are compatible with the rest of the organization.

Self-managed business units are *willing* to work hard and to take the initiative because they are highly motivated. The empowerment to apply the business concepts freely enables the groups to achieve self-actualization, which is the highest level on Maslow's frequently cited pyramid of human needs [10]. We should add that, in a time of uncertainty and distrust, individuals and groups also have a sixth need, that of *self-reliance*, which is one of the prerogatives of self-managed structures.

Self-managed units are *ready* to respond quickly to new challenges provided that the leadership has created a *cultural force-field* that actively and continuously supports dynamic connectivity as a means to deal effectively with the dynamic complexity of the business environment. This is in contrast to the traditional approach where structures are organized by a hierarchy that has to provide the critical mass of energy to drive the organization and which often ends up mired in the nitty-gritty.

Self-managed units are essential to establishing and maintaining an open system, one that can be really effective because it is *focused, fluid, and fast*. The principle is seldom disputed, but implementing the glob-local organization is not always straightforward because it entails a paradigm shift concerning the management style and the organizational structure.

1.4 Paradigm shifts

Einstein said 'No problem can be solved from the same consciousness that created it'. Indeed, switching from the traditional, centrally controlled organization to what we call the glob-local organization entails major changes. Let us consider some of the concepts that can obstruct the establishment and maintenance of effective self-managed units.

1.4.1 Systemic thinking

We have been taught from the beginning of our school years to break problems down into their component parts in order to better analyze them. As a result, we retain a tendency to look at fragments of a problem rather than at the big picture. In other words we see the trees and not the forest.

Global management requires systemic thinking, in other words a global approach that allows people to see how the different pieces of the puzzle fit together. If corporate and senior SBU management cannot focus on the big picture they will not be prepared to distribute the empowerment to self-managed business units.

1.4.2 Trust

Wheatley points out 'We need to be able to trust that something as simple as a clear core of values and vision, kept in motion through continuing dialogue can lead to order' [7]. Senior SBU managers must trust people in the self-managed units. Furthermore they must trust their own ability to steer the whole organization with shared management practices. Only then will they feel comfortable exchanging detailed controls that are tangible and familiar for trust that is intangible and possibly unfamiliar. Of course trust, like communication, works both ways. If leaders do not trust their subordinates, their subordinates will not trust them in return.

1.4.3 Responsibilities without control

Jantsch summed up the issue of control very clearly: 'In the life [of the organization] the issue is not control, but dynamic connectivity' [11]. 'It is the ideas of a business that are controlling', stated Robert Haas CEO of Levy Strauss, 'not some manager with authority'. However, relinquishing control, and distributing empowerment while retaining responsibility may entail a change in leadership style. Once that shift has been successfully completed, it can be observed that, while controlling requires a considerable input of energy from management, empowerment draws the required energy from the members of the self-managed units.

1.5 The management and the methodology

Shared management practices suppose an effective combination of the methodology, the managers, and the means. While the three are interdependent, it is our contention that methodology drives the other two. It is the methodology that enables the enterprise to attract, to select, to motivate, to develop, and – last but not least – to retain the kind of managers that will lead the organization to its most promising future. It should provide the comprehensive and coherent frame of reference that managers need to be effective as individuals and, even more important, as a team.

Of course the right managers will continuously adapt and improve the way they run their business. But, if the existing methodology has built-in rigidities strong enough to perpetuate themselves, the better managers will feel constrained and will migrate to organizations where they can unfold their full potential. *It is often harder to change the methodology than the managers.*

Given a sound methodology and good managers, the enterprise should be able to obtain whatever it needs in terms of tangible and intangible resources in order to fulfill its ambitions. It has been argued that *the limitation of resources is an excuse managers use when they run out of ideas*. This led us to turn Marshall McLuhan's famous 'the media is the message' into the *methodology is the message*. The methodology conveys values and vision, it conditions thinking as well as behavior. It integrates principles and practices and it is one of the most powerful messages senior management can deliver.

To put things in the right perspective, we should distinguish between the following concepts.

- The *methodology* integrates and optimizes the coordination of all the principles and methods deemed necessary to guide and to direct the major mental, behavioral, and action processes. Shared management practices must be based on a methodology.

- The *methods* help manage specific aspects of the business. The best management practices are those methods deemed to be at the leading edge in the management of a given task. A group of methods focusing on the same task can link up, but they will not link up to other methods unless they are connected in the framework of a methodology.

- The *tools and techniques* support the implementation of a specific method.

We stress the importance of making this distinction because of its organizational implications. Corporate and senior SBU management respectively are the architects and the guardians of the methodology; tutorial and services management is the tutor of the methodology; operative SBU management is the owner of methods; and the self-managed units are the users of the tools and techniques. If corporate and senior SBU management do not ensure the integration of methods and tools into a comprehensive, and coherent methodology, their troops will be marching in extended order.

Obviously endowing the enterprise with a high performing methodology is easier said than done. A majority of enterprises seem to tackle the issue from the wrong end. Without guidance from corporate and from senior SBU management, the organization will end up enacting a Tower of Babel of methods, tools, and techniques. Shared management practices cannot take hold on such an unsteady base.

The resulting problem is illustrated by the fact that the management methods and tools have become big business with worldwide annual sales of business publications in excess of $500 million, and yearly billing for management consulting and training that – according to *Business Week* – are well in excess of $50 billion. This led Stefan Stern to write in the May 1994 issue of *International Management* 'More nonsense is written about management than any other subject. Evangelical textbooks proliferate, university courses multiply, and executives hand over large sums to be harangued and cajoled in lecture theatres'.

While it is easy to point at consultants as the culprits for method-mania, let us not forget that the flight to the next best method can also serve as a cover up or as an excuse. There is no better mousetrap as there is no panacea in modern medicine, but apparently the spirit of the alchemist still lingers on. Furthermore, we should not belittle the fact that the various disciplines of management have greatly benefited from the considerable amount of research that has been carried out. Much progress has been made, and, albeit less publicized than technological advances, the new insights into organizational effectiveness are really quite impressive. However, we must point out that the search for a managerial silver bullet has created three types of problems, namely:

- the turnover of tools and techniques has been too fast to be effective;
- the narrow scope of most tools and techniques tend to fragment the organization;
- there is confusion in the terminology used.

1.5.1 The turnover of tools and techniques

'When the master points his finger at the moon, the fool stares at the finger'. Lao Tzu's maxim alludes to the finger as the tool, to the moon as the objective. With these images the philosopher admonished that tools can be useful to implement an objective, however, they cannot serve as a substitute or as a crutch for a missing business concept.

Since 1994, Bain & Co. has conducted an annual survey on the usage of, and overall satisfaction with the most popular management tools. Their billboard chart shows that respondents use only about half of the tools listed, out of which less than half score a reasonable level of satisfaction. It should be noted that the level of satisfaction indicated by the respondents merely reflects subjective opinions, as there is no factual information on the results obtained via the various methods. The Bain survey also shows that some of the management remedies that are widely talked about – like business process reengineering – draw the highest rate of dissatisfaction.

Bain & Co. laconically concluded its 1995 report by saying, 'the use of some tools may be growing faster than their satisfaction scores warrant'. However, such comments have not distracted management from spending millions of dollars on the newest management fad or fashion, nor consultants to promote the next remedy.

In some cases the quick turnover of tools and techniques has not enabled the enterprise to really take advantage of the theory it has introduced. Obviously, an organization cannot be efficient if the methods and tools keep changing. One should also take into account the fact that the lapse of time from the introduction of a new theory until it is adopted and efficiently deployed can be fairly long. For example 'Hoshin planning', introduced in Japan in the mid 1960s, began to be implemented by a few Western corporations in the mid 1980s and is still not widely used. 'Value Based Management', introduced in the early 1980s, is just starting to gain a broader following. 'Core competencies' has been widely talked about since this concept was first published in the *Harvard Business Review* in 1990, but many companies still grapple with its practical application.

Many a theory has proven elusive and its implementation evasive. Not only has the proliferation of management methods and tools unnecessarily burdened budgets but in some cases it has also been disruptive. Focusing on the narrow scope of the application of a tool, distracts us from looking at the global picture. Corporate and senior SBU managers have difficulties digesting the plethora of tools, lose interest, and delegate the matter downwards. Thus, they sidestep their responsibility to set priorities and to provide guidance and support. Personnel sense this situation and have grown increasingly indifferent to the carrousel of 'program-of the-month' announced by management.

1.5.2 The narrow scope of tools and techniques

Managers' choice of tools and techniques is not only complicated by the plethora of methods, but also by the fact that a vast majority of them are highly specialized and only address a particular aspect of management. This not only limits the scope of the tool but also the approach of its user. If all you have is a hammer, you will be looking around for something to hammer on. Managers have been induced to introduce tools and techniques that appear relevant to their function without giving much thought to their compatibility with what other functions are using.

The tunnel vision of specialists focusing on just one aspect of management is inadequate, and distracts them from taking a systemic or global approach. It perpetuates traditional organizational compartmentalization, it blocks the connectivity among the various nodes of the organization, and it stymies the organization's cross-functional effectiveness.

Academics and consultants have left management with an incongruous patchwork of tools and techniques. As a result, different departments of the same enterprise may end up using different methods, different vocabulary, and different consultants! One executive guide lists 25 major management techniques from Activity Based Costing to value chain analysis [12]. Such a list encourages viewing each of these methods as a stand-alone entity. This is misleading. For example Activity Based Costing, benchmarking, total cycle time reduction are parts of process management, which in turn is only one of the pillars of Total Quality Management (TQM).

1.5.3 Loose terminology and quality jargon

Sometimes new products forge new words such as 'Internet', sometimes new concepts force a new meaning onto an existing word. Traditionally the word 'quality' has been associated with the conformity of the product to specifications, and 'the management of quality' was understood as the assurance of conformity to reasonable customer expectations. This narrow and technically oriented interpretation neglects the economic dimension. Some authors have tried to enlarge the meaning of 'quality' but the traditional definition stubbornly remains. We prefer to speak of 'value-added' rather than of 'quality'. Value can be added by product conformity, it can be added by an innovation which goes beyond conformity to expectation, it can be added by saving costs, and so on. As opposed to 'the management of quality', 'the quality of management' should be understood as the value added by the management of all the business enablers that have an impact on the organizational performance, and not merely by ensuring product acceptability.

1.6 The three levels of quality management

'There can be no progress without change, but there can be change with no progress' said Dr Deming. In order to avoid the problems resulting from a patchwork of methods and tools, management has resorted to different models and international standards have been developed to help managers on their journey towards management excellence. We will describe some of the models of quality management and then see whether they provide a basis for the effective implementation of shared management practices.

Taking into account their scope, level of sophistication, the involvement of management, and the results that can be obtained, we can distinguish between the following three types of quality management:

1. an ISO 9001:2000 program leading to registration is implemented in order to satisfy customer demands or to emulate the competition;
2. quality management focused on a continuous process improvement program, *kaizen* style or based on ISO 9004:2000 guidelines;
3. Total Quality Management or TQM is a comprehensive bundle of concepts, methods, and tools that are aimed at sustaining a competitive advantage.

1.6.1 ISO 9000 registration

The International Standards Organisation (ISO) published a family of international standards that can be used to establish and to audit the quality assurance systems of a supplier. Registration according to this standard provides assurance, although not a guarantee, that the supplier has the organizational means to meet customer requirements on a regular basis. Its senior management takes responsibility for the quality assurance system. Operative management and the quality manager of the supplier ensure that the capability of the processes is maintained through adequate procedures and through operator training.

Over a quarter of a million enterprises have obtained a registration to these international standards. Many managers have sought registration either to satisfy pressing or potential customer requirements or just to emulate their competition. We refer to this approach as *reactive* [13]. Professor Bernard Reimann, one of the founding fathers of the Malcolm Baldrige National Quality Award has estimated that an ISO 9001:1994 registration satisfies only one third of the requirements of this quality prize.

Martin Bangemann, commissioner of the European Commission, has warned managers that the registration to the above mentioned standard should not be considered the final destination [14]. In a working paper of 1995, the European Commission reports substantial research and defines its policy on the promotion of quality management [15]. It stated: 'The recourse to the ISO 9000 standards by companies can be regarded as a first step towards overall quality management'.

1.6.2 *Kaizen* and '9000 Pro'

Kaizen is a step-by-step approach the Japanese have been using for continuous process improvement. It is inspired from the old Chinese maxim 'step by step walk a thousand miles'. Imai's book [16] has introduced this concept to the West, but for the most part companies have limited their *kaizen* efforts to delegating to operators the continuous improvement of manufacturing processes.

Taking our cue from the quality policy of the European Commission, we published in 1996 a model of a program that combines: (i) the rigorous guidelines of ISO 9001 to enhance the discipline of the workers; (ii) a system of audits; and (iii) the team-based approach of TQM [13]. We call this pro-active approach '9000 Pro' because, beyond satisfying customer requirements, this program seeks continuous business improvement. Our approach is not limited to the manufacturing environment, as is often the case with *kaizen*.

The '9000 Pro' implies the involvement of the senior management of an enterprise in designing the system of quality management and in the organization of the program. The reviews with the process improvement teams (PIT) provide additional exposure to senior management of what happens on the shop floor. Furthermore, the '9000 Pro' also features the following advantages:

- the ISO 9001:2000 standard and its ISO 9004:2000 guidelines provide a road map that companies starting their trip towards quality management find very useful;
- registration can normally be obtained in 6–18 months. It should not prove too difficult to retain the attention of management and operative personnel for this length of time;
- registration can be obtained by any serious applicant;
- the registration to an internationally recognized standard has some promotional value for the personnel as well as for customers;
- last but not least, the ISO 9001:2000 program raises the awareness of discipline, of the quality of the work and of the quality of the

management as a means to achieve customer satisfaction and competitiveness. Communications, particularly between different functions and units, are improved, and process performance levels are stabilized on a satisfactory level. Provided that registration is not considered the final destination, the '9000 Pro' can serve as a stepping stone towards TQM. However, we do not want to belittle the fact that from '9000 Pro' or *kaizen* to TQM still requires a quantum leap.

1.6.3 Total Quality Management (TQM)

TQM is a management program that can lead an organization to superior performances. It compasses a host of philosophical concepts, a variety of methods, and an extensive toolbox covering far ranging subjects from policy deployment to operational effectiveness, from people to processes, from suppliers to customer relations.

TQM has been around for roughly half a century, and its credentials are quite impressive. Effectively implemented, TQM can improve the bottom line. According to a study conducted at the Georgia Institute of Technology and at the College of William and Mary, the 600 publicly traded winners of some 140 annual quality prizes awarded in the USA by states, private agencies, and corporations for achievements in TQM, have enjoyed, over a five-year period, a stock appreciation 50 percent higher than their industry average and have shown two or three times the growth in operating income, sales, assets, and employment [*Business Week* September 21, 1998]. Studies by the U.S. National Institute of Science and Technology (NIST) confirm the organizational superiority of companies that have been selected for the Baldrige award.

These results and promotion by consultants as well as by governmental and professional associations have encouraged management to introduce TQM. However, many such attempts have failed, and a vast majority of managers have downgraded TQM to the level of *kaizen* or '9000 Pro' or lower. The fact that the label 'TQM' was retained for a downgraded program has discredited this approach.

Much of the disappointment is due to some misunderstanding. To provide clarification we quote Soin [24] who contributed to the introduction of TQM at Hewlett-Packard and who wrote:

> Some of the companies that implemented TQM found this methodology more explicit on the destination than on how to get

there. The array of different precepts, practices, models and methods, tools and techniques has not simplified the task of management, if anything it has made it more cumbersome.

To use our terminology, TQM is not a methodology but an assortment of methods. While these methods are largely compatible, TQM does not provide a road map to integrate the advocated quality management practices into a methodology supportive of shared management practices. Some world-class companies have developed their own methodology and adapted TQM concepts and methods to their culture and to their operational needs. They had the necessary wherewithal to evolve their own approach under names such as Hewlett-Packard's 'Quality Maturity System', 'The Xerox Management Model', and 'The Dana Style Management'. We have been shown Hewlett-Packard's Quality Maturity System with the understanding that this is proprietary information and we have witnessed the substantial efforts they have put into developing and continuing to improve their methodology of management.

1.7 The introduction of a management methodology

Not only have a majority of enterprises been unable to develop a methodology based on the teaching of TQM, but the efforts to introduce some of these methods and tools have met with a number of problems. While they have been widely described in the literature [17, 18, 19, 20], we would like to list some of them as they may be useful for self-assessment.

- Many enterprises have not been able to establish a strong link between strategies and operations. Obviously senior management has not been intimately involved with the application of a methodology. The fact that the implementation of company-wide TQM takes many years has prompted senior management to delegate this program downwards in order to attend to issues considered more urgent. Without direct support from the top, operative management may limit its involvement to providing facilitation and letting the teams get on with their projects. Given the pressures on all levels of the organization, operative management is unlikely to lead to the introduction of a new system unless it can quickly bring tangible results and is easy to implement. TQM does not score high on either of these counts.

- With no integration of the various management methods, there can be no coordinated leadership. We conducted a survey a few years ago and found that for a majority of respondents, the different layers of management focused on their field of responsibilities alone and did not understand very well what the other layers were doing [21].

- Frederick Taylor, the father of scientific management, has had such an influence on management that some of the concepts he introduced a century ago still have an impact today. As a result, some senior managers feel they hold the exclusivity on decision making and they are somewhat reluctant to assess their own performance. There may also be some remnants from Louis XIV's concept of 'divide to reign'. Operative management lowers its view to minding day-to-day operations. TQM advocates distributing empowerment to the person or group actually doing the work, which fosters cross-functional cooperation, and flattens the organizational structure. Obviously, this upsets the hierarchy, which draws its authority and power from its position. In the traditional structure, the attitude summarized by Senge [2] as 'I am my position' fragments the organization into separate compartments, and the involvement and the allegiance of personnel go to their line management rather than to the enterprise as a whole.

- Research has shown that the senior management of Western enterprises focuses on daily issues and spends relatively little time on strategic issues. This is confirmed by a study conducted by Price Waterhouse for the World Bank in 1995 according to which chief executive officers in OECD countries devote less than 3 percent of their time to planning the future of their enterprise [22]. As a result, they may not find the time to conceive and to lead the implementation of a comprehensive methodology of management. It is interesting to note that, as reported by Wheelen and Hunger [23], senior managers of Japanese corporations typically spend 50 percent of their time on business policy. With the benefit of hindsight one can wonder whether that approach has done much better. A golden middle-way would suggest senior management spend one third of its time on business policy, one third on direct contacts with the key actors in the success of the company, and one third on studies and unforeseen issues. Of course in practice these three types of activities are intertwined and difficult to separate.

- In spite of efforts made by academics and consultants, the meaning of the word 'quality' clings obstinately to 'product specifications'. Consequently, 'quality management' is still associated with the control of product specifications. This may have lead to misinterpreting the designation of Total Quality Management: 'total' should be understood as being company-wide; 'quality' as defined by the Baldrige award means added value; 'management', also according to the Baldrige, is measured by 'criteria for performance excellence'.

- Reluctant to introduce the profound changes to traditional management required by TQM, senior management may sometimes resort to an ISO 9001 certification to demonstrate 'quality management'. For however useful or even indispensable it may be, the ISO 9001 is at best a sub-system of TQM.

- For many decades, technological advances have led to an ever-increasing specialization in our education as well as in our profession. As enterprises have grown, the organization has been increasingly fragmented into departments with functional/technical specialization. As a result, our thinking pattern has narrowed to focus on specific techniques or activities. Our ability to think systemically or holistically has been impaired. We can look at a tree and overlook the forest.

- TQM has lost some of its glamour, maybe some of its credibility. Of course past attempts that have partly succeeded or partly failed have left some scars and some biases. Re-introducing this approach after a failed first attempt is an uphill battle that management is not eager to attempt.

- Lower and middle management have been supportive of systems that have improved their own effectiveness and efficiency. Waves of rightsizing have so pruned their ranks that operative management cannot generate the enthusiasm and time required to take on additional programs.

- The process improvement teams (PIT) tend to spend too much time on tools and techniques. Without proper support, their learning and achievements on given projects will not be consolidated and diffused throughout the organization.

- Often TQM has been inadequately introduced. The American Society for Quality published in February 1997 the results of a

survey among *Fortune 500* companies, which identifies the following deficiencies:
- Out of the 95.5 percent of respondents that had introduced a TQM program, 96.7 percent of them delegated problem-solving to task forces, which leads us to suspect that senior management did not really get involved. Not surprisingly, a majority of these enterprises felt that they have achieved only about half of what was expected.
- 80 percent of the managers had insufficient knowledge of the methods.
- Statistical process control tools were only utilized for 30 percent of their potential.
- Recognition to the task forces for their accomplishment is always given by 18 percent of the respondents, often given by 31.5 percent, and seldom or never given by 50.5 percent of these companies. No recognition and no results should come as no surprise.

Admittedly, the array of different precepts, practices, models and methods, tools and techniques promoted by academics and consultants has not simplified the task of management; if anything it has made it more cumbersome! Leading management gurus like Drucker, Deming, and Senge, have been calling for an integrated management methodology based on the principles and practice of TQM as a key to sustain performance excellence.

We have taken the challenge and developed a framework for shared management practices that can integrate the principles and practices of TQM as well as many of the newer management theories that are being developed. We call this framework the Process of Management, or POM.

The POM is an integrative methodology that starts with the policy directives and guidelines, structures the activities concerning the development and the deployment of strategies, helps the coordination of the implementation of the strategies, and finally assesses the performances.

Various mind-maps integrated in the POM can provide a basis of concept and terminology that are prerequisites of shared management practices.

In the next chapter we will set out the structure of the POM that can be used as a road map for the design and implementation of shared management practices or as a reference point to validate the management system already in place. In the subsequent chapters we will discuss the sub-processes of the POM and its building blocks.

1.8 Summary

We have summarized the five major effects that globalization exerts on the business environment. Some advocate a global management with centralized controls, others a local management with local controls. The 'glob-local' organization finds a compromise by enacting global thinking and local acting.

Global thinking is the responsibility of the corporate management but local acting is entrusted to the self-managed units of the strategic business units (SBU). The problems raised by this newer form of organization are clear: how can the corporate management maintain an interactive connection with the SBU management; how can the SBU management maintain an interactive connection with the self-managed units; how can the self-managed units establish interactive connections with each other as necessary. To solve the above enigma, managers have searched for the silver bullet. New methods and new consultants have been brought in. By and large the results have been disappointing and managers have been left toiling with a patchwork of methods, tools, and techniques.

How can organizational connectivity and effectiveness be increased with methods, tools, and techniques that are not connected? The methodology is the integrator of methods, tools, and techniques and the best-in-class have managed to develop their proprietary methodology.

In order to assist those enterprises that do not have a methodology and to enable those that do to validate the system they have in place, we have developed a single, integrated methodology that we call the Process of Management or POM. The POM serves as a basis for shared management practices. While best management practices can increase the efficiency of a particular activity, shared management practices provide a compatible way of working that facilitates communications, cooperation, and fosters collective creativity. In the next chapter we present the methodology of the POM.

■ CHAPTER TWO ■

The Process of Management

The Plan

Best management practices are tools and techniques that can increase the efficiency of a particular activity, but, to increase the effectiveness of the whole enterprise, *shared management practices* are needed. Shared management practices ensure that all the nodes of the organization are interdependently connected and that they are capable of interacting dynamically with a shifting business environment.

Shared management practices require a single, integrated methodology of management, which ensures transparency, understanding, and commitment from the mission statement to the measures of performance.

In order to help management introduce the appropriate methodology or to validate the management system in place, we present in this chapter the Process of Management or POM. It features four interactive sub-processes and several management principles.

The Mind-Maps

- The POM as a road map to doing the right thing right.

- The four sub-processes of the POM.

- The five principles that guide the approach to managing the five business enablers.

Introduction

In the preceding chapter we discussed the glob-local organization, the one that appears best-suited to dealing with the globalizing environment. It gives a high degree of autonomy to the self-managed units so they can deal effectively with the dynamic complexity of the globalizing business environment. We have shown how this can be achieved by introducing shared management practices. It is this framework that enables the different management levels and the different functions to remain interactively connected.

World-class companies have developed such an integrative methodology. Hewlett-Packard, for example, integrates the various functions of management into a proprietary process they call the Process of Management. We are grateful to Hewlett-Packard and to Mr F. Ducheyne, Quality Director Europe, for showing us their approach. The effectiveness of their methodology encouraged us to integrate into a comprehensive process many of the mind-maps we developed in our consulting practice in over a decade. As a result, while pursuing a similar objective, the integrative management process presented here is an original construct that differs conceptually and structurally from Hewlett-Packard's model.

We have developed the Process of Management or POM to assist management implement a comprehensive, coherent, and connective methodology that supports shared management practices. The POM describes the organization of the major managerial tasks as well as their interdependencies, but it does not prescribe how management should run its business. Management can use this construct to check whether the management system in place is satisfactory or use the mind-map provided here to implement whatever improvements are deemed appropriate.

2.1 The Process of Management

Figure 2.1 shows the POM as a comprehensive road map. This process has the following features.

- The POM is a logical construct that integrates business principles and practices into a single, interactive methodology of management. Such a framework, as already mentioned, is a prerequisite for an effective glob-local organization.

28 CONNECTED: CHAPTER TWO

FIGURE 2.1 The Process of Management

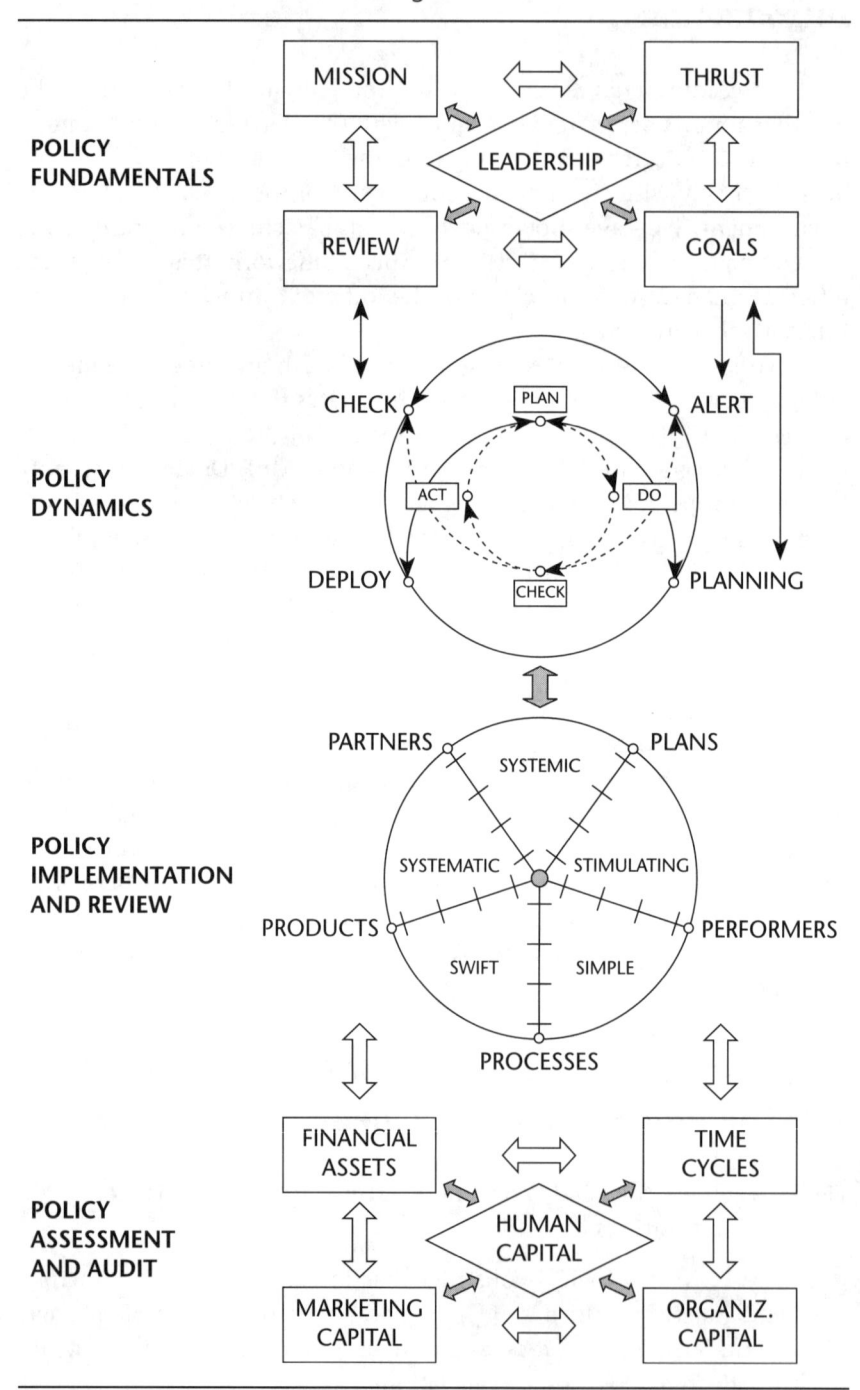

POLICY FUNDAMENTALS

MISSION ⇔ LEADERSHIP ⇔ THRUST
REVIEW ⇔ GOALS

POLICY DYNAMICS

CHECK — PLAN — ALERT
ACT — DO
DEPLOY — CHECK — PLANNING

POLICY IMPLEMENTATION AND REVIEW

PARTNERS — SYSTEMIC — PLANS
SYSTEMATIC — STIMULATING
PRODUCTS — PERFORMERS
SWIFT — SIMPLE
PROCESSES

POLICY ASSESSMENT AND AUDIT

FINANCIAL ASSETS ⇔ TIME CYCLES
HUMAN CAPITAL
MARKETING CAPITAL ⇔ ORGANIZ. CAPITAL

- The POM encompasses four interactive sub-processes. It emphasizes the connectivity of people, of their business unit, and of their tasks. The rational, relational, and emotional/creative elements of management are brought to the fore. This ensures *transparency over the whole process*. Individuals and groups at all levels and in all functions must be able to satisfy their need-to-know concerning 'who is doing what' and 'why we are doing what we are doing'. This is the basis for a level of purposeful understanding, acceptance, and commitment that will trigger cross-functional cooperation and creativity.

- The first two sub-processes of the POM, namely the *Policy Fundamentals* and the *Policy Dynamics* concern the development and the deployment of the business policy. The globalizing environment imposes such a rhythm of change that unless the enterprise is *doing the right thing* it may not have the means to alter its course at the most appropriate time. Its success and even survival are on the line. Corporate and SBU management interact in these sub-processes.

    Two of the four sub-processes of the POM, namely the *Policy Dynamics* and the *Policy Assessment and Audit*, feature close cooperation between the SBU's senior and operative management. The two management levels start by carrying out complementary tasks and then get together to evolve consensual decisions. Structuring these interactions enables a quality of communications and creativity often prevented by hierarchical distance.

- The POM assists management in *doing the thing right* by emphasizing the interdependencies between the five business enablers. Management must get a grip on them in order to leverage the business performance. They include the action plans, the strategic resources or performers, the processes, the products, and the partners (customers and suppliers). We also refer to them as the five <P> and use this alliteration as a memory aid. Furthermore, we suggest that the approach to managing the five business enablers be systemic, stimulating, simple, swift and systematic. These principles can eventually find broader applications as a guide to managerial thinking.

- The last of the four sub-processes of the POM concerns the *Policy Assessment and Audit*. Operative management assesses the effectiveness of the day-to-day business while senior management focuses on auditing the value added by the enterprise during the planning period. The same evaluation criteria are used by senior and operative management. The two approaches are complementary and the two management levels get together to decide whether the enterprise is well positioned to be *doing the right thing right*. Their conclusions may lead senior management to revisit and possibly revise the *Policy Fundamentals* and the *Policy Dynamics*. This closes the loop.

As can be appreciated, the four sub-processes of the POM are interconnected. Furthermore, each of them features several interactive building blocks. We stress the coherence and consistency of this construct because this comprehensive and integrative methodology should not be simplistic, although it can be simple to implement thanks to its logical connectivity.

In addition to an integrative methodology, shared management practices require a common dictionary and common mind-maps to approach important aspects of the business. We will propose the mind-maps that we consider useful for the implementation of the POM.

Hereafter we present an overview of the four sub-processes of the POM and the related management concepts. The *Policy Fundamentals* and the *Policy Dynamics* will be covered in detail in Chapters Three and Four respectively. The business enablers managed in the *Policy Implementation and Review* will be discussed in Chapters Five through Eight, and the *Policy Assessment and Audit* is the subject of Chapter Nine.

2.2 The Policy Fundamentals

The Policy Fundamentals set the basis for business policy and summarize *the purpose and the identity of the enterprise.*

The Policy Fundamentals provide directives to align corporate strategies, SBU strategies, and business units plans and actions with the stated strategic ambitions of the enterprise. They also ensure consistency of purpose and foster identification with the enterprise by all those who contribute to its success. This is particularly important as things around us change so quickly.

Changes in the internal environment can be destabilizing, and wield a particularly strong emotional impact. People need something to hold on to, they need some *continuity* amidst change. This is why Alfred North Whitehead said: 'the art of progress is to preserve order amid change and to preserve change amid order'. Therefore, the Policy Fundamentals should provide a set of business concepts that people can rally around and relate to. They focus on 'who' and 'what' the organization should be, on the collective personality it should have.

Senior management is the architect and the guardian of the Policy Fundamentals. Their periodic review featured in the Policy Assessment and Audit (Chapter Nine) affords an opportunity for introspection and out-of-the-box thinking.

The Policy Fundamentals comprise the following five interactive building blocks:

- the mission, the values and code of behavior, and the strategic biases;
- the strategic thrust, the value chain, the competencies and capabilities;
- the strategic ambitions, the strategic goals, and the road map;
- the processes of resource allocation and empowerment and of review–evaluation–recognition; and
- last but not least, leadership, which is at the center of this management sub-process.

Among the business concepts encompassed in the Policy Fundamentals, we will now consider the following in more detail:

- optimizing the satisfaction of the stakeholders;
- aligning strategy and operations;
- harmonizing global vs. local considerations.

2.2.1 Optimizing stakeholder satisfaction

The ultimate economic and moral justification of any enterprise lies in the satisfaction of its major constituencies or stakeholders. The systemic approach ensures organizational effectiveness in optimizing the satisfaction of all the key constituencies. Schematically we can say that every enterprise has the following stakeholders:

- the customers (buyers, users, and consumers);
- the personnel (including permanent and temporary personnel as well as freelance);
- the critical suppliers of tangible and intangible goods, the allies, the network partners, and the distributors;
- the communities in which the enterprise operates, and the relevant interest groups; and
- last but not least, the shareholders (private and institutional).

The shareholders and the customers are the only stakeholders who provide the money that the enterprise needs to stay in business. The personnel, the critical suppliers, the strategic allies, and the community contribute to the value the enterprise delivers to both the customers and the shareholders. As we will discuss in more detail in Chapter Three, a proactive management defines its constituencies and the business boundaries in its mission statement.

Ideally a proactive management should be able to choose its major stakeholders. It should also be able to decide on the level of satisfaction it wants to offer to each of them and the means to achieve these objectives. Viable alternatives can then be considered, and the business policy and the relevant strategies planned.

Of course, once a business policy has been engaged and long-term commitments have been undertaken, changing the course set for the enterprise may prove difficult, costly and even risky. We should add that management's control over the desired future state of the enterprise is subject to endorsement by its key constituencies, namely the key customers, the personnel, and the shareholders.

It is important to understand the interdependencies among the stakeholders, and more specifically the cause and effect relationships between the factors that drive their satisfaction. Therefore, while customer satisfaction and shareholder value are indeed paramount, no enterprise can afford to neglect any of its stakeholders. All interest groups must be attended to lest the enterprise be ostracized or even find itself stymied. Interest groups have been getting increasingly vocal and, as a former executive of AT&T rightly observed, 'the ultimate bottom line depends on public acceptance'.

Several models have been proposed to help visualize the interdependencies of the main requirements of the various stakeholders. We believe that every enterprise should develop its own model using the information it has available on the requirements of its major stakeholders, their interdependencies, and stakeholders' acceptability of the compromise proposed by management between the various interests.

Several factors can influence the interdependencies among the various stakeholders and management's position; in particular:

- the culture of the sector and its influence on the corporate or internal culture;
- the culture of the region and its influence on the corporate or internal culture;
- the corporate or internal culture;

- the competitive position of the enterprise and the way it plays the rules of the game;

- senior management's ambitions and the pressures exerted by the stakeholders.

Each stakeholder group has a set of requirements and expectations. Often stakeholder groups are composed of sub-groups that can be identified by looking at their nature and at the profile of their requirements and expectations. Admittedly, dealing with the different and apparently diverging interests of several parties is complex. However, this should not deter us from trying to design a systemic model for the optimization of stakeholders' satisfaction, which can be translated into corporate goals and performance indicators.

This process starts by identifying the degree of satisfaction the enterprise should offer to each of the major stakeholder groups. The relevant strategies and the appropriate indicators should then be agreed upon. Here again we stress the *proactive approach* that puts senior management in the driver's seat, consistent with its responsibility of setting the strategic ambitions as well as the performance measures. The determination of the strategic ambition concerning the degree of satisfaction of the stakeholders is a delicate exercise, which probably will need refining over time. Reichheld suggests that the strategic ambition should be placed within a band width or tolerance zone [29]. At one extreme, this zone we will have total loyalty and total commitment of the stakeholders and, at the other extreme, no loyalty and no commitment. Loyalty and commitment have a value to the enterprise but also generate costs. Here again management must find a workable balance.

A proactive management will strive to ensure as broad a tolerance zone as possible, taking advantage of the following factors.

- Stakeholder demands tend to be incremental rather than subject to sudden or unreasonable shifts. Management should be alert to trends in stakeholders' requirements and expectations.

- Increased demands from one stakeholder do not necessarily entail additional demands from the other stakeholders. Sometimes increased demands of one stakeholder group may actually dampen the demands of the other constituencies. For example unavoidable environmental investments will most likely entail squeezed margins that shareholders will accept.

- Stakeholders' requirements and expectations can and should be negotiated. Management should be able to explain its rationale for reaching a compromise between the diverging interests of the various constituencies.

- Stakeholders who take a long-term interest in the enterprise will generally accept reasonable compromises that optimize the level of satisfaction of all the parties concerned. However, in order to obtain understanding, acceptance, and cooperation from the stakeholders, management must ensure the appropriate communication and negotiation.

It must be said that the tolerance zone is continuing to shrink as a result of the increased mobility, volatility, and susceptibility found in both internal and external business environments. Management should regularly monitor the attitude of its constituencies.

At first, creating a model of *balanced stakeholder satisfaction* can be laborious; however, the discussions the process generates, both internally and externally, provide a better insight into stakeholder requirements, and serve as a basis for negotiations. Such a model helps formulate the general business policy and can be communicated to all concerned in the mission statement and in the strategic goals.

The strategic process that enables us to formulate a balanced approach to stakeholders' satisfaction can be structured as follows.

- Identify the major stakeholders, their requirements and expectations, the performance indicators they use, and how they evaluate our performance.

- Identify the interdependencies among the major stakeholder groups, and the influence management can have on their evaluation.

- Identify the interactions among the external influences that can modify their requirements and expectations and affect how they will evaluate our performance.

- Identify the best among alternative balanced policies. In principle they should be consistent with the mission, principles, and vision of the enterprise; in extreme situations, however, even the business fundamentals may have to be revised.

- Deploy roles, responsibilities, and resources as well as performance indicators that will be used in managers' assessment and in senior management audits (see Chapter Nine).

2.2.2 Aligning strategy and operations

Figure 2.2, 'Doing the right thing right', expands on Drucker's model, which illustrates the importance of linking strategy and operations [30]. However, this is easier said than done. We take as a proof the fact that, in a majority of enterprises, one set of people concentrates on strategies and another on implementing them. Arguably this is one of the legacies of Taylorism. But there are some valid reasons that explain the separation of these two tasks of management, as there are no less valid reasons for linking the two.

The mind of the strategist looks far into the foggy future, it devises grand plans based on broad concepts. The mind of the operator focuses on the present, and deals with concrete, day-to-day situations. Many executives as they ascend the organizational pyramid bring along the paradigms that served them well when they were managing operations. Combining strategic thinking and operational orientation in the same person looks like a mission impossible. And yet in practice most people show some disposition for both strategic as well as for operational thinking.

FIGURE 2.2 Doing the right thing right

	DOING THE RIGHT THING	
	NO	YES
YES (Doing things right)	DANGER *INNOVATION*	SUCCESS
NO (Doing things right)	FAILURE	VULNERABLE *IMPROVEMENT*

→ OPERATIONS MANAGEMENT
↓ STRATEGIC MANAGEMENT

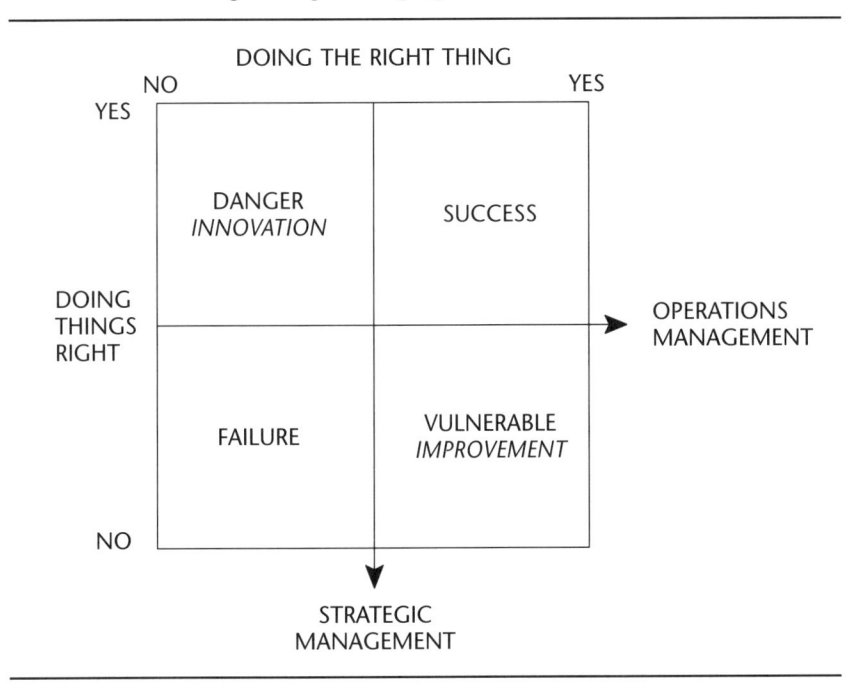

There are good reasons for helping people to develop bivalent competencies, and systemic thinking can help visualize strategy and operations as interactive parts of the same business system. Sun Tzu admonished 'strategy is too important to leave it to the generals' [31]. There are two ways to interpret this statement. Firstly, when generals wage a war, it is the soldiers who die. One may argue that the soldiers have a right to understand why they are dying. Furthermore, if the troops do not understand the strategy they are to carry out, they are unlikely to commit to it. Actually, it is human nature to be afraid and to resist situations that are not well understood. Secondly, generals are too far from the trivial details: the details which are insignificant when taken individually, but create an avalanche when they combine. The analogies to the enterprise are easy to see. We should stress the fact that the soldiers in Sun Tzu's armies 2500 years ago were supposed to obey and execute, while the higher ranks were required to contribute and to create. We will revert in Chapter Five to the role of the intellectual capital contributed by individuals and teams.

Clearly strategies and operations must be aligned. We need a powerful method that facilitates translating strategy into actions, and allows management to feed back to strategy the results obtained with actions. We will present in the next chapter the model of the 'Two Rings', which includes the method we advocate to manage this important link.

2.2.3 Harmonizing global vs. local considerations

The 3M company and ABB have been among the pioneers of the concept *think globally and act locally*. The supply chain, information technology, knowledge management, corporate and financial strategies are among the ones that must be conceived on a global basis in order to drive efficiencies through the economies of size, of scope, of scale, the economy of time, and – as discussed in Chapter One – through the economy of systems.

Sales and marketing as well as human resources are among the strategies that must be planned on a local basis in order efficiently to take into account the different regional regulations and cultures. Corporate, marketing, and financial strategies are examples of global strategies.

Management must find a workable balance between global and local factors of success. This balance is a critical aspect of success for enterprises that have diversified both geographically and sectorially. An incoherent amalgamation of units or a loose federation of local subsidiaries will result in competitive weaknesses that other global players will take advantage of. As mentioned in the previous chapter, many world-class enterprises ensure the connection of the various units through a structure consisting of three levels as illustrated in Figure 1.1.

2.3 The Policy Dynamics

The Policy Dynamics develop and deploy the strategies in accordance with the directives and guidelines of the Policy Fundamentals. While Policy Fundamentals seldom change, the Policy Dynamics, as the name implies, are constantly evolving.

The Policy Dynamics receive the following inputs from the Policy Fundamentals, namely: the strategic goals, the resource allocation and empowerment, and the review–evaluation–reward processes. Furthermore, the leadership drives the Policy Dynamics also taking into account the mission statement and the strategic thrust.

The Policy Dynamics have to connect the internal environment with the external environment, the long and the short range, the senior management with the operative management. In order to present a systemic view of this sub-process and to clarify the formal interactions between the different levels of management, we have developed the model of the 'Two Rings'.

The outer ring features the four major functions of senior management namely 'check–alert–planning–deployment' of the strategies. The inner ring features the 'plan–do–check–act' performed by operative management as it manages the business enablers or the 5 <P> in order to implement the Policy Deployment.

Senior and operative management interact on the planning and on the deployment phases in which priorities as well as the means to reach the targets are agreed upon. The resource allocation follows the priorities, which distinguish between the business breakthrough, the continuous business improvements, the business maintenance, and the special projects.

The Policy Dynamics evolve action plans that are passed on to operative management for implementation and review in the next sub-process of the POM, namely the Policy Implementation and Review.

Among the many business concepts that are encompassed in the Policy Dynamics we would like to consider the following:

- commitment;
- cooperation;
- collective creativity.

As mentioned earlier, the main purpose of the Policy Dynamics is to develop and to deploy strategies. However, unless commitment, cooperation, and collective creativity are generated in the process, there will be no dynamics to the business policy evolved by management. Moss Kanter's 'concept, competence, collaboration' [32] rests on the interaction of rational and relational drivers. In addition, the stimulating approach that we advocate as part of the management principles emphasizes the emotional drivers. Our model, illustrated in Figure 2.3, features the rational and relational factors that drive group dynamics and foster *commitment*, the relational and emotional factors that foster *cooperation*, the rational and emotional factors that generate *creativity*.

Our model is reminiscent of Dr Eric Berne's transactional analysis [33]. The 'adult' is rational, the 'child' is emotional. However, our relational mode does not necessarily fit the 'parent' as pictured by Berne. We also differ in the way we draw behavioral patterns from the interactions between paired elements of our model.

2.3.1 Building commitment

Without commitment people work to rules. When being told or even sold to, the individual or the group are under external pressure and, depending on the situation, opposing internal pressures will build up, acting as a countervailing force. Real commitment can only come from inside the individual because only then can clear barriers or resistance be avoided.

FIGURE 2.3 The behavioral modes

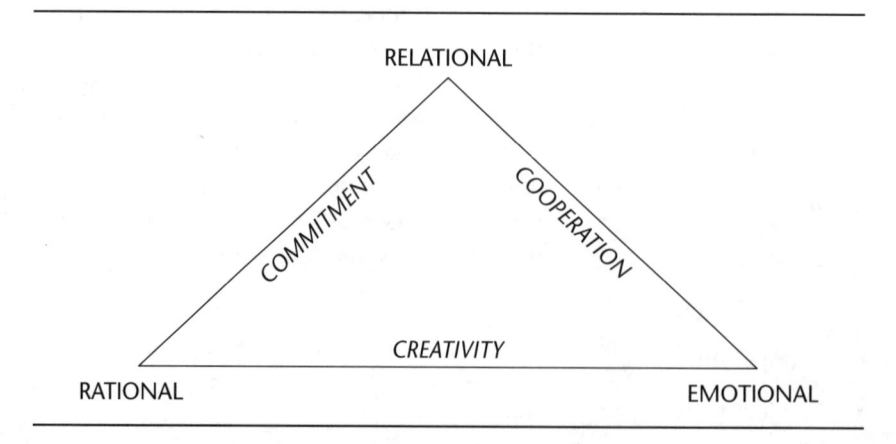

Furthermore, the effects of internal stimuli tend to be stronger and far more durable than external stimuli.

Taking a cue from research done by Stevenson Gumpert [34], we believe that commitment can be obtained by a combination of *vision and confidence* [35]. People can rationalize on a desired future state or a vision. However, there must be congruence between the vision pursued by the organization, and the vision pursued by the individual and by his or her group. Speeches and slogans may exacerbate some emotions, but when things cool down – and that can happen very quickly – the rational side takes over and people revert to their own goals. The distance between personal and organizational vision cannot be allowed to be too big for too long.

Even if the vision is good for the enterprise as well as for its personnel it is not enough to elicit durable commitment. Left-brain vision must be balanced with right-brain confidence. Winning a million dollars in the lottery is easy enough to envision. But the confidence of winning is probably low. As a result, playing the lottery is just a gamble, there is no real commitment behind it.

Figure 2.4 presents schematically alternative combinations of vision and confidence. Vision is fostered by a combination of rational and relational drivers and results in commitment and creativity. Confidence is

FIGURE 2.4 Vision and confidence

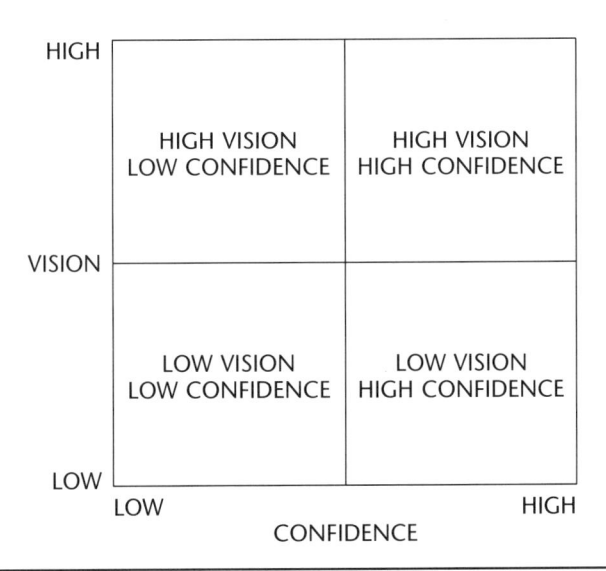

	LOW CONFIDENCE	HIGH CONFIDENCE
HIGH VISION	HIGH VISION / LOW CONFIDENCE	HIGH VISION / HIGH CONFIDENCE
LOW VISION	LOW VISION / LOW CONFIDENCE	LOW VISION / HIGH CONFIDENCE

fostered by a combination of emotional and relational drivers and results in cooperation and to some extent in commitment.

Several methods contribute to building up vision. We discuss some of them in Chapters Three and Four respectively under Policy Fundamentals and Policy Dynamics.

There are several mechanisms used to build up confidence. Group support, trust in the leadership, strategic and organizational consistency over time, past successes and early success are among such mechanisms. Many authors including K. Blanchard, G. Hofstede, and J. Kotter have analyzed aspects of psychological drivers and group dynamics as generators of vision and confidence. However, we cannot discuss the details of this subject here.

2.3.2 Cooperation

By nature man is a sociable being, inclined to cooperate with like-minded people provided there is a commonality of interests, a shared vision, and mutual trust. If there is no commonality of interest and shared vision individuals will tend to go in different directions or to harbor hidden agendas; if there is no trust, circumspection will inhibit cooperation.

As we will show in Chapter Five, senior management is the architect and the guardian of the synergies among the strategies, the systems, the structures, and the style of management. It has to ensure that self-managed units can move freely across functions and hierarchical levels. It should encourage the formation of networks that are focused, fluid, and fast.

Experience shows that it is more important to remove the barriers that obstruct cooperation than it is to promote cooperation. Unhindered, people will tend to cooperate. However, as shown in our research, management style and the review–evaluation–reward process can be powerful drivers of cooperation [36].

2.3.3 Creativity

The books and articles published on the subject of creativity could easily fill a room. A selection are mentioned in the bibliography [37, 38, 39, 41]. For all the models that have been presented, creativity remains an elusive skill. The best management can do is to create a favorable environment.

The POM calls for creativity to develop innovative strategies and to implement innovative solutions. A three-pronged approach is used, namely working with facts, working with ideas, and – last but not least – working in teams. Goal/QPC presents a list of the relevant tools [26].

Working in cross-functional teams, as advocated by Deming, the father of Total Quality Management (TQM), has proven effective in projects of continuous business improvement [42, 43]. Teamwork allows greater scope for idea generation, and a more balanced view on the selection of ideas. Furthermore, the individuals who participate in cross-functional teams become internal sponsors of the required changes and effective facilitators of their implementation. TQM's toolbox assists teams in working with ideas.

The Japanese approach to creativity is essentially a pragmatic one, and the results obtained in the manufacturing area are quite impressive. Toyota, for example, reported averaging as many as 32 suggestions per employee per year in their Japanese plants. Impressive as they may sound, however, such figures need to be qualified: not all of those ideas are resounding innovations or revolutionary invention by a long way. Indeed many, if not most of them, are but the simplest of improvements. Managing creativity – as we will state time and time again – requires a reasonable and productive balance of improvements, innovations, and inventions.

2.4 The Policy Implementation and Review

The Policy Implementation and Review is where the customer value is delivered in accordance with the action plans evolved in the Policy Dynamics.

Frequent reviews are necessary so that corrective measures and improvements can be implemented in good time. In addition we recommend that operative management carries out a *quarterly review* of (i) the results achieved vs. the objectives for each of the business enablers and for their interactions (both lagging indicators of the effect and leading indicators of what causes the effects should be considered); (ii) benchmarks; (iii) the improvement measures; (iv) marketing data and forecasts; (v) as appropriate, the budget and the annual business plan. We return to the quarterly reviews in Chapter Nine.

We have developed the model of the 5 <P> [25] so as to focus management's attention on the interdependencies among the following *business enablers* and on the cross-functional teamwork needed to manage them. The 5 <P> include:

- the Plans for action;
- the Performers or strategic resources;
- the Processes;
- the Products;
- the Partners that include key customers and critical suppliers.

The toolbox of TQM can be used as appropriate to manage the business enablers. Shiba [20] and Brassard [26] are among the many authors who present a wide selection of TQM tools and techniques.

Among the business concepts that are encompassed in the Policy Implementation and Review we will now consider the following:

- the management of all the activities using Deming's 'P–D–C–A' [42];
- the management of the business enablers or the 5 <P>;
- the action plans.

2.4.1 The Deming Wheel or the 'P–D–C–A' model

In his days at Bell Laboratories back in the 1930s, Walter Shewhart – one of the pioneers of statistical process control – recommended that all actions be planned, done, and studied in order to evaluate performances and variances. Actions should then be taken to correct any shortfall and to improve performances. Easy to understand, this approach is also very effective when applied systematically to all types of activities, and at all levels.

Deming translated Shewhart's concept into what is often referred to as the 'Deming Wheel', whereby once an action has gone though these four phases, the cycle starts again. Figure 2.5 shows the 'plan–do–check–act' or 'P–D–C–A' cycle [42].

Deming changed Shewhart's 'study' into 'check'. We prefer Shewhart's terminology. Taken literally, checking refers to quality control's task to make a binary decision on whether a given item meets the standards or not. Study implies a deeper analysis of the cause and effect relationship, and an investigation so that those lessons can be learned and effectively applied. However, Deming's 'P–D–C–A' has now entered managers' dictionaries, and we can retain it with the aforementioned proviso.

In order to take full advantage of the systematic approach of the P–D–C–A, we recommend that it be applied as follows.

THE PROCESS OF MANAGEMENT   43

FIGURE 2.5 The Deming Wheel (continuous business improvement)

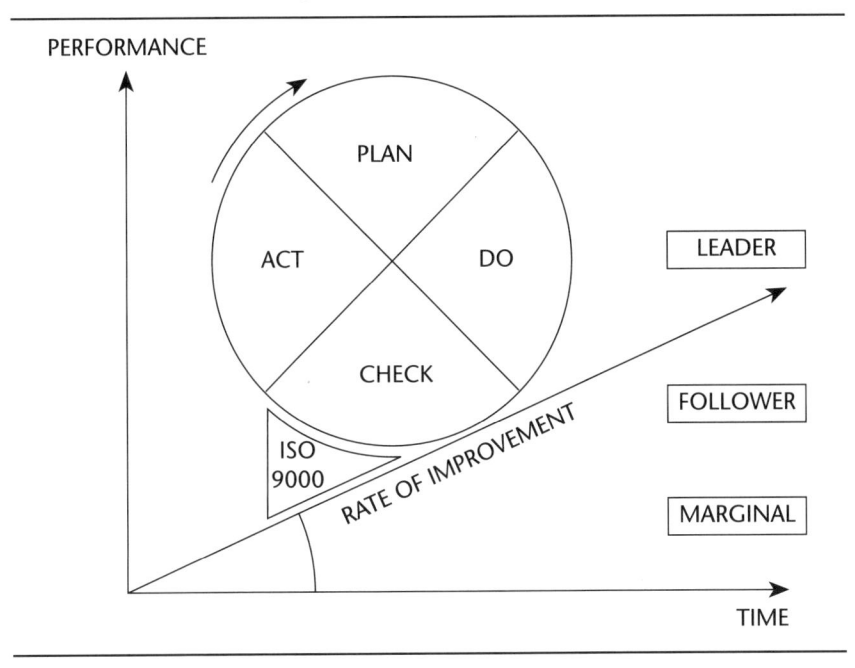

- Every phase of the Deming Wheel should feature objectives, indicators, targets, performance measures, and, whenever applicable, the planned improvements. This also implies that the results of the 'act' phase are measured.

- Every phase of the Deming Wheel should be documented as appropriate to ensure organizational learning and safeguarding of the information. Documentation may protect the enterprise and its personnel in case of liabilities. The international standards of ISO 9001:2000 and the guidelines ISO 9004:2000 are helpful.

- The Deming Wheel supposedly makes a full turn with the completion of each cycle. Before starting a new cycle and commencing the planning of a new cycle, the documentation of all the four phases of the previous cycle should be reviewed, the organizational learning summarized in lessons learned, which should be circulated as appropriate throughout the organization. In practice, the cycles often overlap, as a new one starts before the old one has completed its run.

2.4.2 The five business enablers

Managing in a globalizing environment is full of ambiguities, dilemmas, and surprises. Sometimes, facing a clogged agenda and an overflowing e-mail, managers may recall the famous quote: 'Oh God, give me the serenity to accept those things I cannot change, the courage to change those things that can be changed, and the wisdom to know the difference'. The things that management can change, shape, and act on are the business enablers. As already mentioned, we have identified them as the 5 <P>, as follows.

- The Plans that translate strategies into specific and empowered business or action plans.

- The Performers or strategic resources are invested in processes and in accordance with the plans in order to achieve the planned performance. Our mind-map – discussed in Chapter Five – includes the following performers: financial assets, time cycles and timing, human capital, organizational capital, marketing capital.

- The Processes are the engines that transform the inputs (activities and resources) into outputs. The architecture of processes connects processes of different natures and of different levels in the hierarchy of processes.

- The Products are the goods and services that are delivered to buyers/users/consumers and should in return contribute 'market recognized value'.

- The Partners are the key parties with whom and for whom we work, more specifically the customers (buyers/users/consumers), the distributors, the critical suppliers, and the strategic allies.

The 5 <P> are the mind-map that we use in the Policy Implementation and Review, the third of the four sub-processes of the POM. In order to increase impact and retention, we use alliteration and a small number of items. Figure 2.6 shows our mind-map. Every <P> should be managed according to the Deming Wheel, in other words it should be planned, deployed, its performance checked, and improved on.

The model of the ISO 9001:2000 is quite similar to the one we published in 1993 [25]. However, our model encompasses all the activities of the enterprise while ISO 9000:2000 focuses on the customer value delivery that Porter refers to as 'the primary process' [52]. Furthermore, the aforementioned model, as well as the European Quality Award (EQA), does not dedicate a block for the product, which is merely considered as

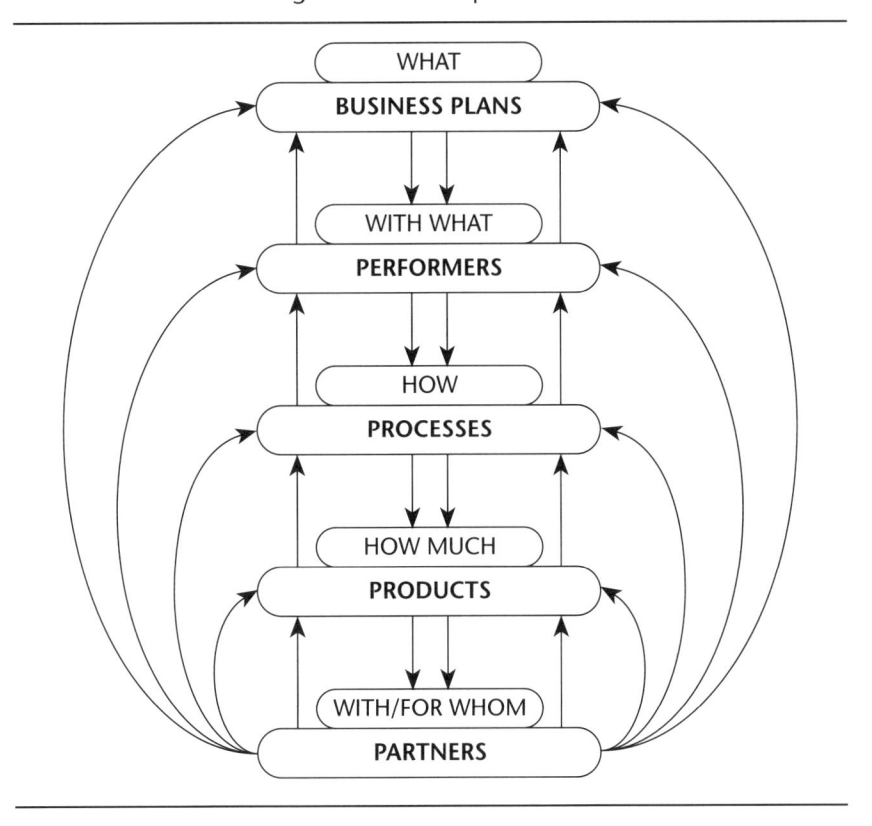

FIGURE 2.6 Connecting the 5 <P> of performance

```
            WHAT
         BUSINESS PLANS
              ↕
           WITH WHAT
           PERFORMERS
              ↕
             HOW
           PROCESSES
              ↕
           HOW MUCH
            PRODUCTS
              ↕
         WITH/FOR WHOM
           PARTNERS
```

an output of processes. We consider the product as a business enabler in its own right. If anything, sometimes managers pay too much attention to the product and neglect some of the other business enablers. We consider all the 5 <P> to be equally important and interactive.

The EQA features a causal relationship between each of the enablers and its results. The Malcolm Baldrige National Quality Award (Baldrige) places its seven enablers in a circle to emphasize the relations between one element and the next. Our mind-map emphasizes the importance of managing the interactions between each of the 5 <P> and all the other business enablers. To stress this point we show the business enablers either in the form of a cascade, as in Figures 2.6 and 2.7, or, like the Baldrige, as a circle as in Figure 2.1

Occasionally we see management focus on reengineering processes without due consideration for personnel, or change policy without aligning processes and structures, or change policy without adapting the

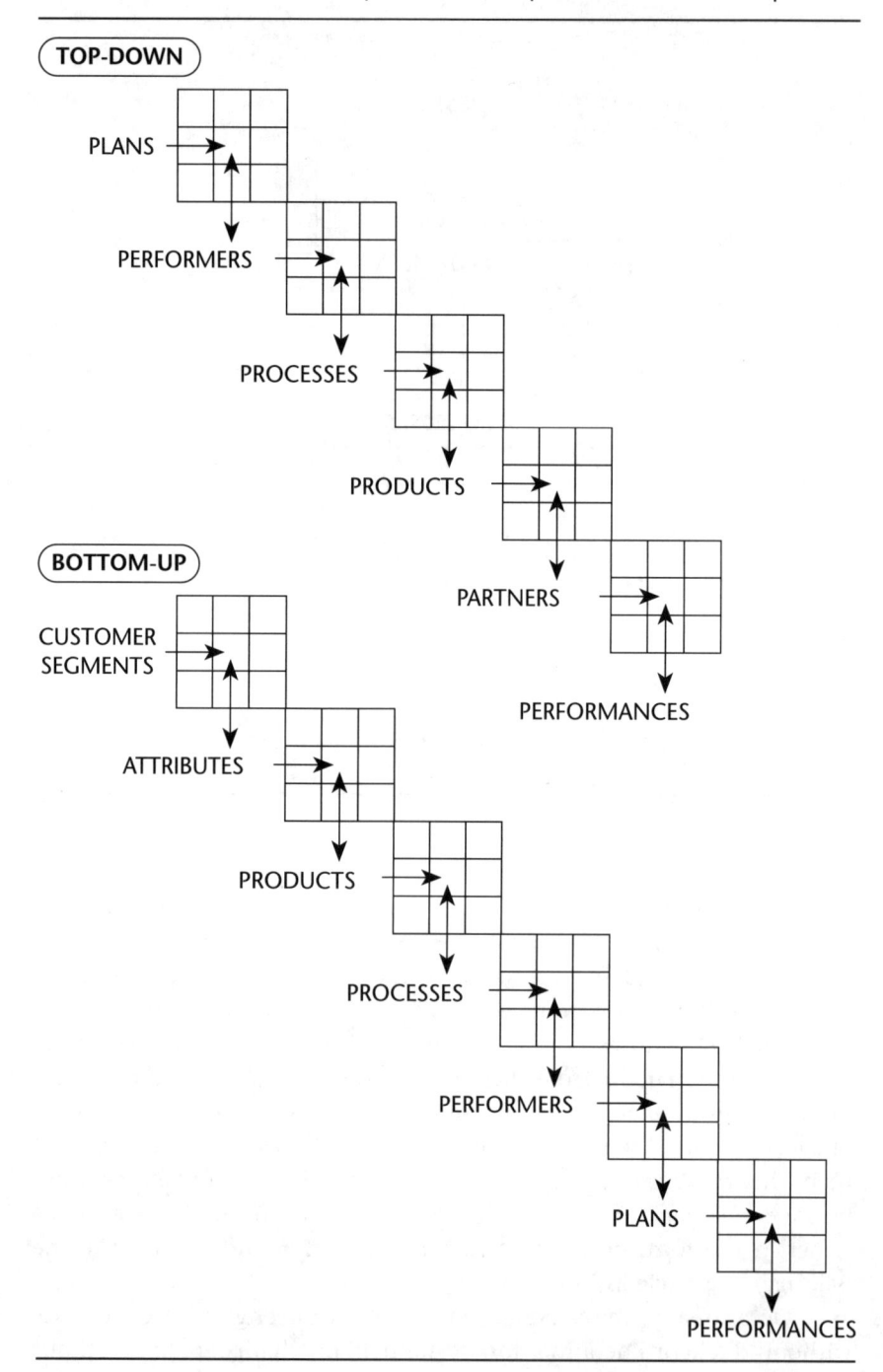

FIGURE 2.7 The 5<P> of performance top-down and bottom-up

style. Examples abound and always result in sub-optimizing performances, sometimes in major problems. As will be discussed in Chapter Nine, this kind of problem can be avoided by using the mind-map of the 5 <P> both in the plans and in their review.

In Figure 2.6 we present the 5 <P> cascading down from policy to partners. Minding the voice of the enterprise, operative management can start with the plans evolved in the Policy Dynamics in order to determine the performers needed and the processes to be employed so as to be able to deliver the products that generate customer satisfaction and revenues.

Figure 2.7 shows the 5 <P> bottom-up, from partners all the way to business plans. Operative management, which must remain very close to the day-to-day customer value delivery, may prefer to start with the relationships with customers and suppliers, then review the competitiveness of the products and work the 5 <P> bottom-up all the way to review the action plans.

We recommend that the process be run from both sides to ensure checks and balances.

2.4.3 The action plans

The complexity of the business means that there are more things to do, less time to do them, and fewer people around after waves of rightsizing. Never before has the old saying *first things first* proven so pertinent.

Experience shows that policy development is just the beginning; the critical part is deploying strategies into action plans, measuring the results, and acting swiftly on the improvements. We believe that the visual display of the progress made on the action plans helps to build alignment and accountability throughout the organization. The reviews of the operations are a powerful enabler of continuous improvements and of organizational learning. Every enterprise should develop its own set of visual displays. A very practical series of tables which is used for visual management is presented by Soin in *Total Quality Control Essentials* [24].

2.5 The Policy Assessment and Audit

We have adopted the concept of performance assessment by operative management as advocated by various models of quality management. In addition the POM features an organizational audit by senior management.

Operative management focuses on assessing the effectiveness and efficiency of the day-to-day management of the 5 <P>. The senior management focuses on auditing the value added by the enterprise by comparing the valuation of the strategic resources at the beginning and at the end of the planning period.

The executives and the board of directors are responsible for the value of the enterprise as reflected in the value of its strategic resources that we refer to as the 'performers'. We have developed an original mind-map for the performers, discussed in Chapter Five. It puts the emphasis on the intangible resources because they are often the most critical success factors in our business environment. We believe that our approach complements the financially oriented *shareholder value*.

This sub-process of the POM requires senior and operative management to start by carrying out tasks separately, and then to convene, to compare notes, and to achieve a consensus on actions for improvement concerning the approach and the deployment of the Process of Management. This is a major review that takes the management team back to basics to ensure that the enterprise is and will be doing the right thing right.

The consultative approach between senior and operative management has already been applied in the 'Two Rings' of Policy Dynamics. Therefore, by the time they get to the assessment and audit, this practice should already be fairly well tuned. Furthermore, the same evaluation criteria are used consistently through the Policy Dynamics, the Policy Implementation and Review, and the Policy Assessment and Audit.

As required by the European Quality Award (EQA), the assessment should include both leading and lagging indicators. However, rather than using the schema of the EQA, namely approach, deployment, scope, and results, we use the following evaluation criteria.

- Check of the effectiveness i.e. results vs. plans.
- Alertness to change and knowledge management.
- Planning for innovation.
- Deployment and efficiencies.

We join Tito Conti who recommends that the process of assessment start with a check of the results obtained [27]. We differ from some of the models of quality management in as far as (i) we emphasize alertness first of all because it presents opportunities for innovation and secondly because it may reveal potential dangers while it is timely to deal with them; (ii) we include innovation as a criteria for all the business enablers; (iii) each of the aforementioned performance evaluation criteria (C–A–P–D) is applied to each of the 5 <P>.

The Policy Assessment and Audit is presented in Chapter Nine. We can now discuss the five principles, which complement the POM and guide the approach concerning the management of the five business enablers.

2.6 The five principles

While tools and techniques need instructions, a comprehensive and integrative methodology such as the POM should be anchored in a few powerful principles that guide people's approach to the management of the business enablers. Eventually principles can become tutors of thought and, with senior management support and enriched by life experience, they will integrate the internal culture of the enterprise.

To facilitate retention of these principles, we use alliterations and limit their number to five. We advocate that management's approach be systemic, stimulating, simple, swift, and systematic. Let us discuss these principles. The sequence in which we consider them reflects a logical order.

2.6.1 The systemic approach

When putting together a puzzle, we start by looking at the whole picture depicted on the box. The next thing we do is to line up the pieces that form the boundaries of the picture. Colors and shapes help us to match the individual pieces so that we can put them together and complete the whole puzzle. The systemic or global approach advocated here bears some analogies with the puzzle. We start by looking at the whole picture, then by identifying the boundaries of the ecosystem. As we will see when discussing processes, staking the boundaries of a system is not so easy.

Next we will try to identify the components and the actors of the system and see how the various forces at play interact. We need to understand what drives what. Finally, we may further refine our picture by looking at the evolution of the business system.

Of course, not all forces interact with all the other forces. When they do, reinforcing loops or balancing loops are initiated. We may also experience delays. A characteristic of the dynamic complexity of our environment, is how frequently the patterns of interactions shift.

Reinforcing loops can be positive or negative, positive when they increase and negative when they decrease the outcome. A well-known example of a positive feedback loop is the one that can be triggered by management recognition, that stimulates the personnel, who in turn become more attentive to the customer. This in its turn produces higher customer satisfaction, which results in increased sales.

Balancing loops can be trickier, they just offset actions when a given limit has been reached. Budgets and business plans can act as balancing loops. In certain cases, managers may prefer not to exceed the business plan in order to avoid the objectives being even tougher for the following period, or to go out and spend all the money allowed by the budget to avoid being allocated a smaller budget in the following year.

Complex systems also feature delays that separate, in time, the effect from its cause and thereby mask the cause and effect relationship.

We can plot these causal loops, and, if we need to go into detail, we can assess whether their effects are weak, medium, or strong. If we want to make a graphic presentation of the system, we can use solid, dotted, or pointed lines to distinguish the different types of feedback loops and delays. We can also use different colors to indicate their strength, and we can use arrows to point out what drives what. In order to visualize the interplay of the different forces we can use the interrelation digraph or the nominal group technique.

The importance of the systemic or global approach cannot be stressed enough. It has become a critical factor in dealing successfully with the dynamic complexity of the global environment. Applied to all activities involving planning and review, the systemic approach prevents overlooking some critical interdependencies of the system and rashly following a strategy which has not been fully thought through. The increasing specialization in all the functions of our organization leads to tunnel vision. Highly focused personnel get trapped in the rut of their own specialized interests, thus accentuating organizational fragmentation to the point that the right hand does not know what the left hand is doing. Management should offset this by teaching profound knowledge of the whole system. Scenario planning – as described by Schwartz [28] – is one of the methods that can be used to understand the spill-over effects of actions planned by any of the players on the whole web of interdependencies.

We should start with a *systemic approach* to put things rationally into perspective. If we de-emotionalize the way we approach a problem, it becomes solvable. Furthermore, a systemic approach is a key to smart strategies. Taking into account the key elements of complex and dynamic situations avoids going into battle without being fully prepared.

2.6.2 The stimulating approach

The next principle, *stimulation*, is important to get *attention, interest, desire* to get involved, and finally *action*. This principle has been taught in marketing courses and anchored by its acronym of AIDA.

2.6.3 The simple and swift approaches

A popular saying that we have slightly modified reads 'keep it simple and swift'. Simple in order to facilitate communication and implementation; swift because the frantic rhythm imposed by global competition does not leave windows of opportunity open for long.

Einstein has been quoted as saying 'everything should be made as simple as possible, but not one bit simpler'. Management is as much of a science as it is an art. Science provides increasingly sophisticated tools to analyze complex situations, but the art is to keep it simple! In order to get a critical mass of people involved, things must be kept simple. Furthermore, as discussed in the previous chapter, it is important that simple directives and guidelines be provided and that empowered individuals or teams be given credit for intelligence, and be allowed to use it to take appropriate initiatives.

'It used to be that the large companies gobbled up the small companies. Now it is the nimble outfit that eats up the sluggish one.' This saying comes up time and time again with different wording but with the same powerful message. While the planning phase needs to be systemic, stimulating, and simple, when it comes to acting, operations must be swift. The windows of opportunity tend to close quickly and often do not re-open.

2.6.4 The systematic approach

The systematic approach ensures competitive efficiencies through the orderly management of the business enablers and their interdependencies. By consistently applying the appropriate method, consistent results should be obtained. This consistency is of comfort to the customer to whom it can mean quality assurance. It is also of comfort to the personnel because, as mentioned earlier, too much change is destabilizing. We must realize, however, that the systematic way we do things can only last as long as we do not find a better way.

2.6.5 The five principles and the five business enablers

Although the five principles are complementary, we realize that it may be too cumbersome, at least initially, to ask operative management to apply all five principles to each of the five business enablers. Therefore, as shown in Figure 2.1, we have framed each of the business enablers between two principles. We then get the following picture.

- Action plans need to be systemic and stimulating. If plans are not systemic something important may get left out. As actions are often taken by cross-functional teams, it is important that the cross-functional synergies be considered. If plans are not stimulating, the human capital – one of the strategic resources deployed by the plans – will not give its very best.

- The performers should be stimulating and simple. Human capital, one of the performers as discussed in Chapter Five, should generate creativity and their output should be simple enough for the organization to understand and to implement.

- The processes should be as simple as possible to be easy to manage. They should also be swift as pertains to time-to-market and timely delivery.

- The products go to satisfy the external customer, the one who pays. Products should be delivered swiftly because customer satisfaction does not wait. The way products are delivered should be systematically right from the first time and every time. The same procedures should be used as long as they are pertinent enough to avoid confusion.

- Last but not least, the external customer should be approached with a systemic view to ensure that all relevant requirements and needs are understood and addressed. As already mentioned above, the customer needs to be attended to in a systematic way: (i) for the sake of the customer's efficiencies; and (ii) for the sake of the customer's comfort.

2.7 Summary

Superior performances can be achieved when the organization is *doing the right thing right*.

The Policy Fundamentals and the Policy Dynamics, which are the first two of the four sub-processes of the Process of Management develop and deploy the business policy to ensure the enterprise is doing the right thing.

The next sub-process of the POM, the Policy Implementation and Review, ensures effective day-to-day management of the five business enablers.

The last of these sub-processes, the Policy Assessment and Audit, assesses the performances in the operations and audits the 'business value'.

All the components of the POM are interactive and provide a comprehensive and cohesive methodology as required to serve as support to shared management practices.

In the next chapter we will discuss the Policy Fundamentals and its building blocks.

CHAPTER THREE

The Policy Fundamentals

The Plan

The Policy Fundamentals serve as a corporate charter that provides consistency of purpose throughout the whole organization. They align all the nodes of the organization in the same direction and ensure that they travel at the same speed. To this end, they act on a combination of rational, relational, and emotional drivers of thought, of behavior, and of action. As they establish a basis for the development and deployment of strategies, the Policy Fundamentals set the *strategic profile* of the enterprise and influence its competitive maneuverability.

The Policy Fundamentals features five interactive building blocks, namely: the mission; the strategic thrust; the strategic ambitions; the resource allocation and empowerment process and the review-evaluation and reward process; and – last but not least – the leadership.

The Mind-Maps

- Mission, values, and strategic biases.
- Strategic thrust, value chain, competencies and capabilities.
- Strategic ambitions, strategic goals, road map.
- Resource allocation and empowerment, review–evaluation–recognition
- Leadership.

Introduction

Since times immemorial, battles have been won or lost depending on the strategy used. Of course the number of soldiers, their training and equipment, the leadership of the officers, are all important factors. But if the strategy is not right, it is all to no avail. Strategy is the approach that sets objectives and priorities, that deploys the resources, and that organizes all the activities. It features reconnoitering and gathering competitive intelligence, scenario and action planning, reviewing and taking corrective action.

In the 1970s management started looking at military strategy for inspiration in order to win the fierce battles fought in the marketplace. More recently globalization has accelerated the shifts in the business environment and, as a result, it has accentuated the importance of smart strategies and of participative planning. However, as applied to business, strategy is a relatively new and evolving discipline. Understandably, some confusion still clouds the subject. Let us therefore start by clarifying the concepts and the terminology we use.

The word 'strategy' is often used to define two different activities, namely *what* the organization should achieve and *how* it should achieve it. There can also be some confusion between the planning done by senior management and the straightforward action plans developed by the operations. We will use the term 'business policy' – *policy* for short – for the big picture as covered by the sub-processes of the POM. We will use the term 'strategies' for action triggers.

3.1 Doing the right thing right

Peter Drucker [30] was among the first authors who emphasized that senior management's first and foremost task is to set the business policy, and to guide the organization towards *doing the right thing*. Doing the right thing means that the organization is doing whatever best serves its interests in the short term as well as in the long term.

As a second priority, it should then ensure that the organization is *doing the thing right*. This means that it is supplying a competitive product, and with a competitive profit margin. However, doing the thing right will ultimately not translate into the right financial results unless it is the right thing to do.

When the market situation changes, the organization may be still doing the thing right, but it may no longer be doing the right thing. This fundamental principle of business is sometimes neglected as enterprises pay more attention to their products and their internal activities than to customers' needs and to the movements of the market. Furthermore, as we have already pointed out, the globalizing environment imposes such a frenzied rhythm of change, that the enterprise that is not doing the right thing may neither have the time nor the means to redirect its efforts.

We can illustrate Drucker's concept of *doing the right thing right* by expanding as follows on the four scenarios already shown in Figure 2.2.

1. If the enterprise does the right thing and does it right it will be *successful*.
2. If it does the right thing but does not do it well enough, the enterprise is *vulnerable* and it will need to improve substantially the quality of its deliverables, in other words the value the customer recognizes. In order to do the thing right, it will have to improve the capabilities of the processes as well as the competencies and the behavior of its personnel.
3. If the enterprise is not doing the right thing, even if it does it very well, it is in real *danger*. It will either have to use its competencies and capabilities in another field, or it will have to develop new competencies and capabilities to innovate its present field of activities. In either case it will have to reinvent its business. This may prove very difficult to achieve, or at least it may be hard to achieve a breakthrough fast enough to avoid being overtaken by the competition. Even giants implode if they are not doing the right thing, or if they cannot adapt in time to a changing market environment.
4. If the enterprise is doing the wrong thing and not doing it very well either, it will be lucky to find a buyer or it will have to *liquidate*.

Doing the right thing right is easier in theory than it is in practice. Some of the management principles that we proposed in the previous chapter as a guide to the management of the business enablers, can also assist senior management as it designs the Policy Fundamentals.

Their approach must be *systemic* in that it must take into account all the relevant pieces of the puzzle and all the different parties. It must be *stimulating* because in order to do the right thing right the organization needs the commitment, cooperation, and creativity of all those who can contribute to the success of the enterprise. Of course, business policy, although not simple to develop, should be simple to understand. Tactics may take the form of a swift response in the marketplace, but policy requires time for development, time for deployment, and time for review: time which senior management must be prepared to invest.

Setting business policy is a complex intellectual and social process. It is an intellectual process that seeks to broaden perceptions and to reframe perspectives. It is a social process that should inspire those taking part and focus them on corporate goals. Policy is not about predicting the future, but about shaping it. *Purposefulness*, *pragmatism* and *perseverance* are the pillars of business policy. By increasing the effectiveness and the efficiencies of the whole process, most organizations should be able to emulate the best-in-class where senior management typically invests in excess of 20 percent of its time on business policy, vs. an average of 3 percent as reported in the previous chapter.

So important is business policy that we distinguish between the Policy Fundamentals, which provide identity and stability to the organization, and the Policy Dynamics, which convert business policy into strategies and steer the actions effectively in the face of emerging opportunities and threats.

In large and diversified corporations, the corporate management sets the Policy Fundamentals and passes them on to the senior management of its strategic business units (SBU). In turn, the senior management of the SBU details the corporate policies as appropriate. Hereafter we place ourselves at the level of the SBU.

3.2 The five building blocks of the Policy Fundamentals

Policy can be airy and all together pretty useless unless it is based on a deep understanding of the spirit and of the ambitions of the enterprise. The English statesman Benjamin Disraeli reportedly stated that 'the secret of success is consistency of purpose'. In order to provide clarity and consistency of purpose, in order to direct all the enterprise's combined energies in the same direction, senior management should lay down the Policy Fundamentals.

Senior management is the architect and the guardian of the Policy Fundamentals, which determine where the organization is going, why it is a desirable destination, what the organization should look like, what it should feel like. These strategic directives and behavioral guidelines also afford an opportunity for introspection and periodic review. They are the basis of business policy and seldom change. We cannot stress enough the importance of the Policy Fundamentals: they help maintain the general course.

The Policy Fundamentals should provide a set of business concepts that people can rally around and relate to. They should provide a frame of reference that is widely shared inside the organization. This is particularly important as things around us change so fast. People need something to hold on to, they need some continuity amid change. Changes in the internal environment can be destabilizing and wield a strong emotional impact. This is why Alfred North Whitehead is quoted as saying 'the art of progress is to preserve order amid change and to preserve change amid order'.

Senior management sets Policy Fundamentals by defining, communicating, and reinforcing five groups of business concepts. As shown in Figure 3.1, these business concepts form a logical sequence and complement and reinforce each other. Let us now review the five interactive building blocks that make up the Policy Fundamentals, namely the mission, the strategic thrust, the strategic ambitions, the resource–allocation–empowerment and the review–evaluation–recognition processes, and the leadership.

FIGURE 3.1 The Policy Fundamentals

```
┌─────────────────┐                    ┌─────────────────────┐
│     Mission     │                    │  Strategic Thrust   │
│     Values      │    ⟵⟶              │    Value chain      │
│     Biases      │                    │  Competencies and   │
│                 │                    │    Capabilities     │
└─────────────────┘                    └─────────────────────┘
           ↕            ↘    ↙            ↕
                      ⟨ LEADERSHIP ⟩
           ↕            ↗    ↖            ↕
┌─────────────────┐                    ┌─────────────────────┐
│ Resource Allocation                  │ Strategic Ambitions │
│ and Empowerment │    ⟵⟶              │  Strategic Goals    │
│ Review Evaluation                    │     Road Map        │
│ and Recognition │                    │                     │
└─────────────────┘                    └─────────────────────┘
```

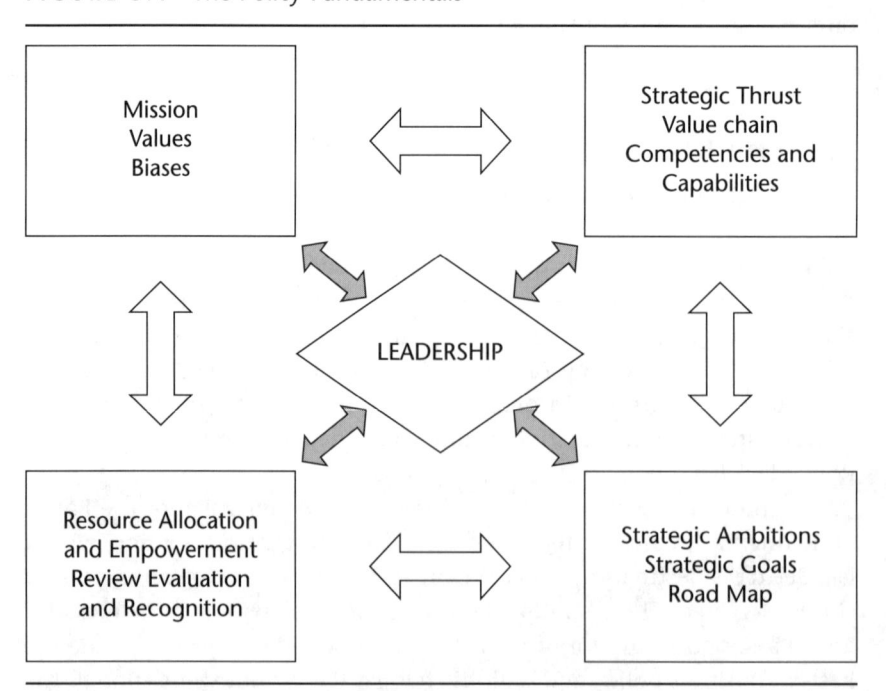

3.3 The mission

3.3.1 The mission statement

In order to clarify and to communicate 'what's my line', 'what is my claim to fame', in order to define the mission of the enterprise, management should organize sessions of introspection. Various groups, at different levels of management and representing the different aspects of the business should answer questions such as the following:

- what is it that we really like to do, what should be our unique value proposition (UVP)?
- who do we really like to do it for, how would we like them to perceive our UVP?
- how do we really like to do it; how should our UVP be measured?
- with whom do we really like to do it, what should be the profile of our personnel, of our suppliers, of our strategic allies?
- what and how much do we want to get out of it, how should the results be measured?

We use the word 'like' to bring out the emotional content which underpins the commitment to the mission. It should almost be unnecessary to emphasize that individuals and groups are at their best when they do what they like and when they like what they do.

As suggested by Kepner and Tregoe [44], for additional clarity, the above-mentioned questions can also be put in the negative. For example we can ask what it is that we really do not like to do, which customers we really are unable to serve competitively. Other questions can be added like where or when do we really feel uncomfortable about doing certain things. We can also ask who we want to compete against, and who we would rather not tackle.

'What' and 'for whom' help us review our marketing positioning. 'What' and 'how' should help us understand the competencies and the capabilities we consider critical. 'With whom' and 'how much' may provide clues on organizational needs. 'How would we like them to perceive our UVP' calls into question the performance measurement system. 'Who should benefit from it' leads us to ponder over a balanced level of satisfaction for the major stakeholders as already discussed in Chapter Two.

The mission statement should be like the fairway on a golf course, wide enough for the good players to choose their placement, with roughs to catch the wayward shots. But, most importantly, clear out-of-bound signs should be posted for the 'no-go' areas in order to avoid serious potential problems. The shifts in the marketplace have thrown into relief the importance of the mission statement. Periodic reviews should be careful to take into account new opportunities and new threats. Many a company has missed major opportunities; some have dropped out of the competitive race by defining too narrowly the line of business or by not adapting it to shifts in the marketplace. Other companies have drawn up a fuzzy mission statement which has allowed them to drift away from their core business.

We believe that simple slogans like 'we want to be the first and the best' are inefficient generalities. The former war-chants of some Japanese corporations, for example Komatsu's 'encircle CAT' or Canon's 'beat Xerox', narrowly focus the firm's attention on one competitor or on one situation. Such mottoes stress a particular policy, but this is not what Policy Fundamentals are all about. Rather than generalities and slogans, deep introspection is required to achieve a shared mission statement.

3.3.2 The corporate values and the code of conduct

Corporate values, or simply values, state what senior management considers important and valuable for the organization. While the mission statement communicates the purpose and the positioning of the enterprise, the value statement should elicit desired behavior by implanting behavioral principles and paradigms. The link between the line of business, the values and the line of conduct is illustrated in the following value statements.

As examples of short value statements with great impact we can mention Honda's 'First Man then Machine' and FedEx's 'People, Service, Profits'. Another good example is Sear's requiring that 'the company be considered a compelling place to shop, a compelling place to work, a compelling place to invest'. Sir Iain Valence, chairman of BT, laid down corporate values in the following: 'We put our customers first, we are professionals, we respect each other, we work as one team, we are committed to continuous improvement'. Statements such as these can be translated into guidelines and supported by management setting a good example.

The combination of mission and value statements and their frequent reinforcement during formal and informal sessions and enable senior management to influence the internal culture of the enterprise.

Consistent with the values, senior management may set out certain rules and procedures, which personnel are expected to follow. The ensuing code of conduct and constraints should also ensure that the enterprise follows applicable national and international guidelines and standards concerning business conduct and business ethics such as those mentioned in the Caux Round Table [45]. The term 'policy' is frequently used in the narrower context of rules concerning organizational conduct.

3.3.3 The strategic biases

On the subject of business policy, management has to deal with many unknowns, and with a variety of inputs and influences. Inputs such as information, intelligence, insights, and intuition are processed with the imagination and the judgment of individuals or of groups. Of course, rarely does management dispose of all the inputs, or only of accurate and timely inputs. *Supposedly, the art of management lies in an ability to make complete sense of limited information, rather than limited sense of complete information.*

The strategic decision-making process can be biased by senior management's view of the relevant business environment, in other words by its paradigms. Provincialism, paternalism and prejudice prevent us from getting to the bottom of situations and of sensitivities.

There are four circles of influences that can shape senior management's paradigms. In the first circle we can observe the interactions among the members of the strategic decision-making unit (DMU). Senior managers' personality and ambitions, their backgrounds, their personal relations – including relations with other members of the strategic DMU – drive these influences. In the second circle we find the internal culture of the organization – often referred to as the corporate culture – which is shaped by the beliefs and by the collective memory of past successes and of past failures. In the third circle there are influences from the culture of the sector and in the fourth circle the culture of the region, both of which infiltrate the organization.

Some of these influences insidiously introduce what we call strategic biases, which may act as filters for opportunities or as a free pass for threats. Strategic biases can distort or block certain inputs, they can alter the importance attached to threats as well as to opportunities. The results can be productive or counterproductive. Visionary and powerful leaders have built business empires by imposing their revolutionary views. Conservative committees have remained neutral observers of the decline and demise of their corporation.

It is hard, not to say impossible, to avoid certain strategic biases. They are like weeds, cut them and they will grow again. What matters is that senior management be aware of its biases as well as of their potential effects on the situation being considered. For this purpose, managers should periodically review the Policy Fundamentals as part of the Policy Assessment and Audit (Chapter Nine). Revisiting past experiences and the related critical success and failure factors enables the management teams to gain a better understanding of the effectiveness of their strategic decision-making process.

Introspection will bring out the strategic biases, and can contribute to improving the decision-making process. We can quote the saying: 'Before you listen to others, listen to yourself. If you do not understand the inner you, you will not be able to relate to what others will tell you'.

An independent consultant should facilitate sessions of introspection because *often the shortest way from you to the inner you, passes through someone else*. In order to uncover senior management's strategic biases, the facilitator should seek to find out the rational, relational, and emotional content of the inputs made by each of the executives participating in a workshop on Policy Fundamentals.

Sessions of introspection should be facilitated at all the different levels of management. Comparison between the outcomes of these workshops should indicate to what extent mission, values, and views are understood and shared throughout the organization. These findings should then be summarized and addressed by senior management in order to improve the strategic decision-making process and its influence at the different levels of management.

Senior management should also periodically revisit the distance between its views concerning the business policy and the internal and external cultures of the enterprise. Chandler points out that, if the distance between business policy and corporate culture becomes too great, the strategic plans will probably fall into a crevice [46]. This is confirmed by an unpublished study undertaken at the Harvard Business School that shows that companies often fail to achieve their objectives because the projects they undertake are not supported by the organizational culture [47]. In Chapter Five we will discuss the kind of culture that supports the management system we advocate.

3.4 The strategic thrust

3.4.1 The strategic thrust

The mission provides a broad outline of the identity and the purpose of the enterprise. The strategic thrust, which is the second building block of the Policy Fundamentals, focuses management's attention on a particular area where it wants to excel. This is where it wants to concentrate its resources so as to develop the superior competencies and capabilities that will sustain a competitive advantage.

Original work on the concept we define as strategic thrust was done by Tregoe and Zimmerman [48] who presented what they called 'the ten driving forces'. We prefer to speak of 'strategic thrust' to avoid confusion with other drivers. As shown in Figure 3.2, we present the strategic thrust in four groups, each encompassing two closely related factors.

The strategic thrust is sometimes reflected in positioning statements. Corning Glass Works' 'Excellence through glass technology' of the

FIGURE 3.2 The strategic thrust, the market lifecycle, and the macro- and mega-trends

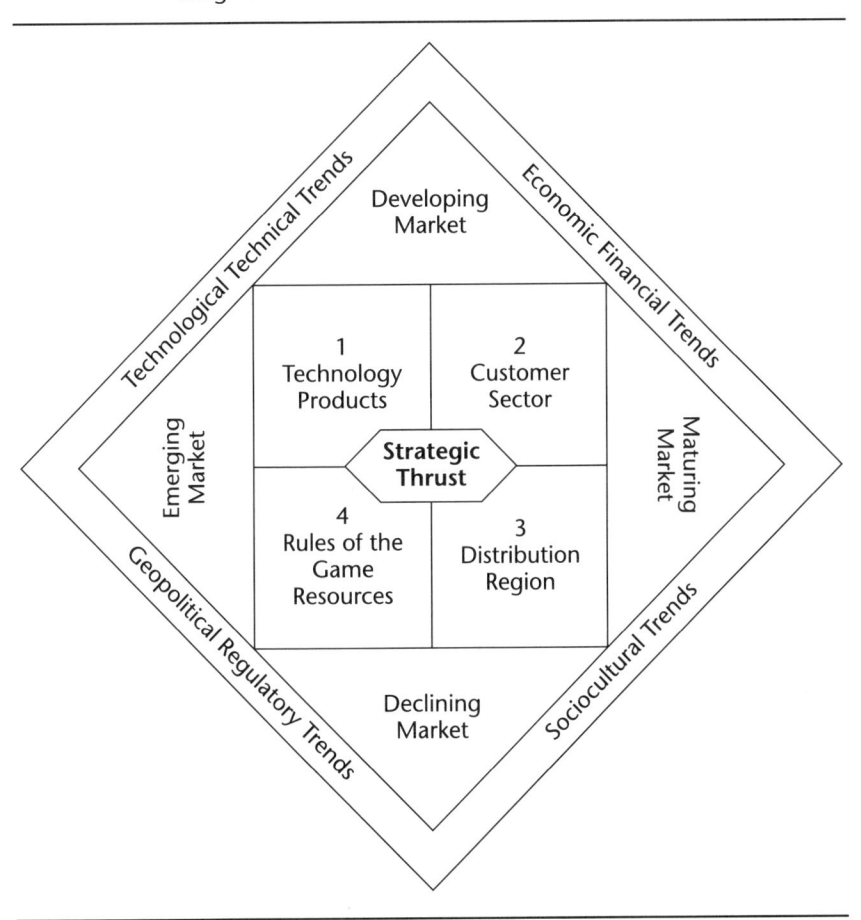

1970s clearly indicated that the company relied on its glass technology to sustain success. Coca-Cola's statement 'Put a bottle of Coke in the reach of every consumer' was a clear indication that distribution, promotion, and regional expertise were its strategic thrust.

Of course, no organization can operate exclusively on one strategic thrust, nor can it be efficient if it spreads its resources thinly across too many strategic thrusts. A combination of one dominant and one complementary strategic thrust is therefore the most practical approach. Often the combination of strategic thrust is the key to achieving competitive superiority. Senior management must identify and communicate the strategic thrust or, as appropriate, the combination of strategic thrusts, that underpins its Policy Fundamentals in order to mobilize all the organization's relevant energies on doing the right thing.

3.4.2 The strategic implications of the strategic thrust

Strategic thrust, the value chain and the critical competencies are closely intertwined. The strategic thrust has a strong influence on the competencies that will be developed and therefore on the links of the value chain where competitive advantages will be sought. Often the selection of the strategic thrust is not the result of a deliberate decision, but rather the fact that *success breeds success* and that management tends to continue to invest future funds on past successes.

Research conducted by Tregoe and Zimmerman [48] and more recently by Galbraith and Kazanjian[49] and by Robert [50], shows that frequently senior management is not sufficiently aware of the strategic thrust adopted and of its effects on the business potential of the enterprise. As a result, the resource allocation remains fuzzy. When the competitive dynamics change, the organization may work even harder on implementing a strategic thrust that is no longer effective. Managers are blinded by the successes of the past and this has led to the now well-known saying *nothing fails like success*.

The strategic thrust can be viewed in connection with the market lifecycles as follows:

- *emerging market* – the strategic thrust is based on technology and new products;
- *developing market* – the strategic thrust is based on customer and sector oriented marketing;

- *maturing market* – the strategic thrust is based on distribution and promotion as well as regional specialization;
- *declining market* – the strategic thrust is based on changing the rules of the game, and on the finance to divest or to strengthen the position through acquisitions.

Of course this is only a schematic view. Markets are emerging because of a new need and, in our supply-side driven economy, new needs are often driven by technologies and the new products that can be offered. Developing markets become very competitive, and the suppliers must get very close to the key customers to provide a customized product and a better service. Maturing markets push suppliers to look for new frontiers, new niches. Declining markets offer reduced volume at reduced margins but they may force the way to renewal and revival. Changing the rules of the game, or a restructuring of the industry are more radical means to modify the economics of a declining market. Occasionally they may even convert a declining market into an emerging market.

In Figure 3.2 we have placed each of the four strategic thrusts between two market lifecycles because every lifecycle harbors the genes of a new cycle, and the strategic thrust and related competencies enable that transition. For example an emerging market may launch the investments in technology and in products that will eventually engender a new market lifecycle, namely a developing market.

It is interesting to note that, as the market lifecycle progresses, the critical competencies change from essentially technical ones to support the product and technology strategic thrust to people-related competencies to support a customer and sector thrust; then to critical contacts and strategic partnering to support distribution channels and regional thrust; and finally to financial means to fund a rules-of-the-game and resources thrust. Understanding the current and the next phase in the market lifecycle and the required critical success factors should enable senior management to make timely preparations for a smooth transition.

Each combination of market lifecycle and of the strategic thrust has a particular risk–reward ratio depending on the sustainable competitive advantage the enterprise can develop. Technology and rules-of-the-game thrusts should afford the greatest competitive advantage because they are the most difficult for competitors to duplicate. A new technology can lead to a proprietary standard, innovative rules-of-the-game may lead to a new form of distribution. In both cases competitors will need time and money to circumvent patents or to duplicate novel ways of doing business.

Therefore the first entrant should enjoy, for a period of time, 'the control of the sandbox' and can even attempt to blanket the market.

Among the external influences, the megatrends and the macrotrends occasionally impose major changes. The *megatrends* affect all parts of the economy and society, while the *macrotrends* affect a particular sector or a combination of interconnected sectors. Megatrends, as shown in Figure 3.2, are likely to cause a major reconfiguration of the value-chain. As a result, they require a considerable amount of rethinking and may compel senior management to change the strategic thrust as well as the composition of critical competencies and core capabilities.

The strategic thrust, and the configuration of competencies and capabilities it engenders, underpin the *competitive maneuverability*, in other words the extent and the speed at which an organization is able to adapt or to change the strategies it is capable of implementing. This is an interesting concept developed by Lele [51], that we apply to the strategic thrust.

First, each strategic thrust entails a particular configuration of critical competencies and core capabilities, which cannot be changed overnight. Secondly, a change in strategic thrust may modify the risk–reward ratio targeted by senior management. Finally, and more importantly, a strategic thrust that has succeeded in the past permeates quite deeply into the internal culture of the organization. The deeper the identification of an enterprise with a given strategic thrust, the more lengthy and laborious the changeover will be from a particular strategic thrust to another. A departure from an established strategic thrust entails a change of competencies and capabilities that most likely will involve restructuring and may meet with substantial resistance within the organization. Furthermore, the image the enterprise has built on the market is strongly tainted by its strategic thrust and a change of image is not necessarily readily accepted by the customer.

3.4.3 The value-chain

Increasingly enterprises revert to Porter's model of the value-chain and focus on excelling on certain links rather than trying to cover the whole chain from end to end [52]. The present and the potential value of the various links of the value-chain should be assessed. Shifts in the marketplace can modify the value added by the various links of the value-chain, they can even modify the configuration of the value-chain. Competitive forces may change the level of critical competencies and core capabilities required as well as their profitability.

Non-core activities can be outsourced to critical suppliers or to strategic partners. The identification of the strategic thrust and of the related configuration of critical competencies and core capabilities helps determine which part of the value-chain the enterprise should concentrate on as well as the customer value delivery.

3.4.4 Critical competencies and core capabilities

Critical competencies are shared skills and know-how that are built up over time to provide a competitive edge over a broad range of value-adding activities. Authors like Hamel and Prahalad [53] and Campbell and Sommers-Luchs [54] brought this concept to management's attention. Critical competencies are the ability and the readiness to put to good use the available skills and know-how in order to maximize the medium- to long-term value of the enterprise's deliverables. A combination of complementary competencies is often necessary to ensure a particularly strong position in the marketplace. Occasionally different critical competencies can block each other as they pull in different directions.

As critical competencies are essentially intangible assets they can be difficult to identify, let alone to evaluate. The following steps may help to identify existing critical competencies:

- an analysis of the success history of the enterprise and, more broadly, of its industrial sector;

- an analysis of the particular links of the value-chain where the most significant developments have been made and that are getting management's attention;

- an analysis of the factors that have sustained the competitiveness of particular links of the value-chain and in particular functions of the enterprise.

Core capabilities are essentially tangible assets that are deployed by the critical competencies to enable the enterprise to deliver value.

Competencies and capabilities are complementary. For example, a critical competency is the knowledge of how to operate a hub-and-spoke type of distribution, the related core capability is the whole infrastructure necessary to operate such a system. If an enterprise only disposes of one of the above-mentioned components, it will have to find a complementary partner. Whether in-house or outsourced, critical competencies and core capabilities must be aligned. Their configuration and potential must adequately support the strategic thrust and the strategic ambitions.

Each strategic thrust requires a synergetic combination of competencies and capabilities to be effective and efficient. As mentioned earlier, no enterprise can afford to dilute its energies on a wide array of competencies or capabilities. This explains the clear trend towards focusing on the core business, and towards outsourcing all peripheral activities.

3.5 The strategic ambitions

3.5.1 The statement of strategic ambitions

Based on the mission and on the strategic thrust, senior management should state the *strategic ambitions* of the enterprise, in other words the desired position the enterprise should achieve by a defined time-horizon, say three to nine years into the future. Of course, the time-horizon or planning period depends on a combination of: (i) the average product lifecycle; (ii) risk-reward ratio; and (iii) the internal culture of the enterprise. Some Japanese corporations used to span 25 years with their strategic plans. Now high-tech companies are happy if they can plan three years ahead.

We prefer using the term 'strategic ambitions' to 'vision' – although the latter is commonly used in the literature and by consultants like Orion International [55]. A vision can be associated with a dream, with something lofty: Martin Luther King had a vision when on August 27, 1963 he declared 'I have a dream . . .' but John F. Kennedy had a strategic ambition when on May 25, 1961 he stated the USA would put a man on the moon within 10 years, and undertook to make it happen.

Visionary managers can be a great asset to the enterprise, however, their individual vision needs to be shared so that it becomes the strategic ambition of the whole organization. Allowing individual visions to ferment in the hotpot of group discussions should provide for a good balance between rational, emotional/creative, and relational drivers. Only if there is such a balance will the strategic ambitions be understood, shared, and committed to.

We have broken down the strategic decision-making process into the following three interactive levels.

1 The *strategic ambitions* translate the mission and the strategic thrust into a desirable state the enterprise should reach at the end of the planning period. They are descriptive and should elicit the ambitious thinking that serves as a basis for the development of strategic goals.

2   The *strategic goals* are quantitative and prescriptive of the level of performance to be attained by the various parts of the organization by the end of each year of the planning period. The road map provides an indication as to the orders of magnitude of achievements at critical junctures over the planning period. As documented by studies presented in *Profit Impact from Marketing Strategies* [56], strategic goals should be focused on the value-added perceived by the customer since this has been found to correlate more significantly than any other factor to the profit margin of private enterprise. They should clearly indicate where the enterprise is going and where the other players are going. The Policy Fundamentals pass on the strategic goals to the next sub-process of the POM, namely the Policy Dynamics.

3   Based on the strategic goals, strategic means to reach these goals are developed in the frame of the Policy Dynamics. The agreed upon strategic means feature the *strategic objectives*, with the pertinent indicators or performance measuring system and the targets to be reached.

Of course, smaller organizations may not need this level of detail, and may interrupt the strategic thinking process to go directly from the strategic ambitions to the strategic objectives.

Breaking down the strategic decision-making process into these three levels, allows us to start with a small, high level group that takes a broad view, looks out at the time-horizon, and focuses on opportunities rather than constraints. Then, step by step, the strategic decision-making process involves more and more people, brings in lower levels of management, and becomes more specific and more detailed until the time-horizon shortens to the next year.

The development of business policy is a long process that should provide a broad scope for strategic thinking. Its premature interruption can drain much of the value-added. We therefore advocate that the strategic ambitions be qualitative and descriptive of the performances to be achieved in terms of size, competitive ranking, and profitability within the targeted sector(s).

The SWOT or strengths–weaknesses–opportunities–threats model is often used. It pegs the organization's strengths against envisioned opportunities. However, it may reduce the strategic ambitions to the existing strengths and to the well-known opportunities. The strategic ambitions should take into account the optimal level of satisfaction that senior management wants to offer to the major stakeholders (see Chapter Two). It should be ambitious, and motivate by generating sufficient confidence. We start with a broad view, looking out in time at opportunities rather than constraints. The dilemma facing management is how to take a fresh and original look at the unknown.

Several techniques help take a broad and bold look at the strategic ambitions. They do not preclude *looking at the future through the rear-view mirror*, but at least they get all the members of the strategic decision-making unit (DMU) involved. For small organizations a structured brainstorming session using the affinity diagram and interrelation diagraph can prove adequate. For larger organizations we advocate using the Delphi technique as described by Wheelen Hunger [23].

The Delphi technique can be applied in the following manner.

- Each of the members of the strategic DMU puts in writing his/her views on the three to five strategic ambitions the enterprise should pursue within their respective time-horizon. The choice of the strategic ambitions should be justified and supported with intelligence as appropriate. At this stage, members should feel free to break away from the mission and the strategic thrust that have been used thus far. They should be encouraged to be innovative, provocative if necessary. These views are then circulated in writing to all the other members of the group.

- Each member takes the time to thoroughly review the inputs received from the other members of the group, and should circulate in writing to all other participants his/her comments on all the inputs received. This helps to prepare for the ensuing meeting.

- When the group convenes to discuss the various components of the strategic ambitions, the cross-fertilization of ideas may uncover strategic biases, contribute new views, and it should evolve meaningful and rich conclusions.

The Delphi technique has some advantages over conventional brainstorming methods.

- It gives the executives a format for a fact-based approach and the time for consideration.

- It generates detailed documentation, which can be useful to gain a better understanding of the various positions taken and eventually to review in detail the decision-making process. Since planning mistakes only show up a long time after they have been made, the documentation produced by the Delphi technique enables learning from hindsight.

- The Delphi technique emphasizes creativity and innovation.

Several *creativity hints* can be used within the framework of the Delphi technique for a creative approach to the strategic ambitions, namely:

- the '5 why technique' attributed to the Japanese quality guru Noriaki Kano who used to ask five times why things are being done the way they are when conducting management audits;
- the 'what if technique' asks what the positive and the negative consequences could be if certain parts of the present system or structure were removed or modified. It is reminiscent of the concept of 'zero budgeting' introduced by Texas Instruments, whereby every year every part of the organizational construct is questioned and must justify its existence;
- 'go to' asks participants to look for related as well as unrelated success stories to find inspiration; internal and external benchmarking fit this concept;
- 'no limits' asks participants to develop strategic ambitions without concern for the availability of the necessary resources or for the limits currently imposed by the current business environment;
- 'pride' in achievements is a powerful stimulator. Participants are asked to imagine what achievements at a given time-horizon would make the live forces of the organization, including its partners, particularly proud of being associated with the enterprise.

These hints can be combined or used in sequence. Senior management should ensure the top-down communication of the strategic ambitions.

3.5.2 The strategic goals and the road map

The strategic goals prescribe what the organization should deliver and who is responsible for doing so.

In order to anchor the strategic goals to a time frame, senior management can outline the major phases leading to attaining the strategic goals. Showing the milestones on the road to the desired future state provide a *sense of urgency* without which the Policy Fundamentals tend to lose their impetus. The road map is a useful communication tool that enables senior management to assist operative management to translate the strategic goals into action plans.

The Delphi technique can be extended from strategic ambitions to cover the strategic goals and their road map. The affinity diagram, the interrelationship diagraph, and the decision matrices are among the tools that can be used to consolidate the various inputs made by senior managers into a workable few.

3.6 The resource allocation and empowerment process (RAE) and the review, evaluation, and recognition process (RER)

The resource allocation and empowerment process or RAE enables the deployment of material and organizational means in order to achieve the strategic goals. The Policy Fundamentals only provide guidance on how, under normal circumstances, the RAE should be managed. It may also indicate how to determine the roles and responsibilities of individuals or groups and how resources should be allocated. Unavoidably, various units and functions will try to pull resources towards their area, so the RAE should set some rules on how the budget-bashing game should be played, and how internal conflicts should be avoided or settled.

The RER is probably the strongest single motivator or, if poorly designed, a diabolical demotivator. You get what you measure is a partial truism. What you really get depends on what you do with those measures. *Eventually you only get what you reward.* This is why the review system and the ensuing recognition system are of capital importance.

Personnel do not operate according to what management says, but according to what personnel believe that management recognizes and rewards. These beliefs, which Peter Scott-Morgan [9] refers to as the 'unwritten rules', stem from the experience that personnel have had as a result of the past implementation of RER. Therefore the 'unwritten rules' are completely logical, albeit not necessarily obvious to management.

The resource allocation and empowerment process (RAE) and the review, evaluation, and recognition systems (RER) are among the most powerful such signals senior management can give on its leadership style. Because they are so powerful, these managerial levers must be handled with great care. They are like a double-edged sword that cuts both ways. Therefore, the Policy Fundamentals must ensure consistency with the other directives and guidelines so as to avoid misunderstandings and conflicts. By entering RAE and RER in the Policy Fundamentals, they become anchored in the organizational charter. They are applicable throughout all the business units of the enterprise, so that they cannot be tampered with by occasional whims. If different RAE and RER need to be applied to a new venture, it is preferable that it be set up as a separate entity until such a time as it can integrate the rest of the organization.

Companies that have launched long-term programs while perceived to reward short-term results have failed. It may take one downsizing to change the unwritten rules that drive the behavior of the personnel. Scott-Morgan led an A. D. Little survey according to which 75 percent of the initiatives to modify the organizational behavior without commensurate support of the RER have failed. He submits that the key factors influencing personnel behavior are:

- carrot and stick, i.e. what is perceived as a reward or a penalty;
- which people have the power to directly enable the personnel to get what is important to them, namely rewards and recognition;
- what triggers the people who have the power to give out rewards or penalties.

RAE and RER should distinguish between business breakthrough and continuous business improvement because, as we will see in the next chapter, they have different priorities. Special longer term projects may require special RAE and RER and need to be given some time to prove or disprove themselves.

The Policy Fundamentals only set the framework of RAE and RER. Their implementation takes place in the Policy Dynamics, which is the next sub-process of the POM.

3.7 The leadership network

A French politician cried out 'how can I lead my people if I do not know where they are going'! As a definition by the negative, this is probably as good as any. If there are no followers it is because there are no leaders. Leadership is felt but it is difficult to describe and impossible to command. And yet, it is a most powerful force field that makes many people and even masses of people move at a particular pace in a particular direction.

Leadership is not a position, it is a role and a process. Leadership establishes and maintains the cultural force-field that translates all the other building blocks of the Policy Fundamentals into reality. Thereby it strongly influences the *corporate culture*, which is the result of the interaction between the internal culture, the relevant culture of the sector, and the relevant culture of the region. However, leadership must also take the corporate culture into account to be credible and effective as it leverages a combination of rational, relational, and emotional drivers of people's behavior to obtain the desired results.

If there was one good formula for leadership style by now it would be known and people would stop buying books on the subject. We can venture to say that the effectiveness of leadership depends on several factors, including the following.

- The interaction of leadership with the other four building blocks of the Policy Fundamentals.

- The alignment of leadership with the competitive situation of the enterprise.

- The interaction of leadership with the internal culture of the organization.

- The interaction of leadership with the relevant culture of the sector.

- The interaction of leadership with the relevant regional culture(s).

- The strength and cohesion of the leadership network.

Returning to the second of the above listed points, we would like to add that leadership influences and is influenced by the position of the enterprise. A healthy and prosperous organization can be led with corporate guidelines and encouragement. An organization that faces tough challenges will need leadership by coaching and facilitation. An enterprise that is embattled and drowning will need an authoritative leadership because the personnel are too shaky to take initiatives and want to be held by the hand.

The last of the above mentioned points should allow us to dissipate some confusion. Sometimes people talk about the leader. One person may serve as a figurehead but no one person, however powerful he or she might be, can move more than a handful of people. It has been observed that a strong individual with a team of between five and seven totally dedicated top managers can complete the turnaround of an enterprise and change the internal culture in five to seven years. To do that, the top team will have to build a network of leaders which will eventually cover all units and all levels.

The leadership network has been referred to as a spiders-web. The big spider sits in the middle of the web. At all the nodes of the next rings of the spider-web, there are little spiders that support and implement the directives and guidelines of the big spider.

The Communist Party in the former Soviet Union is a powerful example of how such networks are organized. The Soviet leadership had placed its peons, sometimes under cover, in all possible places. If their network failed in Eastern Europe it was partly due to the fact that the goals of that top team were self-serving and that their system was used to harass and to command people rather than to encourage them.

It is most indicative that the models of the European Quality Award and of the Malcolm Baldrige National Quality Award start with 'leadership'. We have preferred to place leadership in the center of the mindmap shown in Figure 3.1, to emphasize the fact that leadership enables and is enabled by the other building blocks of the Policy Fundamentals.

3.8 The strategic profile

The five building blocks of the Policy Fundamentals work in concert. The effectiveness of their interactions provides a number of indicators on the strategic maneuverability of the organization including the following:

- the alignment between mission and strategic thrust;
- the alignment between strategic thrust, the value chain, the competencies and the capabilities;
- the alignment of the strategic thrust with the strategic goals;
- the alignment of the strategic goals with the RAE and RER;
- the interaction between the leadership network and the other four building blocks of the Policy Fundamentals.

The configuration of the five building blocks of the Policy Fundamentals and the effectiveness of their interactions sketch what we call the *strategic profile* of the enterprise. As we pointed out earlier, given the fact that the building blocks of the Policy Fundamentals cannot be changed very rapidly, the strategic maneuverability of an enterprise is also a given. Lele [51] and Robert [50] suggest that every organization is limited in its movements, and that if these limitations were properly analyzed, more effective competitive strategies could be evolved. While we agree with this in principle, however, we find that the basis used by the aforementioned authors is too narrow. For example Robert only takes into account Tregoes and Zimmerman's 'ten driving forces' [48]. Neither Robert nor Lele consider the interactions between the building blocks of the Policy Fundamentals.

How companies apply the factors encompassed in these five building blocks can be observed over a period of several years. Their impact on the organization's history of success or failure can be particularly revealing. Nonetheless, their analysis is not easy, nor is it easy to draw conclusions on the appropriate competitive strategies.

We recommend that senior management periodically audits the effectiveness of the Policy Fundamentals of its organization. This can best be done in the frame of a workshop that is facilitated by an independent consultant. Changing elements of Policy Fundamentals is like major surgery – delicate and risky. Should such changes become necessary, it behoves management to allow sufficient time for preparation and implementation so that the organization does not end up in the emergency ward.

3.9 Summary

The Policy Fundamentals can be considered as the charter of the enterprise. They lay down the strategic and behavioral orientations by stating the mission, the strategic thrust, the strategic goals, the resource–allocation–empowerment as well as the review–evaluation–reward processes.

The leadership should be inspired by the Policy Fundamentals and its network should establish the cultural force-field that translates these business concepts into a reality that people perceive, understand, and commit to.

The five building blocks of the Policy Fundamentals are interactive, some like the mission and the review–evaluation–reward system are essentially rational drivers, others, such as the strategic thrust and the strategic ambitions, are essentially emotional/creative drivers, and leadership links them together by acting on relational drivers.

The Policy Fundamentals are the first sub-process of the POM. They make inputs to the next sub-process, which we will discuss in Chapter Four, namely the Policy Dynamics.

■ CHAPTER FOUR ■

The Policy Dynamics

The Plan

The Policy Dynamics can be considered as the engine of the Process of Management or POM. Based on the directives and guidelines from the preceding sub-process of the POM, namely the Policy Fundamentals, the Policy Dynamics evolve the strategic objectives and the strategies and deploy them into action plans that are passed on for implementation.

The Mind-Maps

- 'The two rings' structure the interactions between senior and operative management as they develop the business policy and deploy the pertinent strategies.
- The 'check-alert-planning-deploy' of senior management.
- The five steps of the policy deployment process.

Introduction

Doing the right thing is as essential to sustainable success as it is delicate. It involves developing strategies based on speculation about future opportunities and threats, and deploying these strategies on strengths to be developed and on weaknesses to be corrected. As can be seen, doing the right thing is the result of a very complex and dynamic managerial process, for which we found the term the 'Policy Dynamics' to be quite appropriate.

Academics and consultants have given a lot of thought to this subject, and many models have been proposed to assist managers develop and deploy strategies. The still popular 'Management by Objectives' or MBO was developed in the 1950s. The Japanese evolved 'Management by Policy' or MBP in the 1960s as a substantial improvement over MBO.

MBP has found a limited following in the West. This method is probably too sophisticated and too participative to be introduced as a stand-alone; it must be inserted in an integrative methodology that supports shared management practices, such as the POM.

Based on the principles and practices of MBP, we have developed the Policy Dynamics. They are interconnected with the other sub-processes of our framework. The Policy Dynamics include original mind-maps that harmonize the interactions between different levels and different business units so as to facilitate this highly participative process.

In order to understand the evolution of the management practices concerning the development and the deployment of strategies, we will start by describing in this chapter some of the experiences made with MBO, and then outline the practices of MBP. Based on the lessons from its forerunners, we have developed the Policy Dynamics and introduced the mind-map of the 'Two Rings'. Finally we will present the five steps to implementing the policy deployment process, which structures the deployment of strategies into action plans.

4.1 Management by Objectives (MBO)

Introduced in the 1950s, MBO has become one of the pillars of business planning. It has the undisputed merit of focusing management's attention on objectives, of assigning accountabilities, and of featuring performance reviews that are closely associated with budgeting.

Unfortunately, this method is still impregnated with Taylor's concept whereby senior management plans and checks, and the personnel execute. In recent years MBO has become more participative as the manager may discuss the objectives and the results obtained with each subordinate. However, several shortcomings still mar this method. Let us summarize some of the drawbacks of MBO and then we will see what improvements Management by Policy can offer.

- MBO focuses on *managing individual performances* by ensuring accountability for specific annual objectives. Personnel do not have much say on how the objectives are set, they may not even know why they are important. As Malcolm Knowles pointed out, adults need to understand the relevance of what they are doing in order to take an interest and to learn. Senior management, often not close enough to the operations, may overestimate organizational capabilities, or set too many objectives, or define the objectives too broadly. If MBO carries a merit and demerit system, personnel may end up serving as the scapegoat for poorly set objectives. This situation contradicts the eighth of Deming's 14 precepts, namely drive out fear of punishment [42]. Limited understanding of the strategic objectives and fear of punishment are unlikely to elicit commitment, cooperation, and collective creativity.

- MBO focuses on hard results, mainly *financial year-end results*. It tends to neglect the so-called soft results such as the satisfaction of the personnel, of the suppliers and even of the customers. Occasionally, MBO seems to listen first and foremost to the voice of the hierarchy. Deming's eleventh precept advises us not to base management solely on numerical objectives because this leads to figures fumbling and, as we all know, figures can lie and liars can figure. As concerns the factual basis for the plan, an extensive data-collection strategy is often replaced by a mere extrapolation of past results.

- MBO focuses on results, not on how they are obtained. This contradicts another TQM principle, best described by Professor Kaoru Ishikawa: 'manage the process and let the outcome manage itself'. This led Deming to say: 'Western managers get results any old way, mind not necessary'.

- Managing individual results emphasizes a bilateral relationship of manager to subordinate. As a result, MBO deploys the objectives through hierarchical silos. This does not necessarily encourage teamwork or foster cooperation among the different departments of the organization. This contradicts the ninth of Deming's principles, namely 'break down barriers between departments'.

- Last but not least, MBO does not feature a well-defined planning process or a disciplined methodology of implementation and review. It does not distinguish between business breakthrough, continuous business improvement, and business maintenance. The plans are left to the discretion of senior management. The hierarchy of priorities can become muddled if there is a lack of coordination between different units and different levels, and if everything is a priority, nothing is.

No wonder Deming criticized MBO in his seminal works [42, 43]. But it is interesting to note that also Peter Drucker, one of the early promoters of MBO, joined Deming in the early 1990s and stated that MBO was no longer adequate at a time when the participation of personnel plays such an important role.

4.2 Management by Policy (MBP)

Japanese corporations among the early adopters of Total Quality Management (TQM) were looking to overcome some of the aforementioned shortcomings of MBO. Japanese academics developed in the late 1950s and early 1960s a method they called *Hoshin Kanri* as an improvement over MBO [57, 58]. Bridgestone, Komatsu, and Toyota paved the way by introducing this method in the mid-1960s. This method was found to be so efficient that the early adopters considered it a competitive advantage and kept their experiences as proprietary information.

American corporations, for example Hewlett-Packard, learned about this method through their Japanese venture and introduced it in the mid-1980s. In the early 1990s several books in English described the method [24, 59, 60, 61]. Some Western enterprises followed suit and introduced this method under different names such as *Hoshin* Planning or Management by Policy. We retain 'Management by Policy' or MBP as the most frequently used designation in the West.

In a nutshell, while MBO focuses on objectives and accountabilities, while MBP emphasizes priorities and processes to achieve effective policy deployment.

MBP features the following steps.

- A fact based analysis of strengths–weaknesses–opportunities–threats (SWOT) to understand where the enterprise is going and where the market and the main competitors are going.

- The strategic objectives are prioritized in (i) business breakthrough (BBT) where a quantum leap in the level of performance is required to meet strategic ambitions and innovation or even invention of the business may prove necessary; (ii) continuous business improvement (CBI) that features ongoing improvements; and (iii) business maintenance.

- The BBT objectives – also called *hoshin*, the Japanese expression for a shining metal pointing the direction as in a compass – are given priority over the other strategic objectives. They are cascaded top-down from one management level to the next and then the process is reversed and goes back up for approval, level after level until it reaches top management. Characteristically, the level that determines the strategic objectives leaves it up to the next level to evolve the strategies to achieve the objectives. The level that determines the strategic objectives and the level that is responsible for achieving them exchange intelligence and may negotiate the objective's indicators, the targets, and the required resources. This process, often referred to as 'catchball', is very participative, as people at different levels are involved in all the phases of the 'plan–do–check–act' of the activities entrusted to them.

- The deployment of BBT and of CBI goes all the way down to action plans and the whole process uses some of the graphic tools of TQM to display the progress made. This ensures the transparency of the whole process and also facilitates reviews of leading as well as lagging indicators.

- The BBT and CBI projects are managed by the appointed teams according to the principles and practices of TQM. Owners are empowered for each of the strategies of the BBT and the CBI management projects. Business maintenance is managed according to budgets.

The fact that both the Baldrige Award and the EQA require applicants to demonstrate effective implementation of policy deployment has increased awareness to the value of MBP. However, the number of Western enterprises using MBP remains limited, mainly because it requires a fairly high level of maturity in the implementation of the principles and practices of TQM. We may be facing a vicious circle, whereby many enterprises may not be well enough advanced in TQM to efficiently introduce MBP, but without it they cannot truly achieve TQM maturity.

This situation has led us to revisit and to revise the whole process that develops and deploys business policy. Let us first explain the Policy Dynamics, and then discuss each of its components.

4.3 The Policy Dynamics

As can be seen in Figure 2.1, the Policy Dynamics is one of the sub-processes of the POM.

They convert the broad and long-term directives and guidelines evolved by the Policy Fundamentals into specific and short-term action plans that will be managed in the following sub-process of the POM, namely the Policy Implementation and Review.

In order to accomplish effectively the many, complex tasks involved in this managerial process, we need a comprehensive method that fosters communication, cooperation, and collective creativity and that is well integrated with the other parts of the POM. We outline hereafter how this can be achieved with the Policy Dynamics.

- The Policy Dynamics import the strategic goals and the guidelines concerning the review–evaluation–reward and the resource allocation empowerment processes from the Policy Fundamentals. In turn they feed back to the Policy Fundamentals information on their review and planning steps.

- The Policy Dynamics involve both senior and operative management. We have developed the mind-map the 'Two Rings' to harmonize their interactions as they work together on the development and deployment of the business policy.

- The Policy Dynamics call for fact finding and for creativity to bring out all the actionable alternatives from which those most suitable to achieving the strategic objectives are selected. The Policy Dynamics put great emphasis on alertness and innovation. Alertness is needed to spark innovation. Both alertness and innovation are regularly reviewed.

- The Policy Dynamics deploy the strategies all the way down to action plans. These are given objectives with the pertinent indicators and targets. The implementation of the strategies is entrusted to 'owners' and passed on to the operations for implementation and review in the next sub-process of the POM.

- The Policy Assessment and Audit included in the last sub-process of the POM feature an annual appraisal of the effectiveness and of the efficiencies of the Policy Dynamics.

Compared to MBP, the Policy Dynamics offers the following additional benefits.

- As shown above, the Policy Dynamics are interactively connected with all other sub-processes of our framework for shared management practices, the POM. Management can clearly see the whole itinerary as well as the links between the various activities.

- Within the Policy Dynamics, the connections and the feedback loops among all managerial activities are clearly laid out, thus providing for transparency over the whole process.

- The Policy Dynamics puts a greater emphasis than MBP on the link between the development of the business policy and the deployment of strategies. To help senior management prepare for the development of business policy, we have elaborated on their check and alert activities.

- The mind-map of the 'two rings', featured in Figure 2.1 and expanded in Figure 4.1, structures the activities of both senior and operative management and harmonizes their complementary activities.

- We emphasize the need for innovation in both the planning and the policy deployment. The check and alert steps foster innovative planning by senior management, and the search for actionable alternatives stimulates the creativity of operative management as it develops strategies to achieve the strategic objectives.

- While MBP focuses only on the deployment of the business breakthrough (BBT), we advocate using the same approach – albeit in a simplified version – for continuous business improvement (CBI). This facilitates a linkage between these two management modes.

We will start by describing the mind-map of the 'Two Rings', and then we will discuss the various steps taken by senior and by operative management respectively.

4.4 The 'Two Rings'

Research reported by Wheelen and Hunger [23] and conducted by the author [62] shows that one of the main reasons that strategic plans are poorly implemented is the lack of interaction between the planners and the doers.

Addressing this issue, we have developed the mind-map of the 'Two Rings', which structures the cooperation of senior and operative management on the development and deployment of business policy.

We believe that senior and operative management have a different time-horizon, different priorities, and a different role. Senior management should focus on the big picture and be issue oriented. It should be

FIGURE 4.1 The Policy Dynamics and the model of the 'Two Rings'

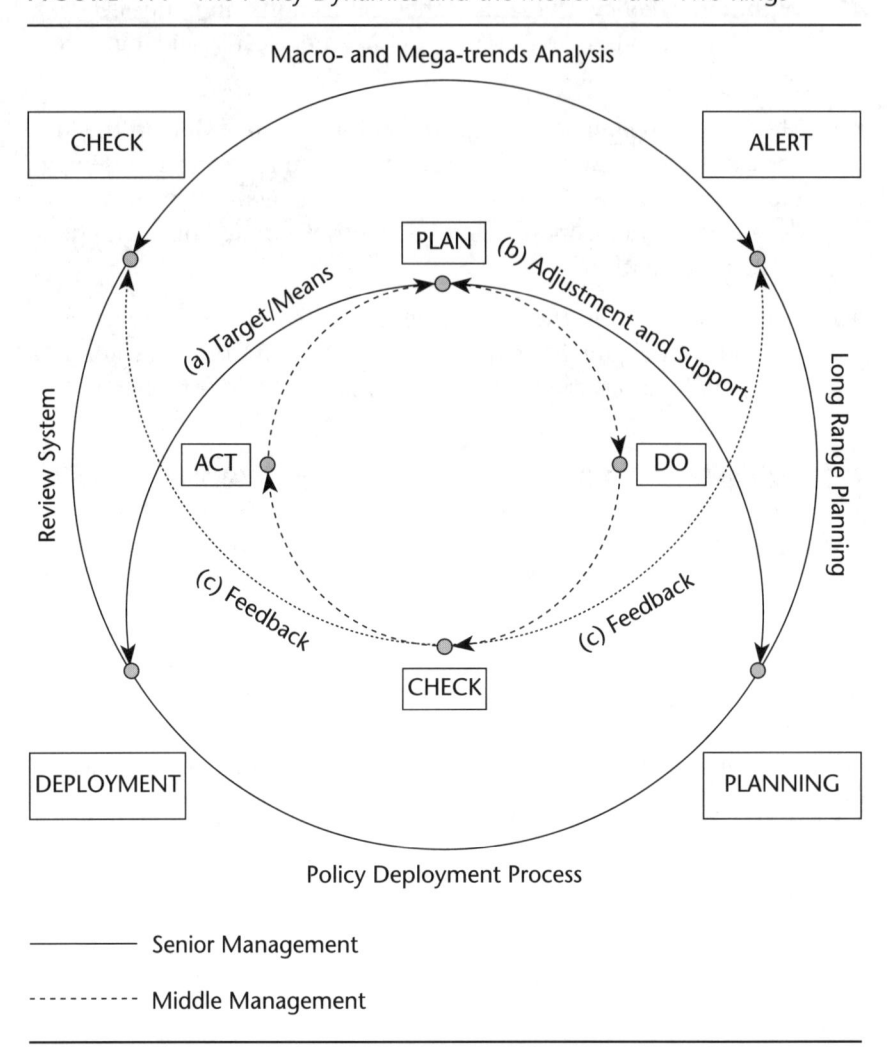

Macro- and Mega-trends Analysis

CHECK — ALERT

PLAN
(a) Target/Means
(b) Adjustment and Support

Review System | Long Range Planning

ACT — DO

(c) Feedback — (c) Feedback

CHECK

DEPLOYMENT — PLANNING

Policy Deployment Process

———— Senior Management
- - - - - - Middle Management

prepared to deal with concepts and with ambiguity. It must ensure that the organization *does the right thing*. Operative management has more in-depth knowledge, and is closer to people and problems. It must ensure that the organization *does the thing right*.

In essence we rejoin Taylor's concern which was to align the tasks with the corresponding competencies. This concept is no longer applicable to the operations where the sophistication of personnel no longer justifies separating the 'plan' and 'check' from the 'do' and 'act'. Yet, Taylor's approach makes sense when applied to the development and deployment of business policy. Consequently, we see senior management, in the outer ring of our mind-map, address the big issues and their long-range implications for the business policy, while operative management, in the inner ring, focuses on the day-to-day implementation. In between these two roles, senior and operative management interact on the policy deployment process.

The outer ring focuses on doing the right thing and features the four tasks that are owned and led by senior management, namely: *check*, *alert*, *plan*, and *deploy the business policy*. *The inner ring* focuses on doing the thing right and features the four tasks that are empowered to and carried out by operative management, namely to *plan*, *do*, *check*, and *act* on all major activities concerning the five business enablers. As can be seen in Figure 4.1, the policy deployment process takes place between the planning and the deployment steps of the outer ring.

The mind-map of the 'Two Rings' presents the following benefits:

- it helps to clarify the formal interactions between senior and operative management and prevents senior management from meddling in the tasks that operative management should be empowered to handle;
- it ensures that the interfaces and feedback loops are carried out in an orderly and systematic manner;
- it helps senior management focus on the high level tasks reserved for the top executives, and frees their time for informal interactions such as *management by walking around*.

We will now discuss the tasks on the outer ring that senior management should lead. Later we will outline the tasks that operative management is empowered to carry out on the inner ring.

4.5 The outer ring

The outer ring features four steps. We will discuss each in turn, considering their purpose, their activities, and summarize their inputs/outputs.

4.5.1 Outer ring step 1: check

Senior management's check serves the double purpose of (i) validating operative management's short-term performance and plans, and (ii) to prepare intelligence for the third step of the outer ring, namely the planning.

The short-term check focuses on checking the performance of the organization vs. the targets set in the policy deployment of the previous year. It analyzes the evolution of the strengths and weaknesses and how they have impacted on the opportunities and threats over the past year. The effectiveness and efficiency of the improvement projects are examined. In the light of this analysis senior management can judge the short-term forecasts produced by operative management.

The internal inputs are mainly provided by the operative management of every business unit as reported in their quarterly reviews (the check step on the inner ring). These reviews show the performance obtained on each of the five business enablers. These data should be supplemented by external benchmarking [63] and by competitive intelligence [64]. In addition, senior management may need to get a feel for the data collected by practicing management by walk around inside the organization and by interviewing key partners. This step should enable senior management to discuss first of all with operative management its corrective and improvement plans, and then to complete its SWOT analysis. The SWOT analysis conducted in the frame of the Policy Dynamics is short- to medium-term while the one carried out in the Policy Fundamentals addresses broad, long-term issues. The two are therefore complementary.

Some of the performance measures used in this check step will be *quantitative* (financial results, share of market, customer complaints and quality reports, productivity, etc.). Other measures will be essentially *qualitative* (the morale of the personnel, the value of intellectual assets, image and goodwill, etc.). There should be a reasonable balance between quantitative and qualitative measures. Frequently the quantitative data show results or *lagging indicators*, which need to be complemented by an analysis of how they have been obtained, i.e. *leading indicators*. The latter can be qualitative data that are soft, somewhat more difficult to evaluate and probably, therefore, sometimes neglected. The chosen selection of quantitative and qualitative results should provide a basis for benchmarking comparisons with the results obtained by other organizations.

Senior management may conduct periodic and systematic checks. These checks emphasize the importance of management reviews, reinforce the Policy Fundamentals, and assist in the training of managers.

The medium-term check that serves as input in the next planning cycle is based on senior management's appraisal of the short-term forecasts made by operative management and also on the periodic monitoring of the macrotrends of the pertinent sectors. For this purpose, with the assistance of operative management and outside advice as appropriate, senior management assesses the outlook of the organizational performance and competitive position of the enterprise by listening carefully to:

- the voice of the customer (buyers and end-users), the voice of the distribution channels that serve the customer, and the sustainable competitive level of satisfaction of their needs and concerns;

- the voice of the market including the economic, financial, social, and regulatory aspects;

- the voice of the personnel and appraising the enhanced value of intellectual capital, as well as the voice of key suppliers and strategic allies;

- the voice of the shareholders, of the board of directors, and of the financial markets;

- the voice of the enterprise, which is an autonomous entity and has its own goals. As pointed out by A. de Geus, each organization has its own needs for survival and success [65].

The selection of these voices must then be aligned with the strategic goals as articulated in the Policy Fundamentals.

We can summarize as follows the inputs/outputs of the check step.

- Senior management receives input concerning the review–evaluation–reward and resource allocation and empowerment processes from the Policy Fundamentals.

- Senior management receives input from the quarterly reviews conducted by the operative management; the inner ring's check step. This way the operative management informs senior management of the outcome of its periodic performance reviews and the corrective/improvement measures planned as a result of those reviews.

- Senior management creates appropriate feedback to operative management as a result of its analysis of the quarterly reviews.

- Senior management creates output to the alert phase of the outer ring in the form of areas of concern that may need to be considered in a broader or longer term context.

- Senior management provide their assessment of the macrotrends as an input to the planning phase of the outer ring.

4.5.2 Outer ring step 2: alert

The alert step is one of the original elements of our mind-map. What will be will be – says a popular song – but by the time it has come to be, it will be too late to prepare for it. In reality, preparing to take advantage of emerging opportunities or threats is taking longer and longer. Therefore, in order to lead the enterprise to a promising future, senior management needs to be alert to early signs of change that might occur in the business environment. Alertness has become crucial in recent turbulent times because *many a false step has been taken by standing still*. Bob Galvin, former CEO of Motorola, recognized the importance of alertness and he also rated his managers on their ability to anticipate trends and to commit to new ways of working.

The check and the alert steps are complementary. The check step focuses on the known environment and consequently has a relatively short time-horizon; the alert step probes as far into the unknown as is possible. The check process goes from inside the enterprise towards the outside; the alert process goes from the outside inwards.

Management should distinguish between passive changes and proactive changes. *Passive changes* are those that cannot be influenced, they must be endured. The alert step can only estimate the probability, shape, extent, and timing of what may happen. The planning step can then take over and devise promotional plans to optimize the benefits from the favorable trends, and draw up preventive and contingency plans to minimize the effects of unfavorable trends. That is about all that can reasonably be expected of management.

Management's greatest opportunity is to initiate *proactive changes*. These are the ones that will enable the enterprise to get to the future first. They will enable the enterprise to set new standards, to dictate the rules of the game, or better yet to blanket the market. The purpose of the alert step is for senior management to dedicate time and resources to optimizing proactive changes. Of course proactive changes can engender exceptionally high stakes. Hence, in order to direct its resources to the right place at the right time, senior management must be very alert to the direction and the speed of change, its drivers, and its key players.

Schematically, and going from the long to the medium range, the *drivers of change* are:

- the megatrends that affect most sectors;
- the macrotrends that affect specific sectors;
- the competitive dynamics that may eventually evolve inside the sector, as described by Porter [52].

Of course regional trends are also relevant but, in a globalizing environment, sectorial considerations generally take precedence.

The *megatrends* are particularly insidious. They are broad and appear far removed from everyday life. Furthermore they evolve so slowly that their progress may go unnoticed. As a result, the cause to effect relation is masked by the delay. When their full potential finally becomes apparent, many a management is taken aback and scrambles to catch up. The transistor, electronic miniaturization, biosciences, digitalization and, more recently, the Internet are just a few examples of technology-driven megatrends. Similar shifts can be found with the other forms of megatrend.

Figure 3.2 shows the four large categories of megatrends, namely (i) technological and technical; (ii) economical and financial; (iii) socio-cultural; and (iv) geo-political and regulatory trends. Within them there are major currents that need to be identified, and their interactions creatively explored. In the same way as water flows are dictated by the law of gravity, megatrends contribute to increasing the satisfaction of the groups that have a critical mass of economical or political power.

Megatrends are difficult to predict and strategic biases can distort management's perception of them. As a result it becomes increasingly difficult to distinguish between foresight and fantasy. Be that as it may, senior management may face the harshest of criticisms if it misses major opportunities or threats, unless it can show that it has dedicated adequate talent, time, and money to remaining alert.

The *macrotrends* tend to have a direct influence on a particular sector. Competitive intelligence is receiving increased attention, although this can no longer be safely limited to the known competitors. Porter's five forces driving industry competition (industry competitors, potential entrants, substitutes, suppliers' power, and buyers' power [52]), while conceptually valid, are increasingly difficult to apply in practice. Networks, strategic alliances, mergers and acquisitions are constantly reconfiguring the competitive forces in the global environment. They cause sudden shifts in the *competitive dynamics*; they affect the margin of maneuverability of competitors and the latitude of responses the competitors are capable of.

The drivers of change present threats and opportunities mixed together. As we have already mentioned, one of the characteristics of globalization is that the various forces at play converge and merge in a somewhat chaotic web.

Peter Drucker took that into account when he identified the ten areas management needs to focus on in order to remain alert, namely: (i) unexpected successes: (ii) unexpected failures; (iii) unexpected external events; (iv) process weakness, or what Rummler and Brache called 'the white space on the organization chart'; (v) changes in industry structure or market; (vi) high growth areas; (vii) converging technologies; (viii) demographic changes; (ix) changes in the perception of facts; and (x) new knowledge [66]. Checklists such as this one can be useful but we prefer to look at the methods management can use to remain alert. We will consider here scenario management, which is mostly reserved for forecasting macrotrends, and then what we call 'trend testing', which considers both mega- and macrotrends.

- *Scenario management* applies military experience to business management. In essence, the macrotrends that affect the sector(s) or that have affected it in the past, are identified; plausible assumptions are made about their evolution, the probability of their occurrence and their impact on the enterprise. For the most important of these trends, strategic plans are formulated that take into account the most likely position and responses of the competition. The construction of scenarios – described by Schwartz – can be fairly sophisticated [28]. The scenarios thus developed enable management to react quickly should one of the envisaged situations occur. This can reduce the risk of making major mistakes or of taking too long to respond to new developments. However, the classic model of scenario management focuses on the macrotrends that are already known in the industry. The problem is that, *since we do not know what we do not know*, we do not know what to look for and may fail to seek the most critical knowledge. This problem is aggravated by the interdependencies of traditionally different sectors and by recombining industry structures.

- *Trend testing*, the approach we advocate, differs from the above-mentioned method. We emphasize out-of-the-box thinking rather than an extrapolation of past trends. We start with the big picture, i.e. with the megatrends, to understand their possible effects on the macrotrends. Then we look for their implications on business policy.

  The experts on the megatrends – mostly recruited outside the organization for additional expertise and objectivity – may use the Delphi technique (already described in Chapter Three under strategic ambitions). The Delphi technique puts on the discussion table a range of views gathered from all the group members. Discussions uncover the common denominator and unveil paradigms as well as diverging opinions.

When a consensus is reached on the megatrends, senior management compare those insights with the macrotrend analysis done for the check step and the research done for the alert step. The ensuing synthesis should focus on (i) the long-term opportunities and threats; (ii) the competencies and capabilities of the organization; and (iii) the strategies. The Delphi technique can be applied again at this stage. A consensus should evolve and the consistency of these conclusions with the Policy Fundamentals should be checked. In case of divergence, the Policy Fundamentals may be called into question.

This process is as important as it is time-consuming. It should be documented for future reference and organizational learning. Trend testing should generate three types of action: (i) an adequate internal communication; (ii) the installation or review of early warning systems capable of magnifying weak signals and preparing competencies in the construction of scenarios; and (iii) a review of the strategic goals established in the Policy Fundamentals.

Should it be desirable to involve larger groups in some of these discussions, the techniques such as those suggested by 'Future Search' might be considered [67].

Trend testing is a way to break the mental attitude that restricts alertness to that which is common place. It should overcome the basic problem which stems from the fact that revolutionary ideas come from a different perspective, tend to conflict with the established paradigms, and risk being blocked by conventional management. Another way to overcome this problem, is for senior management to set up a forum where revolutionary ideas can be expressed, evaluated, and gain funding as appropriate. IBM and Du Pont used to have a high-level committee that would give a fair and friendly hearing to personnel who had potentially important ideas that did not fit the objectives of their hierarchy. Such committees should be staffed by a combination of visionary entrepreneurs who can accept novelty and great communicators who will optimize acceptance of the novelty by a critical mass of people. This cast of characters is neither easy to find nor are such projects easy to fund in times of lean management. Once revolutionary ideas are accepted and funded, the next problem is setting up a separate venture that would allow these ideas to blossom without the administrative burden that encumbers large organizations.

Whichever approach and means are used, the alertness step is well worth the effort.

We can summarize as follows the inputs/outputs of the alert step.

- Senior management receives input from the strategic goals from the Policy Fundamentals.
- Senior management receives input from the check step of the outer ring concerning macrotrends.
- Senior management receives input from the check step of the inner ring when operative management wants to alert them to a new situation.
- Senior management creates output to the planning step.

4.5.3 Outer ring step 3: planning

If you do not know where you are going and how to get there, do not be surprised if you land somewhere else. Christopher Columbus provided a good example. When he set sail he did not know where he was going, during the trip he did not know where he was, then he did not know where he had landed, and when he returned he did not know where he had been. Columbus survived that trip, but managers who do not do a better planning job than that may not be so lucky! This is why, as we repeatedly pointed out, senior management's foremost task is to *set direction*.

Setting direction and pace is part of an intellectual and social process called planning. General Dwight D. Eisenhower stated 'The plan is nothing, planning is everything'. Plans tend to be a static, formal, top-down annual chore. Planning is a continuous and participative process designed to sort out priorities, to set targets and reviews and to empower the right people to do the right job. Once planning has been done at senior management level, detailed action plans can be evolved by operative management.

The purpose of the planning step is to consolidate the inputs from the check and alert steps and from whatever other sources have been made available, and to define strategic objectives. In principle the strategic objectives should be consistent with the directives and guidelines evolved in the Policy Fundamentals. But sound reasons can overturn principles and the same applies to Policy Fundamentals.

The planning process deals with a combination of rational, relational, and emotional factors. Often the balance among these factors is not optimal and, as General de Gaulle pointed out [68], there are too many facts and not enough intuition and creativity. It is preferable that senior management starts with the strategic objectives at the time-horizon, i.e. at the end of the planning period, and works its way back to year one. This approach, sometimes referred to as *reversed logic*, has the advantage of avoiding dabbling with details and of falling into one of the many mind-traps that constrict strategic thinking such as 'not-nowism', 'not invented here', 'it's never been done before', etc.

Furthermore, by developing multi-year planning, senior management communicates to operative management the milestones envisaged in the Policy Fundamentals and its assessment of the organization's capabilities as well as the opportunities. Operative management tends to have a lower time-horizon and needs annual objectives to evolve the appropriate action plans.

The planning step features the following activities.

- Senior management must take a view of the medium range opportunities and threats for the enterprise. Taking into account the strategic goals that have been articulated in the Policy Fundamentals, and the intelligence gathered in the check and the alert steps of the outer ring, senior management should evolve strategic objectives that the enterprise must achieve in the next three or more years.

- Senior management must separate the strategic objectives for:
  - *business breakthrough* (BBT) which includes a few high priority management projects that should enable the enterprise to make a quantum leap ahead and hopefully achieve a substantial competitive advantage. Most likely senior management will find that incremental improvements are insufficient to keep ahead in highly competitive markets and to meet the strategic goals by the end of the planning period. As a result, this gap analysis will show the need for innovation of the business architecture, possibly innovation of the business. *If necessity is the mother of invention, innovation, and improvement planning must deploy that necessity.*
  - *continuous business improvement* (CBI) which should ensure that the organizational performance continues to improve at least as fast, as effectively, and as efficiently as the competition;
  - *business maintenance* (BM) which includes activities of minor importance that can essentially be maintained at the present level of performance and managed by budgets.
    long-term projects such as basic research, new plant construction, etc. which are normally managed outside of the normal structures and have a different time frame.

The identified BBT are given top priority. Their number should be limited to two or three per business unit at any given time so as to sharpen the focus and to provide the necessary resources. Additional breakthrough projects that have been considered should be recorded on a stand-by list. This avoids scrapping suggestions that could very well be considered at a later time. Some of the BBT may be achieved in one year; others may span a period of several years, but should rarely go beyond three years. When a breakthrough has been achieved, it integrates CBI.

Typically CBI accounts for 70–80 percent of the managerial efforts, BBT for 5–10 percent, business maintenance for the remainder. Long-term projects are handled separately.

Senior management should take a systemic view of the various business units, and pay attention to the possible synergies because, as Robert has pointed out [50], competition is increasingly fought between enterprises with their constellation of business units rather than between business units. The CEO plays the role of moderator in the discussions on the planning step, but has the prerogative of the final word on the choice of the vital few BBT, as well as on the strategic objectives for both BBT and CBI.

In order to facilitate their deployment, the strategic objectives need to feature the following points.

- A description of the strategic objective (a noun to identify the subject, a verb to indicate the desired direction).

- A designation of BBT or CBI – in both cases senior management sets stretched objectives but BBT projects should show clear priority over CBI projects.

- Some background leading to the issue with a short explanation of the importance of achieving the strategic goals, and the urgency of the situation. Cost objectives are a catchall category that should be administered with care. They tend to lower the view to the short term, and focus the attention on results rather than the causes.

- Performance indicators as appropriate to assess the evolution of the project. Indicators can be expressed as a percentage, as a quantity or quality, or as a range. There should be *lagging indicators* for the results as well as *leading indicators* for what generates results. Setting indicators must be tied to the objective. Indicators can specify the performance of the business enabler, the business unit, the place, the timeline. Indicators can have an internal focus (personnel and process oriented) or an external focus (customer and supplier oriented).

Setting indicators can be a delicate task. Florida Power & Light provided a classic example of how poor indicators can lead the effort astray. In order to find ways to increase customer satisfaction, this utility company addressed the problem of power failures. It measured the duration of power failures, but in fact customers were frustrated by the frequency of power failures. Two indicators, two causes, and two different remedies.

Indicators should be relevant to the persons responsible for the project, encourage desirable behavior, be easy to determine, capable of graphical display, and should trigger actions in real time. A results monitoring system with early warning signals and triggers ensures that results and, if necessary, appropriate corrective actions are managed in real time. There can be psychological indicators where people's attitudes and behavior are critical. There can be more than one indicator per objective.

- The target should define the performance level to be achieved. Targets must be clear, concise, and quantifiable. Targets may be set on quality, quantity, delay or time cycle, cost, profitability, safety. Targets are deployed top-down.

- The timeline, i.e. the times at which certain levels of performance must be attained.

- The designation of the owner of the strategic objective.

- Guidelines as appropriate (for example on the management system featuring real time visual presentations, techniques and tools that are advisable, early warning systems and triggers in case of problems, etc.). Constraints, if there are any, should be detailed.

We can summarize as follows the inputs/outputs of the planning step.

- Senior management receives input from the strategic goals evolved by the Policy Fundamentals.

- Senior management receives input from the check and alert steps.

- Senior management receives input from the plan step in the inner ring when operative management feels it is useful to show their detailed action plans to senior management, or when it needs to get support.

- Senior management creates output to the plan step in the inner ring when they feel that operative management should receive new knowledge from the big picture.

- Senior management creates output from the planning step to the policy deployment step.

4.5.4 Outer ring step 4: deployment

Research has shown that management often spends a considerable proportion of their time concocting strategies, but not enough time deploying them. As a result, the deployment of the strategies, the last step on the outer ring, has often fallen through the cracks between the levels of the hierarchy. To avoid this problem and based on the practice of MBP, we emphasize the importance of the policy deployment process or PDP, a building block of the Policy Dynamics.

The policy deployment process incorporates the following features.

- As illustrated in Figure 4.1, the PDP makes the link between the planning and the deployment steps of the outer ring. The action plans will be deployed onto the action step of the inner ring, the ring that is entrusted to the operative management.

- The fact that operative management is closely involved together with senior management on the PDP ensures that their point of view is duly taken into consideration and that they are really committed to achieving the strategic objectives entrusted to them.

- The PDP also ensures visibility and manageability of all activities.

- The PDP is a highly participative process that stimulates the creativity and interaction among the participants at various levels and in different units. It gets different people talking to each other.

As shown in Figure 4.2, the PDP can be pictured as a fountain with three dishes. The water gushes from the top and falls into the first dish. When that dish is filled, the water overflows onto a second and larger dish. Finally when the second dish is filled, the water overflows onto the third and last dish from where it is collected and pumped back up to the top through an internal pipe.

Taking this image, we can visualize that the PDP works in two dimensions: *vertically* top-down and bottom-up, and *horizontally* or cross-functionally as the water falling into a dish spreads before overflowing to the next dish. We will outline the principles of vertical and horizontal deployment before going on to discuss the five steps of the PDP.

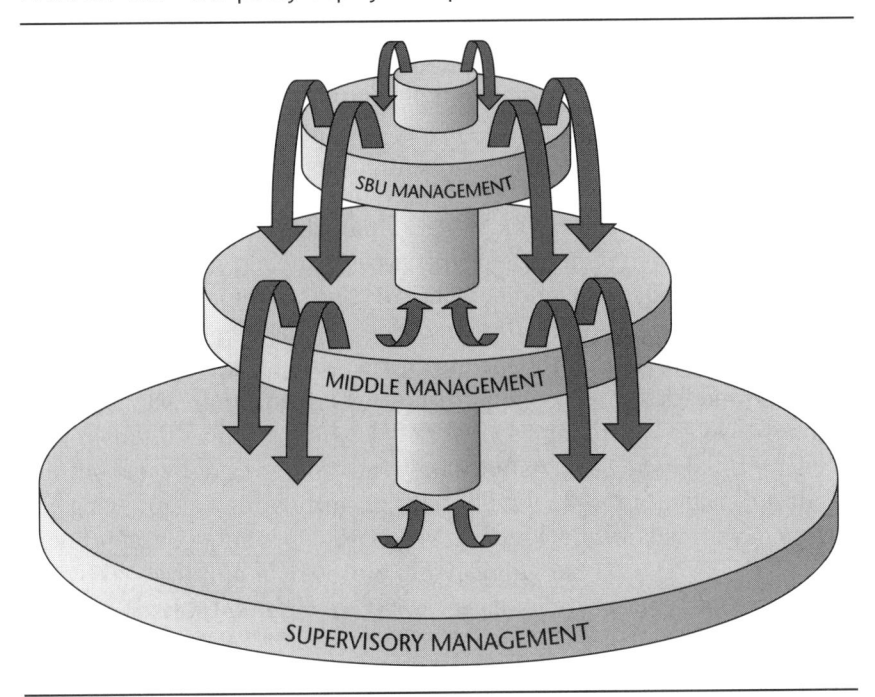

FIGURE 4.2 The policy deployment process

[Diagram showing three tiered levels: SBU MANAGEMENT at the top, MIDDLE MANAGEMENT in the middle, and SUPERVISORY MANAGEMENT at the bottom, with arrows indicating downward and upward flow between levels.]

The *vertical deployment* of the PDP works first top-down and then bottom-up. As shown in Figure 4.3, the PDP typically involves the three management levels of the SBU, namely the senior management and the two levels of the operative management, which we call middle management and supervisory management. The higher the hierarchical level, the fewer the people, the broader the issues covered. Conversely, as we go down the ladder, the number of people involved becomes greater and the scope narrower.

The PDP structures the collaboration between the various management levels as follows. Every level takes ownership for the strategic objectives that it sets, but it can empower the next level to devise and to implement the strategies. This contributes to making the PDP a highly participative and stimulating process. Let us give an overview of how these interactions work.

In the first level of management, the senior SBU management or 'N' lay out *the first level strategic objectives* for the management projects, concerning respectively the business breakthrough and the continuous business improvement. 'N' empowers the next hierarchical level, i.e.

FIGURE 4.3 The policy deployment

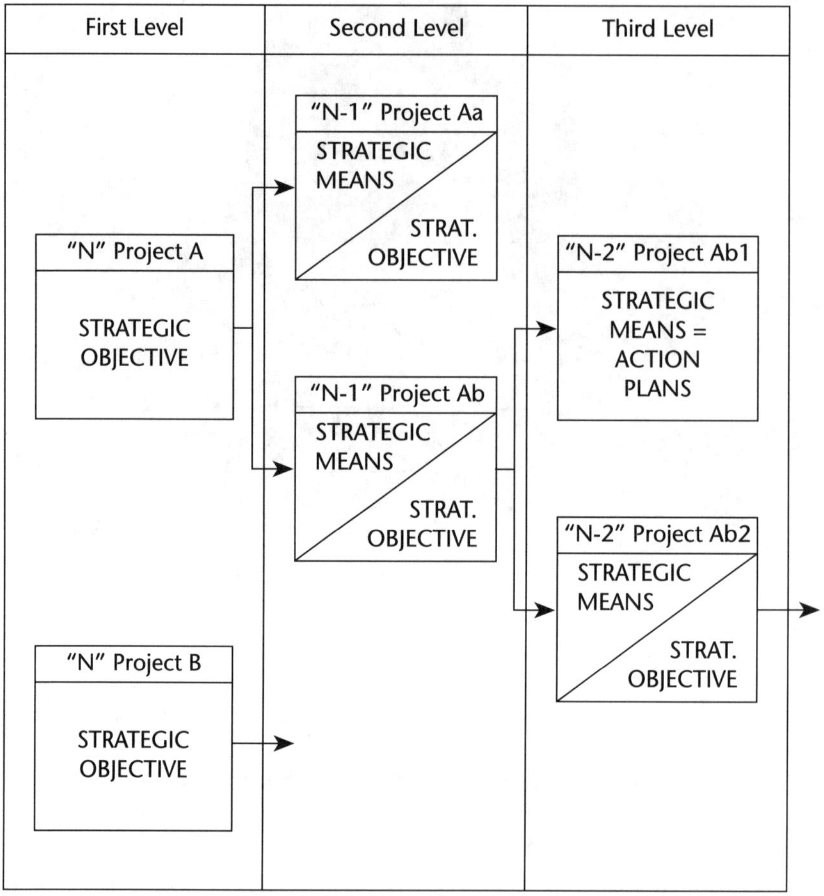

First Level	Second Level	Third Level
"N" Project A — STRATEGIC OBJECTIVE	"N-1" Project Aa — STRATEGIC MEANS / STRAT. OBJECTIVE	"N-2" Project Ab1 — STRATEGIC MEANS = ACTION PLANS
	"N-1" Project Ab — STRATEGIC MEANS / STRAT. OBJECTIVE	"N-2" Project Ab2 — STRATEGIC MEANS / STRAT. OBJECTIVE
"N" Project B — STRATEGIC OBJECTIVE		

middle management or 'N-1', to develop the strategies to attain the first level strategic objectives.

In the second level, the 'N-1' managers and their teams have to generate collective creativity in order to come up with many *actionable alternatives* from which the best strategies will be selected. Having selected the strategies, the 'N-1' managers can set *the second level of strategic objectives,* which are passed down to the next level, i.e. to the supervisory management or 'N-2'.

In the third level, the 'N-2' managers are empowered by 'N-1' to devise the strategies to implement the second level strategic objectives.

Normally, 'N-2' can translate the strategies it has developed into detailed action plans. Should this not be possible, an additional layer of deployment may become necessary. The top-down deployment of the business policy interrupts when the strategies can be translated into action plans that are empowered and for which a performance measurement system is planned.

We illustrate the deployment process schematically in Figure 4.3. Senior management has evolved two business breakthrough projects, namely 'A' and 'B', for which the corresponding strategic objectives have been set. As we follow project 'B', we see that senior management empowers two middle managers. The first middle manager develops the strategies 'Aa' and sets its strategic objectives and related strategies, which he/she can handle so that no further deployment is needed. The second middle manager develops the strategies 'Ab', for which he/she develops the second level strategic objectives, and deploys them onto the next level or 'N-2'. The supervisory manager 'N-2' that takes on the second level strategic objectives 'Ab1' can convert his/her strategies in action plans. The supervisory manager who takes on the second level strategic objectives 'Ab2' needs to deploy his/her strategic objectives down to the next level.

When the policy deployment has been deployed all the way down in specific action plans, the direction of the process is reversed and the flow moves back up for approval by the next level up in the hierarchy. Bottom-up, the resources are negotiated between the level that owns the strategic objectives and the level that is empowered to develop and to implement the pertinent strategies. These negotiations between the hierarchical levels are often referred to as 'catchball'. They make the whole process transparent and improve the understanding and trust between the different levels. Eventually the top level can approve the policy deployment process and launch its implementation.

The horizontal deployment of the PDP takes place at the various levels of the operative management, in our schematic example at the second and third level. In a vast majority of cases, the strategies cannot be dealt with effectively and efficiently by one unit or group. Let us bear in mind that no one unit or function can alone deliver value to the customer. A cross-functional cooperation is therefore required. The cross-functional cooperation is placed under the leadership of the respective owner of strategic objectives. He/she will organize cross-functional groups that will discuss the cross-functional strategies and come to an agreement on the distribution of the roles, responsibilities and resources among the units and individuals involved.

The negotiations across functions and business units are also referred to as 'catchball'. They are very important and well worth the time invested. They make the whole process transparent and improve the understanding and trust between the different units.

Whenever the corporation encompasses several strategic business units (SBU), corporate management sets the strategic objectives and the senior management of each of the SBU has to develop the strategies to attain them. The senior management of the SBU then deploys its strategic objectives onto the levels of its operative management as discussed above.

Having taken an aerial view of the policy deployment process, we can now get into some of the details of its working.

4.5.5 The 5 steps of the policy deployment process

(a) First level deployment: from senior management ('N') to middle management ('N-1')

'N' establishes the first level strategic objectives for business breakthrough (BBT) and for continuous business improvement (CBI). These strategic objectives are set on an annual basis for a planning period of one to three years. Senior management launches the program and communicates an overview to all the managers.

'N' deploys the first level strategic objectives onto the 'middle' managers ('N-1') who are empowered to develop the strategies to achieve them. This approach is similar to the classic search for the cause and effect relationship. In problem solving we know the effect, namely the problem, and look for the causes. Here the objective is known and the strategies to achieve it have to be found.

(b) Second level deployment by the middle management ('N-1')

1   *Developing actionable alternatives*
     In order to come up with the best possible strategies, the 'N-1' managers and their teams will have to be collectively creative in order to develop *actionable alternatives* from which the best strategies will be selected. Brainstorming is a practical tool to get all the intelligence, ideas, and imagination out and displayed on the wall. The 'N-1' managers can organize a think-team that includes members of their unit as well as members of other units to put the necessary cross-functional cooperation into gear. Outside partners (key customers or critical suppliers) can be invited to participate. Such creative sessions are enjoyable and are conducive

to cooperation and commitment. For efficiency's sake, we recommend that the group does not exceed seven people.

For each of the strategic objectives, the brainstorming can be structured using the Ishikwa fishbone diagram. The strategic objective is placed at the end of the horizontal arrow, and the 5 <P> or business enablers provide the headings for the diagonal arrows starting with the partners and ending with the plans. This approach emphasizes the voice of the customer. Furthermore, throwing into relief the interdependencies among the 5 <P> helps the participants visualize opportunities for economies of scale, scope, space, time and systems. We recommend that for each business enabler the actionable alternatives be classified as small improvements, big improvements or innovation. The owner of strategic objectives or the facilitator of the workshop can call the attention of the participants on the distribution of creativity and the degree of improvement among the alternatives. If necessary, he/she may call for another round of brainstorming. All the actionable alternatives should be visually displayed and should be numbered for future reference.

For a first screening, the members of the think-team can plot the actionable alternatives on a 9-square matrix, featuring on the vertical axis the expected impact each actionable alternative will have on achieving the pertinent strategic objective (high–medium–low) and on the horizontal axis, the anticipated feasibility of implementing the actionable alternative (high–medium–low). Placing color-coded self-adhesive dots on the listed actionable alternatives, or using the nominal group technique, helps summarize the group's opinions. The actionable alternatives that score high or medium on both impact and feasibility are retained. Alternatives that have not been retained should be listed and filed for future reference.

At the end of the session, the leader of the think-team should determine: (i) what additional intelligence will be required; (ii) whether the group has been sufficiently alert to trends and likely shifts; (iii) whether there has been sufficient innovative spirit in the proposed issues; (iv) whether the outcome of the brainstorming provides an adequate basis for planning; (v) who should participate in the next step of the deployment process; and (vi) what preparation and arrangements should be made for the next meeting.

2. *Selection of the strategies by the 'N-1' managers*
Each of the 'N-1' managers needs to select the most effective and efficient among the actionable alternatives that passed the first screening. Effectiveness, robustness, efficiency, flexibility, time-

cycles, and synergies are among the criteria that can be used for the final selection of the strategies.

The evolution of the situation over the planned period, competitive maneuverability and responses should also be adequately taken into account. Plotting the critical success factors and the critical failure factors against the critical competencies and core capabilities help ensure the organization has the necessary means to implement the strategies. For the most likely scenarios, preventive and contingency plans should be formulated for potential problems and promotional plans should be evolved for potential opportunities.

Data are brought to bear as appropriate. In this step the think-team may be somewhat smaller than in the previous one as – except for allies – external partners may not be invited to participate. However, cross-functional representation is highly desirable.

At the end of this step, the 'N-1' managers will have selected the strategies to reach the strategic objectives of the first level, and will have collected a fair amount of useful intelligence on the relevant <P>.

3 *Deploying the strategies cross-functionally*

Three simple matrices can help visualize the horizontal deployment. The first one plots the strategies against the pertinent processes, the second matrix plots the pertinent processes against the relevant departments/units and the last matrix plots the department against the resources required by the pertinent processes. At the end of the cross-functional consultation, the 'N-1' managers will have finalized the strategies and their cross-functional deployment, and: (i) the potential problems will have been identified; (ii) the solutions and resources agreed upon; and (iii) the cross-functional actors should be in agreement on who does what, when, and with what. The expected impact of each of the retained strategies on the relevant strategic objective should be quantified; field force analysis can be used to plan the management of the identified potential implementation problems. The empowerment should have been determined.

4 *Interim review by 'N-1' with 'N'*

At this stage, the 'N-1' managers may review their strategies and next level strategic objectives with senior management. Such interim reports keep senior management informed and supportive.

5 *Deployment*

Having determined the second level strategic objectives, the 'N-1' managers can empower their implementation horizontally and, as appropriate, on the next level, namely 'N-2' or the 'supervisory' management.

(c) Third level deployment: supervisory management 'N-2'

1 *Development of action plans*
   The 'N-2' managers need to develop the strategies to achieve the second level strategic objectives developed by 'N-1'. Whenever possible these strategies become specific action plans in this level of the policy deployment process. In some cases an additional level of deployment may be necessary.
   In most cases in this level, the strategies also have to be deployed cross-functionally. The same approach can be used as was suggested for the cross-functional deployment of the first level strategic means.
2 *Checking the effectiveness of the action plans with key partners*
   As appropriate, the 'N-2' managers can contact their key external interfaces, such as key customers or critical suppliers, in order to test and to improve on the drafted action plans.

(d) Bottom-up negotiations

1 *Catchball 'N-2' and 'N-1'*
   The 'N-2' managers present their action plans and the required resources to 'N-1' and there is a negotiation in order to come to an understanding. As mentioned earlier, this type of interaction is often called 'catchball' because the issues are tossed back and forth. Compromises may have to be reached or, failing that, 'N-2' may have to go back to the drawing board.
2 *Catchball 'N-1' and 'N'*
   The 'N-1' managers review the strategic deployment all the way down to the action plans with 'N' and negotiate budgetary and other issues. This level of 'catchball' should lead to an agreement on the whole policy deployment process.

(e) Deployment of the Policy

1 *RAP and RER*
   'N' finalizes all the strategic objectives and strategies ensuring their synergies. 'N' establishes resource allocation empowerment (RAE), as well as the review evaluation and reporting (RER). Normally the PDP is done on a yearly basis for a planning period of one to three years.

2. *Go-ahead*
   'N' gives the go-ahead to 'N-1' who in turn can give the go-ahead to 'N-2'. The visual based management system is put in place to monitor the results as the planned actions are implemented.
3. *Visual based management*
   The PDP supports visual based management, in other words, the display of progress made on each of the major strategies towards achieving the pertinent strategic objectives. Visual based management can enhance productivity by: (i) calling management's attention on deviations from the plotted course and triggering prompt actions; and by (ii) motivating personnel by displaying the progress made. The tree diagram displays the strategic deployment. For each of the major strategies a simple time-chart can show for each period (month, week, day) the progress made vs. the plans. This type of presentation leads to the 'flag system' used by companies like Komatsu and described by Akao [58].

4.5.6 The deployment of continuous business improvement

The deployment process for CBI is quite similar to the one used for BBT, however, the latter, which is given top priority, is more detailed in both deployment and review. It is advisable to keep the progress made on both CBI and BBT in front of people by making use of graphical tools.

Personnel who are not involved in BBT should not feel that their work is less important. BBT may be the butter but CBI is the bread. Ultimately the two go together.

We can summarize as follows the inputs/outputs of the deployment step.

- Senior management receives input from the planning step on the outer ring.
- Senior management creates output to the plan step on the inner ring to deploy the action plans.

4.6 The inner ring

We have discussed in some detail the activities on the outer ring of our mind-map and we have mentioned that the action moves from the deployment on the outer ring to the action plans on the inner ring. Let us briefly review the inner ring.

The inner ring focuses on the five business enablers or the 5 <P>, namely:

- the action Plans;
- the 'Performers' or strategic resources;
- the Processes;
- the Products;
- the key Partners which include the customers and critical suppliers.

Operative management must lead four activities, namely:

- translating the action plans into detailed actions for each of the units or groups concerned;
- ensuring efficient execution of the plans;
- checking and documenting results on a monthly or quarterly basis unless a special situation occurs in order to determine the appropriate short-term corrective or improvement actions – tables can be used to document the progress and icons can be posted to indicate whether the results are acceptable, or to issue early warnings, or to call for corrective actions;
- ensuring that the corrective and improvement actions are planned and taken, and the learning consolidated and diffused as appropriate throughout the organization.

On the inner ring, the act step is entrusted to the competent level of management in operations, who should be empowered to take the appropriate corrective or improvement actions. Unless warranted by a special situation, senior management should not meddle with the tasks on the inner ring, or it will be trapped in micro-management. However, our mind-map provides the following points where senior and operative management interface in *two-way feedback loops* namely:

- As we have seen, having completed the planning step, senior management interfaces with operative management in the frame of the policy deployment process. This process, detailed earlier in this chapter, features a series of interactions between senior management and operative management referred to as 'catch-ball'.

- When operative management has finalized its action plans – at the plan step of the inner ring – it informs senior management who may be called upon to provide support or additional resources, or who may require adjustments to the plans made by middle management.

- 'It is a bad plan that admits no modification', said Roman statesman Publius Syrus. Changes in the marketplace that are encountered by operative management are discussed with senior management in order to agree on the necessary changes in the strategic objectives or in the strategic means.

- The periodic progress assessment made by operative management – i.e. the check phase on the inner ring – is copied to senior management who enters these inputs in its check and alert phase, on the outer ring. As appropriate, discussions between senior and operative management will ensue.

4.7 Implementing the Policy Dynamics

The PDP should be implemented in parallel for the BBT and for the CBI. However, the implementation of CBI requires less time and, to a larger extent, it can be delegated to the personnel in the operations. CBI thrives on ideas that are developed on a fairly regular basis, while the strategies for BBT are usually developed at the beginning of the planning period.

The PDP is a systematic process. The organizations that have successfully implemented 'Management by Policy' – the method on which PDP is based – have developed a set of tables to display and to monitor the deployment of the strategies and their respective action-plans. The set of tables used by Hewlett-Packard, for example, is shown in Soin's *Total Quality Control Essentials* [24].

We believe management can take a cue from other people's models but that it should develop its own tables depending on the level of sophistication and discipline in the organization. However, too many tools and too many tables tend to slow or even prevent the adoption of a management method such as the policy deployment process. A middle of the road approach should be found between the Japanese way that requires a lot of visual aids to compensate for their linguistic communication difficulties, and the Western way that typically makes insufficient use of them.

Senior management must be aware that the PDP requires an investment in time by busy managers, but that results will be reaped when the process has matured. The Conference Board of Canada [60] reported that when Xerox introduced Management by Policy, in the first year some units encountered some difficulties, in the second year all units managed to finalize their deployment within two months, and that in the third year significant benefits were obtained in terms of (i) organizational effectiveness; (ii) intellectual capital; and (iii) documentation of the policy deployment process. Most of the companies we have worked with, after an introductory period of one to three years, complete the five steps of the PDP in two months and all agree that the PDP is well worth the effort.

The 'catchball' procedure is particularly effective in achieving involvement and commitment, by empowering different levels of management to contribute to the vertical, horizontal, and timeline alignment of the organization. Last but not least, the interactions on strategic issues enable management to assess the competencies and the capabilities that are available. In our opinion, the combination of analytical, creative, and interpersonal skills displayed during these sessions provide in most cases as efficient a measure of managerial potential as the assessment centers.

The PDP implements the management principles we have described in Chapter Two, as managers have to think systemically, stimulate people at all levels through participation, and act systematically as they implement corporate goals through effective daily work. However, until this method is well established, the PDP cannot claim to be simple or swift.

It is suggested that before introducing the PDP, senior management, assisted by a consultant, starts by mapping out their present planning process to become aware of the deficiencies as well as the strongholds of their system. To do otherwise would be to put the solution in front of the problem and the benefits of the Policy Dynamics could be obscured.

The following list identifies some of the deficiencies most likely to surface during a critical review of the present planning system.

- Plans are disconnected from their implementation.
- A lack of commitment by management and a lack of discipline by the personnel.
- Operative management does not participate in the planning process.
- Plans focus on financial results not on customer satisfaction.

- Plans state objectives but are not explicit about the strategies required to achieve them.
- There is no connection between the short and the long term.
- There is no mechanism in place for real time reviews.
- Plans are not based on data (plans without data are just another opinion).
- Senior management is too distant from the operations and does not realize that the devil lies in the detail.
- There is no common dictionary across the different levels and functions.
- Problems in horizontal and vertical alignment, i.e. cross-functional barriers and hierarchical structure obstruct cooperation.
- Objectives are cast in stone before strategies are developed on how to achieve them.
- The existence of several unconnected plans.
- Findings of one planning cycle not incorporated in the next cycle.

We should also point out certain problems that should be avoided when introducing PDP.

- Not enough discussion at the catchball levels.
- Too many breakthrough projects as people keep adding new priorities.
- Reviews are too frequent.
- Reviews are not incorporated into the plans.
- Management does not check capabilities, and targets are overly ambitious.
- Insufficient time is allowed to persons involved in the planning process.
- Inadequate data collection and data interpretation strategies.
- The last level of the deployment is not an action or task.
- Senior management is too tactical, and the objectives for the BBT are not of a level sufficient to generate a business breakthrough.

- Deployment does not go down as far as activities or processes and resources.

- Having made a full turn, the outer wheel of the 'Two Rings' gets senior and operative management to agree on the action plans, yet actions are not taken or are then delayed.

- There is confusion between targets and means.

- There is no measure of performance.

- The actionable alternatives reflect strategic biases resulting from an emphasis on just one strategic thrust.

4.8 Summary

The Policy Dynamics form the powerful engine of the POM. They provide a link between the Policy Fundamentals and the Policy Implementation and Review by converting broad and long-term directives and guidelines into specific short-term action plans.

The mind-map of the 'Two Rings' structures the activities performed by senior and operative management as they develop and deploy the strategies to achieve the business policy. Business breakthrough (BBT) projects are given first priority, continuous business improvement (CBI) second priority; business maintenance has to come at the bottom of the list.

On the outer ring, senior management responsible for *doing the right thing*:

- *Checks* the results

- Is *alert* to possible future changes

- Evolves the *planning*, and

- *Deploys* the ensuing strategies.

On the inner wheel operative management, responsible for *doing the right thing*, ensures that:

- Action *plans* are *done* and *checked*, and that

- Actions are taken to implement the appropriate improvements or corrections.

The policy deployment process (PDP), which links the planning and deployment tasks, deploys strategic objectives through the interactions of two to three management levels. The characteristic of this deployment is that the level that sets the strategic objectives delegates to the next level, which receives the objectives, the task to determine how these objectives are going to be met. This method not only opens up creativity but also fosters cross-functional involvement and commitment at the different managerial levels.

The Policy Dynamics is not only an efficient method to develop and to deploy strategies but also an excellent tool to get people talking to one another about what is important for the business and to reinforce mutual respect and cooperation.

In the next chapters we will cover the business enablers. However, having discussed the action plans, we can focus in the next chapter on the following enabler, namely the strategic resources or performers. We will limit our presentation of the enablers to a selection of mind-maps – including some original ones – that we believe can contribute to the successful implementation of shared management practices.

■ CHAPTER FIVE ■

The performers

The Plan

The strategic resources are critical contributors to the performance of the enterprise. This is why we call them the 'performers'. We present an original configuration of five interactive performers, which include financial assets, time cycles and timing, the human capital, the organizational capital, and the marketing capital.

Clearly our emphasis will be on the intangible performers and notably on the 'human capital' and on 'organizational capital' because they are the most critical in today's globalizing environment.

Our research on the management of intangibles is ongoing but we can point to some of the mind-maps that we have developed.

The Mind-Maps

- The process of human capital.
- Communities of practice.
- The five drivers of organizational behavior.
- The marketing capital.

Introduction

The Policy Implementation and Review, the third of the sub-processes of the POM, focuses on *doing the thing right* as it manages the five business enablers. We touched on the first of these 5 <P>, namely the action plans, in the previous chapter. The performers are the next <P>, and we cover in this chapter the mind-maps we consider useful to set a basis for the framework that supports shared management practices.

As mentioned in Chapter Two and illustrated in Figure 2.6, the 5 <P> are interdependent. The action plans, which are deployed in the Policy Dynamics but implemented in the Policy Implementation and Review, put into gear the performers, the processes, and the supplier-partners in order to deliver value to the customer.

The management of the strategic resources is done at both corporate level and the level of the strategic business units (SBU). At both levels, management has to ensure purposeful allocation of the strategic resources. For the purpose of the presentation of our mind-maps, we will concentrate on the SBU.

5.1 The five performers

The classic economists of last century defined the resources as *labor, land*, and *money*. Of course this definition is no longer meaningful.

Manual labor has largely been replaced by machines, robots, and by computer aided systems. Land has become less important as a production factor than the infrastructure and logistics, local regulations, and local labor cost. Money of course is as important as ever, but it has taken a great variety of forms including 'virtual' ones, as is the case for derivatives.

Labor, land, and money are tangible resources. Yet, as mentioned in Chapter Two, the intangible resources have become the dominant factor of performance given the dynamic complexity of our business environment. On that account, we felt that the concept of strategic resources had to be revisited. This led us to develop the mind-map shown in Figure 5.1, which includes the following performers:

- the financial assets;
- the time cycles and the timing of actions;
- the 'human capital' or the genius of people;
- the 'organizational capital' consists of the drivers of organizational behavior that foster and support the human capital;
- the 'marketing capital' comprises various intangible and tangible assets such as customer capital, brand capital, distributor network, and logistics facilities.

FIGURE 5.1 The five performers

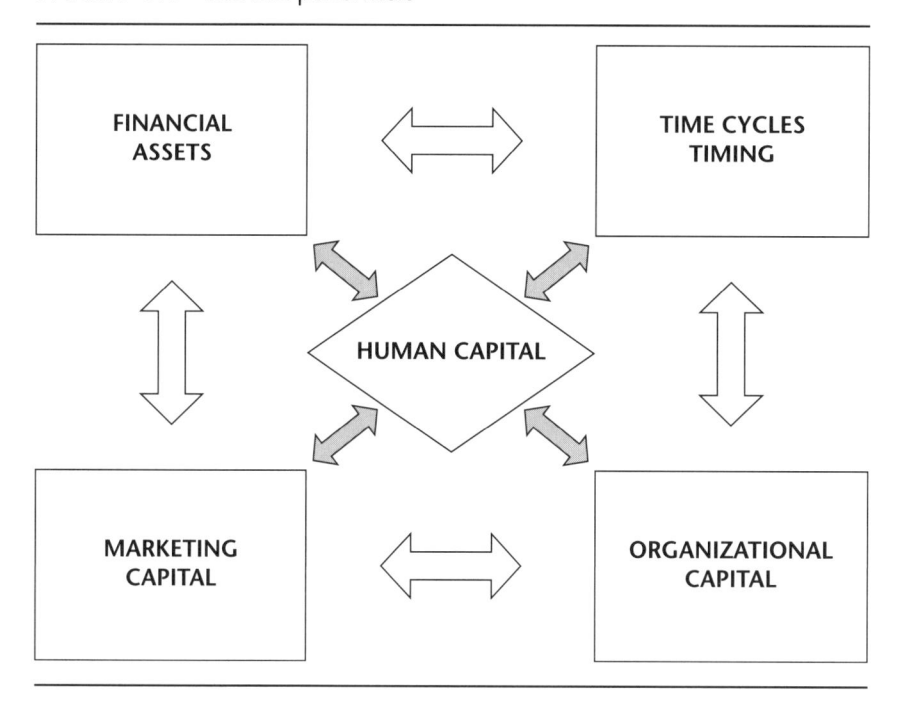

[Diagram: Financial Assets, Time Cycles/Timing, Marketing Capital, Organizational Capital arranged around a central Human Capital diamond, with bidirectional arrows connecting them.]

In the following sub-chapters we will discuss each of the five performers.

5.2 The financial assets

Financial assets as defined here encompass all that is shown in monetary terms in traditional accounting. The management of these assets uses tools such as Value Based Management, financial accounting, industrial accounting, and Activity Based Management.

According to the definition we provided in Chapter Three, the financial assets are a *core capability*, which enables other strategic resources to perform. For example, money is needed to attract and retain brilliant people, facilities are required to put manufacturing competencies to good use.

While indispensable, financial assets only generate advantages for a limited period of time because the competition can acquire and even improve on them. The management of financial assets is well documented in the literature, and we do not need to dwell on this subject here.

Traditionally management has measured the performance of financial assets in terms of return on investment and return on equity. Stern and Stewart introduced a broader concept known as *shareholder value* [72], which has become a performance criterion in the wake of the restructuring of sectors and the ensuing mergers and acquisitions and the increasing requirements of corporate governance.

5.3 Time cycles and timing

We all know that *time is money*, but often we have been more careful about managing money than managing time. Unlike money, time is not a fungible and repetitive resource. Literature on the subject is fairly scarce [73, 74, 75]. We will cover only selected aspects of this strategic resource.

We need to manage the time cycles of activities encompassed in processes as well as the lifecycles of given phenomena or situations such as market lifecycle, product lifecycle. The more time processes take, the more money they take as well. Some of the aspects of managing process time cycles will be discussed in Chapter Six.

Hereafter, some pointers concerning time-cycles and timing.

- In the *external environment*, time cycles have increasingly become a critical success factor in the competitive race. In many sectors innovation has become the driving force. The adage 'first come first served' is applicable as there is little time to take a good share of the market. Time-to-market has become an important key, particularly if the first dominant player can set standards that will put followers at a disadvantage. We could say that the last entrants into the market are most likely to be the first to leave it.

- In the *internal environment* time cycles are no less important. The time cycle of key processes, be they mental such as in decision making or be they operational such as time to delivery, is part of organizational responsiveness. Developing and deploying strategies, time-to-market, getting money from the market back to the treasury all takes time. The ability to reduce time cycles in the various activities, the early recognition of threats, the ability to seize windows of opportunity when they open, are critical competencies. Effective management of time cycles in the internal environment enables management to choose the *timing*, in other words to pick the most favorable moment to launch certain actions.

- *Individuals and teams* have to manage the time cycles of their four daily activities. As shown in Figure 5.2, we think, work, socialize, and rest. There should be a reasonable balance between these four activities taking into account personality and situation. In the long run, imbalances are inherently inefficient. Furthermore, the timing of the different activities can also play a significant role. For example, research has shown that most people tend to be more creative between 9 and 12 a.m., and therefore this time-slot should be reserved for creative work rather than routine exercises.

5.4 Intellectual capital

If you cannot work harder, work smarter! After several decades of rationalization, rightsizing, and reengineering, most of the obvious

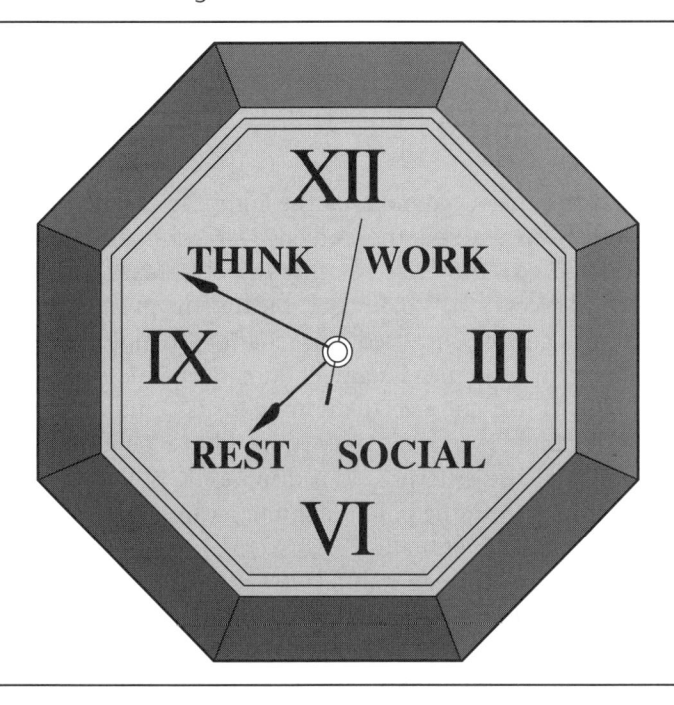

FIGURE 5.2 The timing of time

dysfunctions have been corrected. Now smart players must resort to *improvement, innovation,* and *invention* in order to get ahead of the pack and to enjoy higher profitability.

John Kenneth Galbraith coined the term 'intellectual capital' back in 1956, but the realization of the importance of this intangible asset is quite recent and has been brought to the attention of managers by authors such as Stewart [76] and Edvinsson [77]. With their seminal publication of 1994, Hamel and Prahalad [53] had already alerted management to the importance of managing the critical competencies which are a result of intellectual capital.

The stock market has learned to recognize the difference between financial assets and the genius of people, albeit that the latter is not shown in accounting statements. As a case in point, investors are now paying several hundred times earnings for the stock of enterprises that innovate services on the Internet.

The literature lumps together under 'intellectual capital' both human and organizational capital. 'Human capital' is the know-how of the people. 'Organizational capital' consists of the organizational drivers that support human capital. These two intangible assets are complementary and interdependent. However, these performers are inherently different and lumping them together diffuses and confuses their interactions.

5.5 Human Capital

At the award distribution ceremony of the European Quality Award 1997, Professor Nordstrom startled the audience of eminent representatives from business and government by stating that Karl Marx was right when he declared 'workers will own the means of producing wealth'! Deliberately provocative, he used this citation to point out that the critical wealth of the enterprise, namely human capital, is in the mind of the people. This is not quite accurate: we consider human capital to be the knowledge and know-how that people have deposited with the enterprise and that the enterprise can dispose of. Whatever remains in peoples' minds is, at best, the potential human capital that the enterprise may be able to extract eventually.

We have placed human capital at the center of our mind-map because of the importance of its interactions with all the other performers. As we try to do systematically throughout this book, we start by clarifying our dictionary. Available information is overflowing;

selecting the part that is relevant to given activities becomes intelligence. The part of intelligence that is made available in a usable form becomes knowledge. Knowledge, of course, is important but we consider it as an inert raw material. *Human capital* (HC) is the genius of people used to convert that raw material into a strategic resource or performer.

Being an intangible asset, HC is hard to define other than by some of its diverse manifestations. Schematically we could say that it encompasses various forms of know-how or skills such as: the know-how to get knowledge, the know-how to use knowledge, the know-how to coach knowledge, the know-how to use knowledge in other areas, and, last but not least, the know-how to create new knowledge.

These various forms of know-how can be applied to technical, relational, and mental processes, or, most likely, to a combination of them. HC must be aligned with the other strategic resources in order to maximize its effectiveness when applied to the business enablers.

Human capital cannot flourish on barren ground. Among the resources needed to develop it, a sound basis of knowledge and know-how is necessary. It should also not be forgotten that continuous management support is required. Many companies have recognized that the *more you know, the more you learn, and the more you create, the more creative you become*. The theory of the *learning curve*, originally developed for the manufacturing environment, takes on a new dimension when applied to HC. Thus, an enterprise that achieves a competitive edge based on its HC will be a difficult one for competitors to catch up with because it will continue to ride the learning curve better, faster, and probably more cheaply than its competition. This explains the massive investments enterprises make to keep developing their knowledge base and HC.

Among such investments, for example, is the creation of the position of 'knowledge manager' responsible for managing the development and diffusion of knowledge and of know-how across organizational boundaries. The tutorial and shared services management – discussed in Chapter Two – can act as or assist the knowledge manager and contribute to the cross-pollination of HC between the various business units within the SBU or among the SBU.

Management support of HC is engendered by the business policy and the ensuing strategic objectives that should provide guidance in the following areas.

- The Policy Fundamentals outline the *critical competencies* needed in order to attain the strategic ambitions. The critical competencies purposefully package the required human capital.

- The Policy Dynamics determine the appropriate distribution of human capital and the ensuing critical competencies among the 5 <P> taking into account (i) the strategic objectives vs. the competitive position of the enterprise; (ii) the time cycles of human capital formation vs. the market lifecycles; and (iii) the potential return on investment.

  As emphasized on a number of different occasions, there needs to be a balance in the level of sophistication of these business enablers. Often innovations or inventions are focused on existing new products that without adequate innovation of policy, processes, and partner relationships are no more than a flash in the pan. The British developed antibiotics, the jet engine, the scanner, and sonar, but, unable to match their technological competencies with adequate production and marketing skills, they have been unable to retain a dominant position with these inventions.

- Based on the strategic objectives that have been evolved, management can determine the persons and the groups that should generate human capital, state the expected results, provide adequate material and organizational resources.

- Whenever an enterprise is a constellation of different strategic business units, the critical competencies developed by the different units should be available to the whole enterprise. All business units can then draw from the wealth of available competencies and combine or recombine its elements as required. This point needs to be stressed because on the global market it is not the individual business units that compete but the whole enterprise that leverages its gamut of competencies.

5.5.1 The human capital contributed by individuals and by teams

Human capital can be generated by individuals or by teams.

Individuals obtain inputs, translate them into their own intellectual pictures, process them, and then they may communicate them with their own vocabulary. Individuals can be particularly creative, but they may not be interested in or capable of sharing their knowledge and their know-how. In addition, the 'prima donna' syndrome tends to thwart the creativity of others. The scope of the HC produced by individuals is limited to their field of interest and competencies. Thus, the HC developed in isolation by individuals may be valid for craftsmen and artists, but it is increasingly inadequate for organizations that deal with interconnected subjects and a complex environment.

While the personnel of the enterprise are the primary generators of HC, people outside the organization may have substantial contributions to make. Customers can make valuable inputs on the use of the products; key suppliers have competencies that are complementary to the ones of their client.

As they say *two heads are better than one* and increasingly management looks to teams for the development and for the deployment of human capital. Cross-functional teams are best placed to take advantage of the opportunities that exist at the intersection of different technologies or of different functions. It takes variety to manage variety.

During their work on projects, be they business breakthrough or continuous business improvement or long range projects, teams can play an important role in the development and in the deployment of human capital.

- Teams encourage individuals to participate and to share their knowledge and know-how.

- Teams are more efficient in the documentation of the human capital developed. This is extremely important. It is only by documenting, cataloguing, filing, and safeguarding it that human capital truly becomes the property of the enterprise and that it can be retrieved and distributed. Human capital that remains in the head of individuals leaves the enterprise with them.

- The objectives of teams are more balanced and closer to the ones of the enterprise than the ones of individuals who may have hidden agendas of their own.

- According to Dr Mansfield, an industrial psychologist, people tend to act according to the image they have of themselves and to a self-imposed role-play. This conditions their behavior. The interpersonal dynamics of a team can liberate the energies of the participants or push them into a psychological trap. Team leadership therefore plays a major role in the productivity of the team.

- Teams generally cope better than individuals with high levels of creative tension. The intellectual process can take time, patience and perseverance. Team spirit can overcome some of the frustrations that arise or moderate exaggerated enthusiasm. As a result, a team's output tends to be more balanced and more practical than the human capital produced by individuals.

- When it comes to communicating and to implementing new knowledge and know-how, teams can be more forceful and more efficient than individuals.

In order to be efficient and to generate a good level of HC, teams require a significant level of input particularly in the early phases of setting objectives and means, team building, start-up, and, later, review.

Ideally the composition of the team should be based on the compatibility and on the complementarity of character of the participants. In practice, teams are often composed on the basis of professional experience or availability rather than after a thorough analysis of psychological profiles. We have used psychological tests, proposed, for example, by Dr Belbin [78], and Mergerison and McCann [79]:

- to enable team members to identify their own psychological profile;
- to help them to sketch the profile of their team;
- to help them to identify the ideal profile that the team should have for the given task;
- to determine the strengths and weaknesses of their team as compared to the ideal profile;
- to conceive and implement whatever actionable measures are deemed appropriate.

New teams tend to go through a series of phases described as forming, storming, norming, performing, transforming. Obviously there will be no breakthrough without breakdown, and *teams must to learn to disagree without becoming disagreeable*. In order to perform, teams need:

- clear objectives, indicators and targets, empowerment and resources, reviews;
- leadership
  - to stabilize the environment, to foster identity and belonging,
  - to activate group dynamics by organizing a rich flow of intelligence and feedback,
  - to promote diversity of opinion,
  - to maintain a sense of urgency and focus on priorities and goals.
- to share information, responsibilities, resources and recognition.

The greater the involvement of teams in the development and in the deployment of knowledge and of know-how, the greater their level of motivation on Maslow's pyramid [10], and the greater their identity with their task and with their organization. Winslow submits that when over 50 percent of the personnel are involved in teamwork, a cultural change is likely to take place [80]. We should add that the more teams are involved in using and in developing human capital, the deeper the cultural change will be.

5.5.2 The communities of practice

Towards the end of the 1990s, the focused, fluid, and fast networks have taken a somewhat innovative form, which may be a sign of things to come. They are known as the 'communities of practice'.

In order to circulate human capital above sectorial, regional, and organizational barriers, increasingly the personnel of global enterprises resort to *communities of practice*. They are formed by groups of people who share a common interest or problem and who are willing to exchange knowledge, expertise and experiences. Most of these knowledge-networks are self-starters within the enterprise, occasionally they also involve representatives from critical suppliers or from key customers. Some of these groups may be physically present, others are virtual and use information technology to communicate.

Management is beginning to recognize the value of the communities of practice and to provide support and resources. Sometimes management may take a proactive approach and encourage the launch of knowledge-networks as a means to progress more efficiently on a given business project. It can take the following steps.

- Leadership should state the mission and the means of the community of practice to be set up. It can identify the most competent persons and encourage them to join the community of practice. It can ensure that the hierarchy contributes the necessary resource allocation and empowerment. Leadership should provide a review–evaluation–reward system that is compatible with the contribution as well as with similar systems applicable throughout the enterprise. The results and rewards obtained by the communities of practice should be communicated throughout the enterprise – without disclosing proprietary intelligence – for the purpose of stimulating the launch of other communities of practice.

- The community of practice should be supported by facilitators who will (i) coach its members and to make inputs into the network, to obtain outputs, to apply them, and to provide feedback; (ii) provide assistance in obtaining needed resources including information technology, systems for filing, safeguarding, and retrieval of the knowledge, such as a powerful search engine; (iii) provide coordination as needed for the development and deployment of human capital; (iv) evaluate the contribution, the timeline or frequency, and the volume of the human capital produced; (v) assist as called for in the launch of other communities of practice.

Although the Internet and various Intranets are changing attitudes towards virtual communities, the absence of physical contact among the participants poses some problems, particularly at the time of launch and until the participants in the community of practice are well broken-in. The following advice can be given when launching a community of practice.

- Competent facilitators should be appointed from the very start. In self-starting teams facilitators are elected by the members of the community of practice. Whenever the leadership suggests that a community be set up, it may put forward persons to fill the role of facilitator, but total acceptance of this person by all members of the community is vital. The facilitator must be senior enough to be able to help with the hierarchy and to judge the value of the organizational capital produced.

- Whenever appropriate, a core group should be formed from the outset. It gathers together a small group from among the most interested or knowledgeable of its members in order to get the community underway. The personal presence of the core members is essential to launch a community of practice. It is within the core group that a communication base is agreed upon, including the dictionary, the objectives and scope, the communication channels and procedures, the process, and – whenever appropriate – the performance indicators.

- In order to optimize the effectiveness of the physical meetings and to limit travel expenses, key individuals can be selected – possibly among the core members – who will act as relay and interface with other members of the community. However, the potential value of the output of a community of practice should amply justify some travel expenses as well as investment of time and organizational capital.

- Periodic reviews should be organized to enable members of the community of practice to check the progress made and, as called for, report the outcome to management.

5.6 The process of human capital

We have stressed the scope and the importance of human capital or HC. We have also pointed out that it is an intangible asset. The obvious question concerns how it can be managed. How can the rational, emotional, relational energies produced during this mental process be fostered and directed?

In order to understand some of the mechanisms of HC we can use the mind-map that we have adopted for process management. After all, human capital is a result of a mental process. Our approach to process management is discussed in the next chapter but we can outline its essence here.

Five elements enable the management of a process; they are the objectives, the empowerment, the architecture, the targets and schedules, and the assessment of the outcome. These elements are interdependent. Processes have an input and an output. In between there is a flow of substance, which, in the case of HC is primarily accounted for by knowledge and by know-how. Figure 5.3 helps us to visualize the management and flow of the HC process.

Of course the mind-map described here is meant as a managerial aid on complex HC processes such as those involved in major projects.

We will discuss first the five elements of process management and then the five elements of process flow.

5.6.1 The management of the HC process

(a) The objectives

Every important HC process should deliver results commensurate with the objectives set for the given project. Depending on the level of sophistication of the project to which the HC process is applied, the objectives can call for different levels of HC, namely improvement, innovation, or invention.

The more sophisticated the HC process, the more difficult it becomes to set objectives other than by broadly stated goals. As personnel progress on their project, they may be able to refine the goals and to redefine the objectives of the HC process.

FIGURE 5.3 The process of human capital

THE MANAGEMENT	THE FLOW
OBJECTIVES Setting project objectives connected with strategic objectives.	**PROCEDURE** What, when, where, who, how, how much.
EMPOWERMENT Management empowers self-managed team and allocates resources.	**INPUT** Information, ideas, insights, intuition, intelligence, knowledge.
ARCHITECTURE The design of the process is entrusted to the empowered people. Indicators are set.	**SKILL BASED RESOURCES** Technical, interpersonal, analytical/decision making, creative, visionary.
TARGETS & SCHEDULES Targets, schedules and reviews are set and reviewed as appropriate.	**KNOW-HOW BASED ACTIVITIES** Know-how to get knowledge, to use knowledge, know-how to coach knowledge, know-how to use knowledge in different applications, create knowledge.
ASSESSMENT The assessment of leading and lagging indicators is entrusted to the self-managed team and reviewed with management.	**OUTPUT** Improvements, innovation, invention.

(b) Empowerment

Whether initiated by management or by the self-managed unit, the HC process will require resources. In the case of major projects involving substantial HC processes, empowerment by the hierarchy is a must. It allocates resources and clears the road from internal roadblocks.

The distribution of the roles, resources, and responsibilities among the team members should be agreed upon.

(c) Architecture

Most likely the architecture will show the intertwining of many sub-processes. The various processes, their interdependencies, their main steps should be mapped out to facilitate understanding. As is the case for most sophisticated, cross-functional processes, the boundaries should be clearly marked and who does what agreed upon.

(d) Indicators and targets

It is not always possible or even appropriate to try and harness an HC process with indicators, targets, and deadlines. It may restrain people's creativity. However, for larger projects, such as R&D, some form of control may be applied, possibly using intermediate indicators and targets.

(e) Performance assessment

As already mentioned, the HC process is driven by a combination of rational, relational, and emotional factors. Leading indicators can be used to measure how the team dynamics has performed and how the combination of these different drivers has worked out.

Lagging indicators will measure the results obtained. This can be fairly straightforward if it has been possible to define clear objectives. However, the spill-over effects of HC processes can be as important as the planned outcome. The spill-over can be particularly difficult to measure because of time delays and the involvement of different units.

5.6.2 The flow of the HC process

Figure 5.3 shows also the five elements of the process flow.

1. *Procedures* pertain to all the components of the process flow including how procedures should be established, documented, and checked.
2. The *input* is mentioned in order of increasing importance. Information has to be screened for relevance and, if possible, accuracy in order to become intelligence. Information, ideas, insights, and intuition are raw materials for intelligence. Intelligence as applied to a meaningful purpose becomes knowledge.
3. *Various resources* are necessary to put the HC process into gear. As far as the skills-based resources are concerned we should mention technical skills, interpersonal skills, analytical and decision making skills, and creative and visionary skills. There is an obvious

connection between the objective of the project, the inputs available and the skills-based resources that should be employed.
4 The *activities* are often the most visible part of the process flow. However, they are only useful to the extent that they deploy the resources effectively and efficiently.
5 The *output* should achieve the objectives that have been set for improvement, innovation, and invention.

The following hints may help the management of the HC processes. We would recommend making connections between (i) the various elements of the process management and the various elements of the process flow; and (ii) the various elements of the process flow. For more detailed explanation of these suggestions see Chapter Six.

5.6.3 Creativity

As shown in Figure 5.3, improvements, innovations, or even inventions are among the outputs of HC processes. In order to produce such outputs, the most valuable among the skills-based resources is the creativity. The fact that we no longer live in the Stone Age is due to human creativity having improved, innovated, and invented better ways. Creativity is the highest return we can get on the human capital invested.

As Peter Drucker puts it 'Every organization needs one critical competency: innovation. And every organization needs a way to record and appraise its innovative performance'. According to D.A. Glaser 'Creativity in science requires five main resources: extensive knowledge of previous work, the imagination to form new ideas, the intuition to be able to eliminate bad ideas quickly, the wisdom to visualize the consequences of promising new ideas, and the professional skills required to turn ideas into detailed actions. Creative work is risky since it involves untested elements at almost every step'. A desire to materialize the vision ignites the process, while apprehension and apathy extinguish it.

Creativity is the most ethereal component of HC. As should be expected, it is difficult to manage, and in fact, to a large extent, it should be left to manage itself. Management must enable creativity by providing the required moral and material support. Of course for larger projects management needs to set priorities and allocate resources. However, unlike tangible assets that are ruled by essentially rational decision processes, creativity is fueled by emotions which the leadership network should channel and support. Creative forces enjoy recombining, rearranging, and reinventing and, as has been proven by Walton,

Bloomberg, Dell and other pioneers, they revolutionize major sectors of activity.

Authors have offered a wide variety of methods to stimulate the creativity of human capital. Beanstock suggested we look at what is happening around us and classify what has retained our attention in *what's good, what's bad, what's interesting*. According to this researcher, these groups of items probably suggest opportunities for innovation. De Bono came up with the six thinking hats [38]; Drucker identified seven sources of creativity [66]; we mentioned in Chapter Three some of the approaches we use to stimulate creativity.

It is difficult to find creative people; it is difficult to find a good way to stimulate creativity. However, the greatest difficulty is to find a good combination of the people, the method, and the situation.

5.7 Organizational capital (OC)

Studies indicate that just about any individual, any team, is potentially capable of producing human capital. The nature, the volume of the output, and the level of its sophistication will vary.

The Curies did their seminal work in the ESPCI, a physics research center in the heart of Paris. The facilities have hardly changed since and utilize only small equipment. In spite of its seemingly modest means, this laboratory has been registering an average of 40 patents per year and has produced Nobel Prize winners in pure physics. Is it the spirit of the Curies that motivates creative research or is it that the institute does not mind hiring maverick researchers and gives them reasonable freedom?

Human capital or HC needs to be supported not only by financial assets but also by another intangible asset, not shown in traditional accounting, namely what the literature calls the structural capital. We prefer the term *organizational capital* (OC) to avoid confusion with the organizational structures that focus on the reporting relationships. Organizational capital is to human capital what a well-fertilized soil is to a plant, i.e. a prerequisite to its strong development.

As we have seen, management needs HC to achieve its strategic ambitions. The paradox is that it cannot create it. What it can and must do is to create the conditions that are conducive to the production of HC. For this purpose, management can shape the drivers of organizational behavior that influence the rational, emotional/creative, and relational behavioral modes already shown in Figure 2.3. It is the drivers of organizational behavior and their synergies that generate commitment

FIGURE 5.4 The five enablers of organizational capital

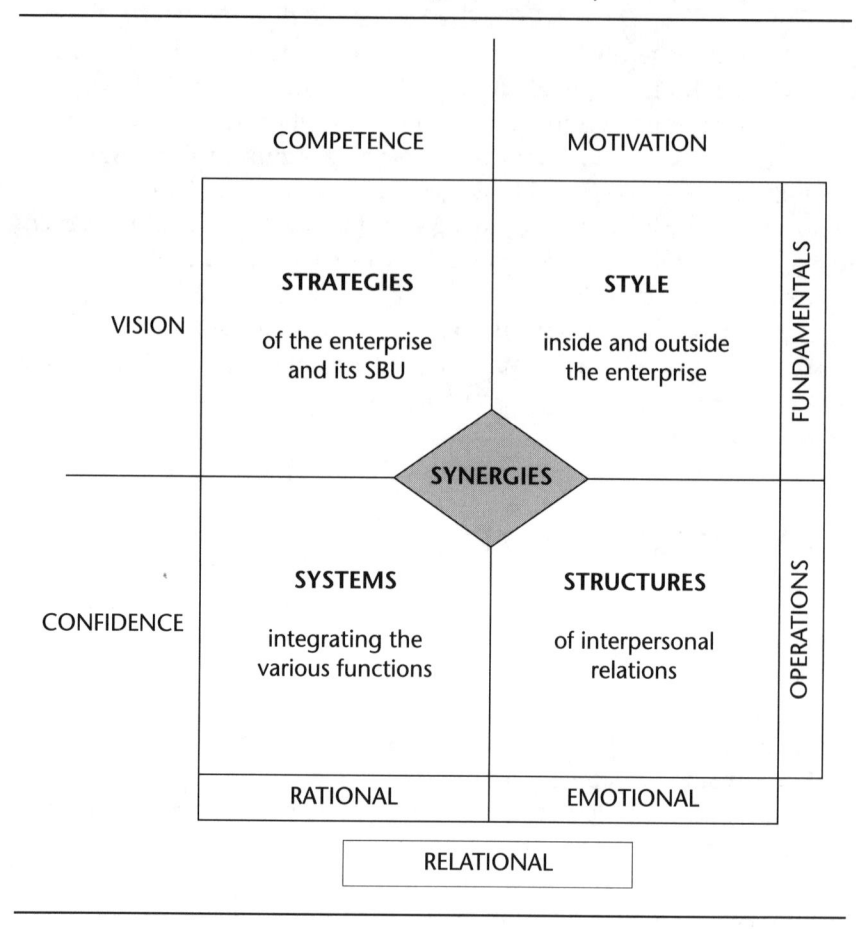

```
                    COMPETENCE          MOTIVATION
                  ┌─────────────────┬─────────────────┐
                  │                 │                 │
                  │   STRATEGIES    │     STYLE       │   F
                  │                 │                 │   U
          VISION  │ of the enterprise│ inside and outside│ N
                  │   and its SBU   │  the enterprise │   D
                  │                 │                 │   A
                  │              ◆ SYNERGIES ◆        │   M
                  │                 │                 │   E
                  │                 │                 │   N
                  │                 │                 │   T
                  │    SYSTEMS      │   STRUCTURES    │   A
                  │                 │                 │   L
                  │ integrating the │ of interpersonal│   S
       CONFIDENCE │ various functions│    relations   │
                  │                 │                 │   O
                  │                 │                 │   P
                  │                 │                 │   E
                  ├─────────────────┼─────────────────┤   R
                    RATIONAL            EMOTIONAL         A
                                                         T
                          ┌──────────────┐               I
                          │  RELATIONAL  │               O
                          └──────────────┘               N
                                                         S
```

which in turn will generate the cooperation that fuels collective creativity.

In order to understand the drivers of organizational behavior we have developed the mind-map shown in Figure 5.4. [35, 81]. Together these drivers of organizational behavior constitute the organizational capital.

In order to facilitate the retention of this mind-map, we use alliteration and we speak of the five <S> of organizational capital, which are Strategy, Systems, Structures, Style, and their Synergies. Senior management is the architect of the aforementioned drivers of organizational behavior, and the leadership network is their tutor. We will discuss how each of these 5 <S> contributes to the OC of the enterprise, and for more details we refer to Chapter Two 'Cooperation'.

1. The *strategies* should provide an understanding of why things are important. Strategies should elicit commitment. Without commitment why bother.
2. The *systems* – we include in this definition all the processes and procedures of the enterprise – should provide confidence. For example the policy deployment process described in Chapter Four aids understanding of who does what and its overview shows that everything is planned out and under control. Various processes tie in with policy deployment. Resource allocation and empowerment ensures the necessary means are available.
3. The *structures* of the organization should facilitate rather than burden activities. Management is the architect of the structures, it can change them. We have discussed in earlier chapters the open space that lets focused, fast, and fluid networks trace pathways to make the appropriate connections. Management systems concern the human resources. *Before having the right product and the right processes we must have the right people.* This saying, attributed to Toyota, recognizes the fact that the enterprise needs to recruit, to motivate, to train, and to retain the right people. The review–evaluation–reward process that is managed by the structures, i.e. hierarchy, should be motivating. Motivation liberates emotional energies, and HC and creativity in particular consume a considerable amount of these energies.
4. The *style* of the enterprise as defined here is a combination of the internal or corporate culture, the culture of the sector, and the culture of the region whereby the country of origin of the enterprise seems to remain prominent even in multinational organizations. The management can exert a positive influence on the style. It can contribute to harmonizing the internal and external components of that style so that it fosters productivity and creativity. As already pointed out, management should take notice of the unwritten rules of the game and fill the gap, if there is one, with the style. Management can plant and reinforce symbols – tangible signs that illustrate style. Strategies and structures are live demonstrations of style. One of the most powerful of symbols may be the example that management sets day in and day out.
5. *Synergies* exist between the aforementioned drivers of organizational behavior. Gaps between the 5 <S> are crevasses into which vision, confidence, competencies, and motivation are in danger of taking a fatal fall.

We can now elaborate on the drivers of organizational behavior.

The *vision* is built on the synergies between strategies and style. Vision requires belief that the strategic objectives are worthwhile and that they are compatible with the style of the enterprise. Strategies are essentially a rational driver of behavior, the style of the enterprise is essentially an emotional one. If the strategies break out of the comfort zone created by the style, the vision will easily be shattered. Chandler [46] was concerned with the distance between strategy and structures. After waves of rationalization, restructuring, and revitalization the structures have become as mobile as the office partitions, which can be moved without causing undue concern. On the contrary, the corporate style has deep roots.

The vision needs to be buttressed by *confidence*. Confidence is built on the synergies between the systems – a rational/relational driver – and structures – an emotional/relational driver. Systems and structures provide confidence that the organization is capable of attaining the envisaged results. Confidence is achieved when people believe that the systems in place are supportive of the strategies, and the structures are compatible with the style.

A high level of vision and confidence are a prerequisite to fully utilizing competencies and motivation.

Competencies are deployed by rational drivers, namely the strategy and the appropriate systems to put it into action. *Motivation* or the 'sparkle factor' as some call it, is driven by emotional/relational factors, namely style and structures. As Juran [17] pointed out, competency without motivation relies on routine achievements where the hit rate is the greatest and the risk the smallest. Motivation without competency leads to the smallest hit rate and the greatest risk.

Style and structures should enable motivation. They can, however, be de-motivators if the style is very traditional and risk-averse, and the structures are rigid and highly hierarchical. Motivation is a result of sensible and clear priorities, the intensive involvement of management, and a good review–evaluation–reward and resource allocation and empowerment systems. Edvinsson suggests that rewards should be given *when the impossible is made possible* [77]. We prefer that rewards should be made as an encouragement as soon as good performances are achieved. Eli Goldratt's precept is applicable worldwide, namely: *tell me how you will measure me and I will tell you how I will behave.* As can be seen, the review–evaluation–reward process is a major motivational factor. We recognize its importance and consequently have placed this issue among the Policy Fundamentals.

The structures, in other words the way interpersonal relations are organized, also play a major role in the motivation of personnel.

Organization charts that focus on positions rather than on the rapport people have to one another are passé. Matrix organizations that put two heads in command of the same job disperse ownership and lengthen the decision making process. Loose, recombining networks of competencies, teams that represent a microcosm of functional, interpersonal, and intercultural competencies are the most stimulating and high performing forms of organizational capital.

It is essential to break through organizational barriers and install what we call *open space* to encourage personnel to take the initiative and to provide for a reasonable tolerance of error [81]. When France's former President François Mitterand visited Silicon Valley to find out their secret of success, Steve Jobs, then CEO of Apple Corporation said 'we tolerate failure'. Better yet, some companies have instituted procedures for new product introduction that feature a safety net at all phases of the project and that limit the cost of failure.

5.8 Marketing capital

The activities deployed on the market should enable the enterprise to build another intangible asset not shown in traditional accounting but one that is taken into account in the appraisal of the worth of an organization.

This asset is often called *goodwill* and it is guesstimated with a lump sum. However, we can be a little more precise by introducing the concept of 'marketing capital' which encompasses the following factors.

- The 'customer capital', which estimates the future potential of the customer base in terms of business as well as learning. The valuation of this intangible asset will be discussed in Chapter Eight.

- The 'brand capital', which goes beyond the existing customer base and the existing product line. It enables the enterprise to pull new customers into old applications and old customers into new applications on the basis of the credentials acquired by the brand. Brand extension is an effective lever in the case of new product introduction, however, levers also have their limitations. The value of the brand is connected, in many cases very closely connected, with the image of the producer or vendor. The more sophisticated the product or some aspects of its value delivery chain, the more the customer will seek assurance in the credibility of the producer or vendor.

- Market position is a broader concept based on share of the market which impacts on the economies of scale and possibly economies of systems.

- The infrastructure, including logistics facilities, the distribution network, and its facilities.

- Influential, local contacts that have been built up over the years and in certain countries and in certain sectors are critical success factors in their own right.

We will return to marketing capital in Chapter Eight where we explore relationships with key customers.

5.9 Summary

We have identified five strategic resources that have a major impact on the performance of the enterprise, and called them the 'performers'.

In Chapter One we pointed out that the intangible strategic resources have become the determinant factor. They are like the bottom of the iceberg, the large part that supports the smaller, but visible, tip of the iceberg.

We covered very superficially the financial assets, introducing original mind-maps concerning time cycles and marketing capital. However, the focus has been on human capital and on its support, namely organizational capital.

We illustrated an approach based on process management to get a better understanding of the workings of human capital on large projects and discussed a relatively new but potentially very interesting form of circulating human capital, the communities of practice.

Organizational capital can be developed by shaping and managing the five drivers of organizational behavior. We presented an original mind-map of the drivers of organizational behavior, throwing into relief their impact on vision/confidence, and on competencies/motivation.

Finally we described 'marketing capital', which is a broader and more clearly defined concept than the traditional one of goodwill.

■ CHAPTER SIX ■

The processes

The Plan

Processes are the third of the business enablers or the 5 <P>, which are managed in the Policy Implementation and Review. The action plans put into motion the performers, the suppliers, and the processes in order to deliver a value that the customer will recognize.

The Mind-Maps

- The hierarchy of processes.
- The ten elements of process management.
- The 5 <D> of process management and innovation.

Introduction

In the seventeenth century, Antonio Stradivari reached unsurpassed mastery in violin making. To this day no one knows what he did or how he did it. That was his 'black box' and when he died he took it with him. The process and the 'know-how' contained in that 'black box' have been lost.

As organizations become more complex and more participative, management must open up these 'black boxes' and turn them into processes. From input to output, all the elements of the process must be transparent, measurable, and therefore manageable.

Process management has become a major management tool and much has already been written on this subject. In this chapter we will focus on a few mind-maps that we consider useful for the implementation of shared management practices.

6.1 The hierarchy of the processes

The International Standards Organisation (ISO) dictionary 8402 § 1.2. defines processes as 'a set of resources and activities that transform the inputs into outputs'. This broad concept enables us to consider that everything is a process. Indeed, processes come in all sizes and shapes. There are manual and mental processes, physical and psychological processes, simple and sophisticated processes, repetitive and exceptional processes. For all their variety, all processes have the following points in common.

- All processes are designed to produce the planned outputs by adding value to specified inputs.

- All processes have the same basic architecture.

- All processes can be mapped so as to visualize their interconnections and to facilitate their analysis.

- Process performance can and should be measured.

- Procedures, documentation, and personnel training can stabilize processes. Processes can be compared, corrected, improved on, innovated, and new processes can be invented.

An organization puts into gear a complex network featuring hundreds of different processes. These processes cannot work in isolation because no single process is capable of delivering value to the customer or to any of the other stakeholders. Processes form networks within a *hierarchy of processes* whereby, like the Russian dolls, the processes of different hierarchies fit into one another.

Depending on their hierarchical level, we distinguish between mega-processes, macro-processes, midi-processes or business processes, and micro-processes.

The first level, which we call the *mega-process*, is the frame that encompasses all the processes of the enterprise. Processes generated from outside impact the mega-process and conversely some of the processes generated by the enterprise are directed outwards. Senior management is the architect of the mega-process and must see to the effectiveness of the interdependencies of the processes of the next level of hierarchy.

On the next level we have the *macro-processes*. We distinguish between five types of macro-processes, as illustrated in Figure 6.1.

1. The *strategic macro-processes* encompass the management activities described in the Policy Fundamentals, the Policy Dynamics, and in the Policy Assessment and Audit.
2. The *resource allocation and empowerment* (RAE) and the *review-evaluation-reward* (RER) are extremely important processes, whose guidelines are established in the Policy Fundamentals. They interact with all the other macro-processes. So we have placed them at the center of our mind-map.
3. The *social macro-processes* relate to the administration of the human resources. Concern for personnel must underpin all managerial activities. Therefore social processes are intertwined in the network of processes. Social processes are designed by human resource specialists, but require the approval of senior management.
4. The *support macro-processes* concern the administration of the enterprise. As is the case for the social processes, they are intertwined in the network of processes. However, unless their development is kept in check, they grow like poison ivy at the expense of the plant they grow on. The support processes are designed by specialists in information technology, in finance and accounting, in security and safety, etc. Approval of operative management and in some cases senior management is required.
5. The *customer value delivery* (CVD) features a horizontal chain of processes that go from the external supplier to the external customer (buyer or user/consumer) adding competitive value that the customer and the market should recognize. This macro-process starts outside the mega-process and ends outside. The CVD is driven by the strategic macro-processes, supported by the resource allocation empowerment as well as by the review–evaluation–reward processes. The activities of the CVD take place in the Policy Implementation and Review sub-process of the POM. Operative management is responsible for the design and for the effectiveness and efficiencies of the processes of the CVD.

Figure 6.1 illustrates the fact that (i) all macro-processes are interconnected; (ii) there is a vertical axis from business policy and its strategies to the CVD; (iii) the RAE and RER processes interact with the other processes; (iv) the social and support processes concern the internal

FIGURE 6.1 The five macro-processes

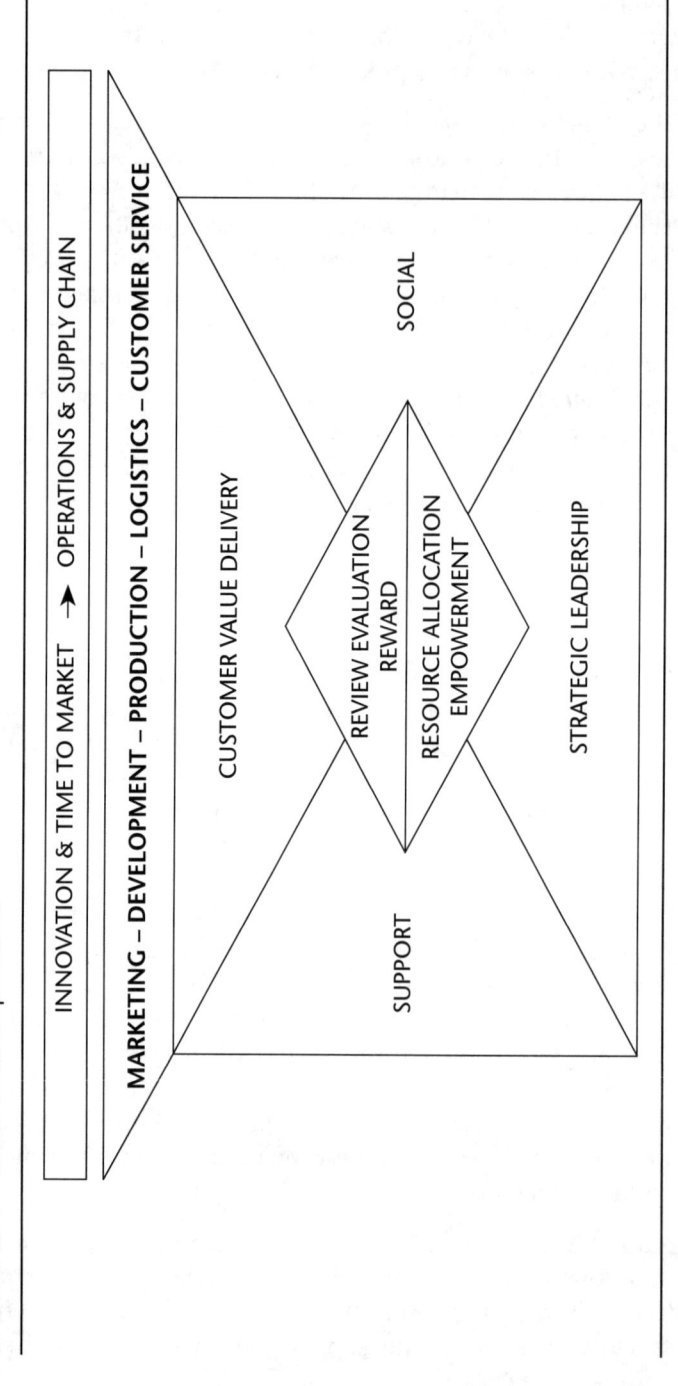

INNOVATION & TIME TO MARKET → OPERATIONS & SUPPLY CHAIN

MARKETING – DEVELOPMENT – PRODUCTION – LOGISTICS – CUSTOMER SERVICE

CUSTOMER VALUE DELIVERY

SOCIAL

REVIEW EVALUATION REWARD

RESOURCE ALLOCATION EMPOWERMENT

SUPPORT

STRATEGIC LEADERSHIP

administration; and (v) that all aforementioned macro-processes serve as support to the CVD which is where the money is made.

The tutorial and services management mentioned in Chapter Two contribute to the social processes where they act as coach, and to the support processes where they provide shared services to various departments and strategic business units (SBU).

When designing the architecture of the macro-processes, senior management starts with the strategic macro-processes. It will use the Policy Fundamentals to point everybody in the same direction, and the Policy Dynamics to deploy the strategic objectives onto the customer value delivery and design the architecture of the value-chain. Finally, it will outline the appropriate social, and support processes. Following the guidelines for RAE and RER set out in the Policy Fundamentals, senior management designates an owner for each of the macro-processes, ensures their collegial cooperation and responsibilities, and provides for an adequate distribution and circulation of the competencies and capabilities.

Senior management can use a block chart to visualize the interactions among the macro-processes. Discussion by senior management with the macro-process leaders shown on the block chart will reveal the inputs, the outputs, and the value added, as well as internal problems such as frictions – which we call *hot-spots*, and occasionally the *black holes* when nobody knows for sure what happens.

Together, senior and operative management will estimate the value added, the competitiveness, and the future prospects as they concern the various macro-processes and the next level of processes namely the *midi-processes*.

Based on the review of the concepts concerning the strategic thrust, the value chain, the competencies and capabilities developed in the Policy Fundamentals, and based on the knowledge evolved in the Policy Dynamics planning step, senior management will decide which part of the network of processes needs to be strengthened, what should be improved/innovated/invented, what should be outsourced, and what should be discontinued.

In the following step of the Policy Dynamics, namely the deployment, the strategic objectives, the empowerment, and the resources will be deployed over the midi-processes. The hierarchy of processes is generally reflected in the hierarchy of *process owners*. Increasingly process owners are given cross-functional empowerment so as to overcome departmental and functional barriers.

The detailed plans concerning the next level of processes, namely the *micro-processes* will be turned over to the next sub-process of the POM, the Policy Implementation and Review.

As can be seen, senior management plays a major role in the concept of the whole architecture of the macro-processes. It must ensure that the appropriate connections between the various macro-processes are in place before the system is turned on. Otherwise, as with loose electrical wires, a short-circuit is possible. Deming surprised his audience when he stated that 85 percent of an enterprise's dysfunctions are attributable to management. Considering the fact that senior management is responsible for designing the configuration of the processes and for the implementation of the POM and that operative management is responsible for the effectiveness and efficiencies of the network of processes, Deming's point is perfectly plausible. If human error accounts for 15 percent or more of the cost of dysfunctions, reasons may be found in the management of human resources, i.e. in the social macro-process, which senior management has approved.

Of course the architecture of the processes is not a simple task. The rush into business process reengineering has provided many examples of misalignment of macro-processes. In some cases the point of view of the personnel has been completely forgotten, in other cases the supporting system has not been properly aligned, in yet other cases the process engineers focused on just one of the links in the value chain and overlooked the big picture.

Of all the processes, it is the customer value delivery process that has attracted most of the attention and rightly so. We will now consider aspects of the management of this macro-process.

6.2 The customer value delivery process

The customer value delivery (CVD) process makes the link between the internal and the external environment; it makes the link between external suppliers and external customers; it is the one that justifies all the other processes. On the flowchart of the POM shown in Figure 2.1, the CVD takes place in the Policy Implementation and Review. This macro-process breaks down into sub-processes or *midi-processes* sometimes referred to as business processes, where we include the following functions, namely:

- marketing;
- R&D;
- production;

- logistics;
- sales and customer service.

The international standard ISO 9001:2000 does not separate marketing from sales and customer service. We do because these functions require different approaches and different competencies [13]. They also happen at different stages of the CVD. Marketing starts the CVD by looking for opportunities that will satisfy both the objectives of the enterprise as well as the needs of the customer. Sales and customer service normally close the CVD cycle by placing the available products on the market.

The midi-processes encompass more detailed processes, which are of the next level of hierarchy and which we call *micro-processes*.

The best way to visualize the networking and interactions of processes is to map them out. As shown in Figure 6.2, the *chain of processes* goes from the external supplier to the external customer. Every link of the chain of processes must add value according to objectives so as to enable the enterprise to deliver to the customer at the end of the chain the *unique value proposition* that has been planned and for which strategic objectives are deployed in the Policy Dynamics.

The customer determines the *service level agreement* (SLA), in other words his expectations concerning the characteristics of the unique value

FIGURE 6.2 The chain of processes

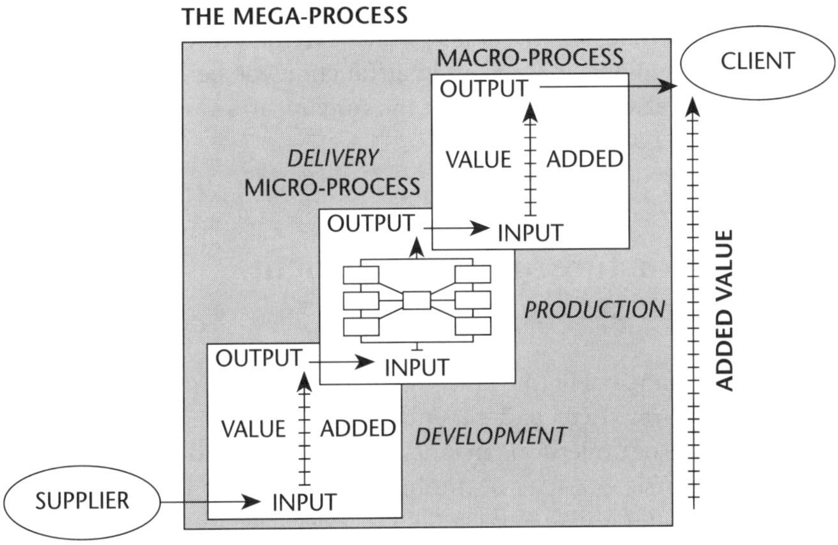

proposition. Drawn from the SLA, requirements are passed on up the chain of processes, link after link all the way back to the external supplier.

Throughout the chain of processes of the CVD, a great variety of connections are established between *internal provider* and *internal user*. The 4 × 100-meter relay run, illustrates the delicate relationship between internal provider and internal users. Running fast is to no avail if the baton is not passed efficiently to the next runner. An inefficient transfer of the baton will result in a loss of time and aggravation that will impair the good efforts produced by the runners.

We reserve the word 'customer' for the one who pays for the product, and the word 'supplier' for the external partners. Often enough, the relationship between internal user and internal provider is less efficient that the one the organization entertains with its customers and its external suppliers.

First, the external customer pays and judges the value received. The internal user often does not see the cost to the enterprise of the value delivered by the internal provider. Secondly, the internal supplier often has a de facto monopoly. As long as the internal user receives the same delivery its efficiency and competitiveness may not get called into question. Last but not least, focusing people's attention on just the next link of the chain lowers their horizon to a set of tasks rather than to participating in the satisfaction of the customer. This can be insidious as it limits commitment and creativity to one link of a possibly long chain of events, it encourages personnel to specialize and therefore reduces their versatility and mobility. We strongly advocate getting personnel out of their little box inside the organization and to have them interface occasionally with external suppliers and external customers. Furthermore, we recommend that all internal functions be benchmarked with comparable deliverables outside the organization and, whenever appropriate, to be outsourced.

6.3 The structure and management of processes

Processes are comparable to engines. They consist of many moving parts, they consume resources and produce output. The mechanism of the processes has to be understood in order to ensure their proper functioning.

We emphasized at the beginning of this chapter that, in spite of their diversity, and unlike engines, all processes have the same structure. In order to manage them we have to understand their structure. For this

FIGURE 6.3 The ten elements of a process

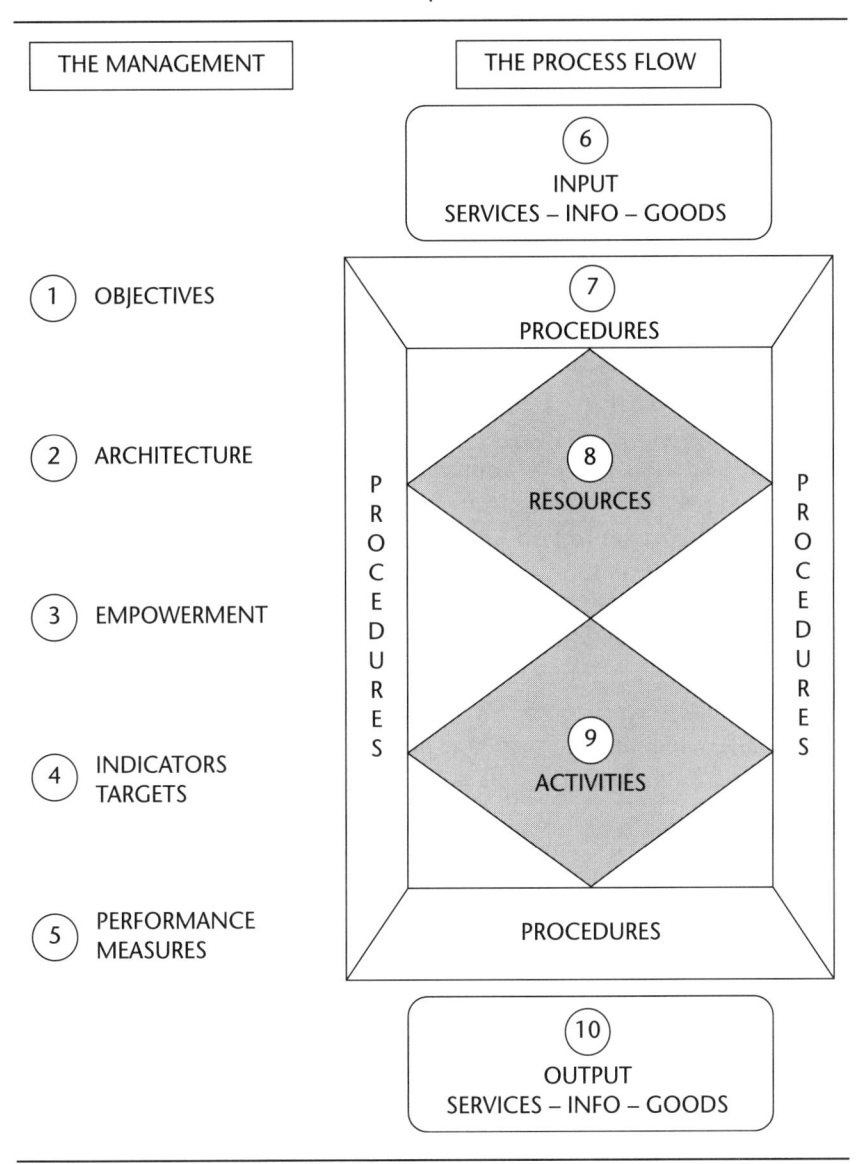

```
THE MANAGEMENT              THE PROCESS FLOW

                                    (6)
                                   INPUT
                            SERVICES – INFO – GOODS

  (1) OBJECTIVES                    (7)
                                 PROCEDURES

  (2) ARCHITECTURE      P           (8)           P
                        R        RESOURCES        R
                        O                         O
                        C                         C
                        E                         E
  (3) EMPOWERMENT       D                         D
                        U                         U
                        R                         R
                        E           (9)           E
                        S        ACTIVITIES       S
  (4) INDICATORS
      TARGETS

  (5) PERFORMANCE              PROCEDURES
      MEASURES

                                   (10)
                                  OUTPUT
                            SERVICES – INFO – GOODS
```

purpose, we have developed the mind-map shown in Figure 6.3, which features five elements pertinent to their management, and the five elements that concern the process flow. As we will see below in the subsection entitled 'Managing process efficiencies and effectiveness' the five elements of process management and the five elements of process flow are interactive, and through these interactions we can manage their efficiencies and effectiveness.

6.3.1 The five elements of the management system

(a) Objectives

Each process should have its *objectives*, which are stated as a noun describing the subject, a verb indicating the direction. Setting objectives is not easy. They must be specific enough to be understood, yet broad enough not to limit scope and ambitions.

Kepner and Tregoe propose a model for setting objectives, which brings into focus the pertinent guidelines and constraints by identifying *results to be achieved, results to be avoided, resources to be used* and *resources to be protected* [44]. For communication's sake, the objectives should also be clarified with background information on the *seriousness*, the *urgency* and the *trend* of the situation.

The level of *priority of the process* should be clear and consistent with the strategic objectives deployed in the Policy Dynamics. As we pointed out in Chapter Four, processes involving a business breakthrough (BBT) take priority over processes concerning continuous business improvement (CBI), which in turn may take precedence over processes relating to business maintenance. The following ten questions help to define the objective.

- Who are my customers/ internal users?
- What are their needs and expectations?
- How do they rate the importance of their various needs and expectations?
- What product configuration are we supplying (directly or indirectly) to them?
- What criteria do they use to evaluate the product configuration we are supplying?
- What is their present level of satisfaction? how has it evolved?
- How do they evaluate major competitor's alternatives?
- What processes are involved in delivering the subject output?
- What parts of our organization are involved? what do they contribute?

- What performance standards have we set for the subject process? how well are we meeting our standards? are our performance standards adequate and competitive?

(b) The architecture

Consistent with the objectives that have been set for the process, the owner who is normally of the management level that corresponds to the hierarchical level of the process, designs the architecture of the process and its boundaries as well as the connections to other processes inside and outside the organization. However, this can rarely be done in isolation because the various processes are interconnected and often they involve several units cross-functionally. Furthermore, higher level processes should deploy their objectives on lower level processes or on processes in other functions. If the architecture is not effective, processes will not be efficient.

In practice, organizations are constructed piece by piece in response to particular needs, hierarchical ambitions, or competitive situations. As a result, rather than a cohesive architecture, the organization struggles with a patchwork of processes. The Policy Assessment and Audit – discussed in Chapter Nine – may feature an in-depth review of the whole construction of processes starting with the macro-processes concerning the customer value delivery process and its sub-processes.

(c) Empowerment

The Policy Fundamentals set the directives and guidelines for empowerment. Every process should have an 'owner' who is empowered to use the allocated resources and to manage the process in order to meet the objectives. The ownership of the macro-processes and of the major midi-processes is established by senior and operative management during the policy deployment process of the Policy Dynamics. Ownership of processes of lower hierarchical order is assigned by operative management.

(d) Indicators and targets

While objectives are descriptive and qualitative, the indicators and targets are prescriptive and quantitative of the results to be obtained and how they should be measured. Setting indicators requires a good understanding of the situation and of how the results should be measured whereupon targets can be set. The importance of measuring the performance of the processes cannot be stressed enough. *What gets measured, gets done.*

Popular belief has it that performance measures are a constraint. This is a remnant of Taylorism where supervisors looked over the shoulder of the operators and punished them if the performance they were responsible for fell short of expectations. Today the approach is quite different. The performance measures and the corrective measures are entrusted to the process owner and to his/her team.

There are different measurement systems. The simplest one, easily remembered by the acronym STEPS, measures the *specifications*, the *time* cycle, the *efficiency*/costs, the *production* volume, and *safety*. A more sophisticated approach measures performance according to the following criteria.

- The effectiveness of satisfying requirements using a customer satisfaction index or percentage of deliveries that conform to customer expectations (E).

- The robustness of the process or control of variations using statistical process control (R).

- The efficiency in controlling costs using cost per unit and other indicators (E).

- The flexibility of supply is a very important criteria when satisfying changing requirements. Pertinent indicators include the measurement of the time and cost of model changes, the time and cost of changing delivery schedules, etc. (F).

- Time cycle indicators may use the time cycle flowcharts discussed later in this chapter (T).

- The transferability of the process and of its improvements when the enterprise operates the same or similar processes in different locations. Enterprises that have similar operations in different locations may want to ensure the transferability of the design and management of key processes. It is advisable to simplify as much as possible the processes that are likely to be transferred at some point in time. The next step would be to document the process flow and its management system in words and drawings, and to load the information onto an Intranet. Cultural barriers have to be recognized, and care has to be taken to avoid expressions and images that have a strong local content and that could easily be misinterpreted (T).

Last but not least, let us emphasize the value of establishing and constantly updating a *database* on process performances and on process improvements, classified for easy retrieval and comparison. This database provides an ongoing baseline for internal benchmarking as well as cross-fertilization of improvement ideas by the pertinent community of practice. Regular contributors to the database may find themselves forming communities of practice in dedicated fields. Some recognition should be given to those who offer valuable inputs to the database as well as to those who get results using them. The recognition could be based on a composite measure of the value of the input, frequency of inputs, timeliness of the input.

The five levers of process management can be applied to each of the five elements of the process flow.

6.3.2 The five elements of the process flow

Figure 6.3 also shows the following five elements of the process flow.

1. *Procedures* frame and stabilize the various parts of the process. The ISO 9001:2000 and 9004:2000 provide respectively an international standard and guidelines on how procedures should be established, documented, communicated, coached, and reviewed [13].
2. *Inputs* include a combination of goods, information, and services. The value of the inputs should be known.
3. *Resources* include personnel time, equipment time, money. For the purpose of managing the process flow, the resources should be easy to convert into monetary terms.
4. *Activities* can also be converted into people-time and therefore into monetary terms. We cannot miss this opportunity to remind the reader that activities serve no other purpose than to deploy the allocated resources to achieve the given objective.
5. *Outputs* include a combination of goods, information, and services. The value of the outputs should be measured and known.

The process flow can best be visualized and reviewed using a *flowchart*, which:

- gives a visual display of the elements of the flow;
- shows the roles and relationships between the steps and departments involved;

- helps to locate areas for improvement, and areas where data should be collected and investigated;
- helps to place performance measures;
- helps to compare information as in benchmarking, also helps with training new personnel and documenting the process.

There are different types of flowcharts. The following list itemizes some of the most popular versions of this tool.

- The *block chart* shows an aerial view on all the components of a macro-process, i.e. the midi-processes. As already mentioned it is a most useful tool when management designs or reviews the overall process architecture.
- The *ANSI flowchart*, is the most frequently adopted tool to show the activities/tasks as well as the decision steps that occur within the boundaries of the process. It uses the symbols proposed by the American National Standards Institute. A useful variant of this tool shows how the activities flow through the various functions and units or through different locations. It aids visualization and eliminates wasteful back and forth movements.
- The *time cycle flowchart* uses symbols BS 3138 of the British Standards Institute and throws into relief the time spent on the various activities.

Unquestionably the flowchart is a most useful tool, which – as is the case for most graphical tools – is neither as difficult as feared nor as simple as hoped for. At least initially, professional facilitation should be provided. Goal/QPC [25] and AT&T [82] provide concise instructions on the use of this tool.

6.3.3 Managing process efficiencies and effectiveness

(a) Managing process costs

In order to be effective and efficient, the process should be as error free as possible. GIRFTET is the acronym sometimes used to exhort personnel to 'get it right the first time and every time'. Juran [17] and Crosby [18] and other authors have emphasized that the *cost of internal and of external failures* substantially exceeds the *cost of prevention and the cost of quality control*. Oakland [19] reports that the cost of failures – often referred to as the 'cost of non-quality' – can account for 10–15 percent of total cost in manufacturing and 30–40 percent in the service sector.

Some failures become apparent through customer complaints, field failures, missed delivery delays, guarantee costs, repair prior to shipment, product recalls, products returned by the customer, etc. However, most of the cost of failures results in *hidden costs*, hidden not by personnel but by the cost accounting system. Such costs include lost customers, unrecorded customer complaints, rework, bad supplies, missing specification, unnecessary line changes, excessive inventory, poor planning, cost of debugging products, etc.

In a manufacturing environment the causes of failure are relatively easy to detect because they tend to stack up pretty quickly. In the administrative environment the causes of failures are subtler. The fact that 'things have always been done this way around here' allows people to assume that the process is efficient. However, in times of change, 'the same old way' is seldom a guarantee of efficiency.

Activity Based Costing/Activity Based Management, also known under the acronym ABC/ABM, are powerful methods to manage costs and efficiencies [69, 70, 71].

As mentioned earlier, the time cycle flowchart helps estimate the time taken by the various activities. The activities can be categorized as (i) customer value-added; (ii) organizational value-added; and (iii) no value-added or waste. The BS 3138 symbols distinguish the various categories of activity so that they may be visualized on the flowchart. From the customer's point of view, delays, storage, and internal transfers, are considered no value-added. Some analysts also put into this category, appraisal, decisions, and even prevention. According to these criteria, it is not unusual to find that activities recognized as value-adding by the customer only account for 5–15 percent of total cycle time.

These kind of data have the merit of getting senior and operative management's attention, but it summarily discounts as 'no value-added', activities that are ineluctable in the operations such as transfers, decisions, quality controls. To be credible, a careful examination of what is and what is not no value-added should precede a time cycle analysis.

A Pareto chart helps to visualize the breakdown of the aforementioned groups of activity, and management can use it as an indicator of areas in need of improvement.

Tending to be focused on financial results, management occasionally attempts to focus process management only on cost reductions. However, Hitoshi Kume reminds us that 'the goal of management is to increase profits not just to reduce costs' [83]. Mature products will have low costs and low profitability, while innovative products will have high costs, greater variances, and initially even a high failure rate, and nonetheless high profitability. This led Soin to suggest that management should concentrate on improving those processes that have been identified as having strategic importance rather than launching an all-out effort on collecting costs data [24]. The process objectives set in the frame of the policy deployment process of the Policy Dynamics serve that purpose.

(b) Checking effectiveness and efficiency

We have already pointed out that the difficulties in setting process boundaries are due to the fact that the processes are interconnected and intertwined. The five levers of process management and the five elements of the process flow are interactive. This mind-map can be quite useful for a quick check of process effectiveness and efficiency.

First, each of the levers of process management can be applied to each of the elements of the process flow. For example we may evaluate a procedure that locks up a process by asking how does it contribute to the objective, to the architecture, to the empowerment, and to the measurement system of the process?

Secondly, the effectiveness and efficiencies of the interactions between the various elements of the process flow can be analyzed. For example the relation of resources used to output will point to the level of efficiencies.

Thirdly, whenever measuring the effectiveness and efficiency of a process the following sequence of steps is suggested.

1. One should start by comparing the output of the process with the target that has been set.
2. The next step may be to check the variance of process performance over a reasonable period of time.
3. The inputs should be checked. A change of supplier or a change in the material are likely sources of problems.
4. The next thing to look into is the resources and to check whether they are wisely used.
5. Last but not least, the flow and the rationale for the activities deployed should be checked.

More sophisticated tools are available should a deeper analysis be required, or the root cause of problems be detected. When looking for the cause of a problem that occurs in repetitive, routine type processes, it often pays to look for what has changed since the first observation of the given problem. Based on this observation, Kepner and Tregoe [44] developed a fairly sophisticated method to identify the root cause. Statistical process control and variance analysis are widely used tools to keep processes under control.

Motorola is a strong proponent of a method based on the statistical notion of *Six Sigma* (3.4 defects per million parts produced) to drive both the targets as well as the results obtained in the manufacturing and in some of the simple and repetitive administrative processes. GE and Allied Signal are among the companies that have followed suit. This method is gaining some popularity, but most companies that claim to use this method only apply Six Sigma as an indicator to control mass manufacturing processes.

We feel that the ten elements of the process as shown in Figure 6.3. provide a useful guide to process management.

6.4 Process performance improvement

Processes are like engines, they are designed to achieve a certain planned performance; to do so they must be operated properly, and periodically checked because they can become out of order. Should this be the case a complete overhaul will be necessary. The internal combustion engine was developed 100 years ago and yet, year after year, improvements continue to be made, sometimes even substantial improvements. Likewise, there seem to be no limits to process performance improvements. As illustrated by the Deming Wheel in Figure 2.5, the competitive race is often won by the enterprise which improves faster than its competitors.

There are several levels of process improvement, namely:

- correction of sporadic process dysfunctions;
- correction of systematic process dysfunctions;
- continuous process improvement *kaizen* style;
- process simplification;
- process-architecture innovation.

6.4.1 Correction of sporadic process dysfunctions

Sporadic process dysfunctions are due to occasional external factors. Operative management should set up an early warning system and must envisage preventive or contingency measures to deal with recurring sporadic causes.

6.4.2 Correction of systematic process dysfunctions

Processes can get out of order in the same way as a motor and, whenever such a situation arises, the empowered team should take the necessary corrective measures to bring the process performance back to the planned level.

Process performance measures should be taken of the output and, whenever possible, measure of the input to the process should also be taken. If at all possible they should be taken in real time and visually displayed. The performance of repetitive processes can be monitored in real time thanks to statistical process control. As a rule of thumb, when the statistical process controls show seven dots in the same direction in a row, of whichever way, it is the signal that the process is running out of control and that operative management attention is required.

6.4.3 Continuous process improvement *kaizen* style

Leading Japanese corporations, inspired by the old Chinese saying *step by step walk a thousand miles*, have taught their process teams to come up with continuous suggestions for process improvements. *Kaizen* puts more emphasis on the number and frequency of improvements than on the impact any one improvement may have on results. The merit of this approach is that continuous process improvements (i) are quite easy to implement and cause no disruption to the operations; (ii) generally do not require massive investments in terms of capital and training or involve the risk of upsetting the whole process; and (iii) keep the team really committed because they are continuously involved with their process.

Whenever dealing with more complex processes, cross-functional teams are put to work, ideally composed of representatives of the internal provider and the internal user. Sometimes these cross-functional teams include representatives of the customer or of the supplier. Complementary competencies are critical to process improvement. If continuous process improvement is extended to all macro-processes, we speak of *continuous business improvement*.

It was Imai's work [16] which brought the *kaizen* concept to the West. The best-in-class have taken advantage of this concept to enhance their efforts towards continuous business improvement. This has contributed to increasing awareness of the management of quality. However, many companies have limited their *kaizen* program to making continuous small improvements in their manufacturing environment.

6.4.4 Process simplification

Over time, new procedures are added, new processes are introduced, some of the levers of process management are changed. Furthermore, new managers bring new ideas and sometimes speedy solutions. As a result the process architecture becomes overly complicated or even incongruous.

The process team or a cross-functional team should seek to eliminate duplications and unnecessary controls, and automate manual operations. The opportunities for process simplification are legion. The following list itemizes a small selection.

- *Bureaucracy*. Remedies include reducing the amount of paper being passed around, reducing the number of meetings, reducing the interfaces, reducing excessive controls, etc.

- *Rationalization* and value analysis. Remedies include eliminating redundant tasks, redistributing the work, optimizing the workflow, reducing the number of manipulations/process steps, eliminating bottle-necks, standardizing whenever appropriate, making tasks easier to perform, fool-proofing, etc.

- *Improvement of the time cycles*. Remedies include replacing sequential with concurrent work, reducing interruptions of the work flow, changing the order of activities, reducing the movement of people and materials, utilizing just-in-time, etc.

- *Optimization of the use of resources*. Areas for consideration include investing in productive technologies, switching from a push to a pull production line, optimizing the productivity of the equipment, optimizing the use of space, etc.

- *Partnership*. Among the many strategies available are outsourcing non-core activities, optimizing the flow of information with suppliers, distributors, customers, etc.

Process simplification can be entrusted to the natural team, in other words to the people who are involved with the process. Generally process simplification followed by *kaizen* is adequate to achieve the goals of continuous business improvement. This approach should be considered seriously before attempting to redesign a process.

6.4.5 Process architecture innovation

Simplification may prove insufficient to achieve more ambitious objectives such as business breakthrough (BBT). While simplification does not change the process structure, process innovation – as the name implies – requires a radical departure.

In the mid-1980s when some American corporations were badly battered by Japanese competition, continuous improvement and process simplification were clearly too little too late. Given the size of their competitive disadvantage, the problem could be likened to *facing a jump over a 10 foot ditch: it would be no good trying to do it in 10 one foot steps*. As a result, several corporations decided to take one big jump, with the risks that would entail.

Hammer and Champy introduced the term 'business process reengineering' and induced many organizations to launch such programs to regain competitiveness [84]. The use of the word 'engineering' was probably indicative of the fact that processes were considered, like engines, as something to be entrusted to technically minded engineers. This resulted in a narrow approach that occasionally neglected the human side of enterprise, and sometimes even neglected the customer. We prefer to speak of architecture because it takes into account the people and the *whole* process architecture rather than just *a* process. We also prefer to speak of innovation as opposed to reengineering. In English the word 'reengineering' contains the element 'engine' suggesting a mechanistic approach. Interestingly enough, the term originally comes from the French 'ingenieurie' the root of which is genius. Anyway, since English is the language of world business, we will speak of architecture.

Now, process architecture innovation is part of the management arsenal of the best-in-class. It is done in the frame of business breakthrough projects (BBT) which are decided in the planning step of the Policy Dynamics. At least initially, business process reengineering was done once and for all. Now, the best-in-class have two to three BBT projects under way at any given time.

BBT may be necessary to shed inertia and indolence, to leapfrog the competition, to enter new areas of opportunity. As mentioned in Chapter Four, it is essential that all the connections and interactions between the area to be innovated and the rest of the organization be well planned and well understood. As repeatedly emphasized, in the organization all of its business enablers are interconnected. Touch one part and the whole structure may come tumbling down. BBT projects are entrusted to a high-level group that has a broad knowledge of the business, and is deemed capable of coming up with creative and practical ideas.

While continuous business improvement and process simplification start with the existing situation and seek improvements, process innovation often starts with the breakthrough objective and a blank piece of paper. Creativity tools such as the ones mentioned in the previous chapters are used. The blueprint for breakthrough has to be tested for feasibility and compatibility in order to avoid mistakes that can be extremely costly. The implementation of the BBT has to be carefully thought out. It has to be smoothly implemented in order not to magnify unnecessarily internal and external resistance. Finally, the learning acquired on each of the BBT projects should serve the projects that will follow.

6.5 Managing process improvement project by project

Process improvement, whether in the form of a correction, a simplification, or an innovation of the architecture is carried out on a project by project basis. While the objectives, the means, and the composition of the project team vary, many of the same principles and techniques are applicable. The project team goes through the following five steps or the 5 <D> of process management and innovation:

- definition of the project and composition of the mission statement;
- diagnosis of the improvement opportunity;
- discovery of the best solution(s);
- deployment of the approved improvements;
- diffusion of the learning.

6.5.1 Definition of the project and the mission statement

The selection and the definition of the process to be improved are the responsibility of the process owner. The improvement objectives of business processes that have a high impact on the strategic objectives are defined in the policy deployment process. For all other processes, the process owner will take the initiative to determine the objectives of the project.

Based on the background and process objectives, a team will be formed and a mission statement issued. The appointed team will expand on the mission statement so that it covers the following points:

- title of the project, name of the project owner;
- background information, definition of the problem/opportunity and how it has been discovered, the point of view of the customer or of the internal user;
- if available, what has been done about this situation in the past and with what results;
- the boundaries of the process (top and bottom as well as lateral boundaries if appropriate);
- objectives, indicators, and targets for the improvement;
- data collection strategy, process management techniques and visual tools of process management to be applied [26];
- distribution of roles, responsibilities, and resources;
- action plans and schedules.

The purpose of writing down the mission statement is to ensure clarification of the project. The performance improvement team (PIT) should review the statement with the process owner and, whenever appropriate, with representatives of senior management i.e. the steering committee. However, the team would be well advised to leave the door open to renegotiating any part of the mission statement at a later time if necessary. The mission statement could be illustrated with storyboarding, which shows the tools to be used at the various steps of the project.

The PIT starts by mapping out the process at a high level within the agreed boundaries before detailing it with additional flowcharts. The PIT may find that, as pointed out by R. Henkoff, the hardest part of process management is figuring out where the process begins and where it ends. The process boundaries should not be dictated by hierarchical responsibilities but by the needs of the customer or by the internal user. As a result, the process boundaries may have to be redefined.

Whenever available, the indicators, the targets, and the performances should be shown for each of the processes. It should not be necessary at this stage to go into the details of the individual tasks which comprise the process. Should intelligence not be readily available, it will have to be collected in the next step of the project.

6.5.2 Diagnosis of the problems and of the improvement opportunities

The members of the PIT have to establish a detailed flowchart or process-map. The data collected on all the five elements of the process flow as illustrated in Figure 6.3 should enable a preliminary identification of the improvement opportunities. Statistical process control provides hard data that have to be complemented by soft data such as customer surveys, customer complaints, and competitive intelligence.

The major technique used to analyze problems is the determination of cause and effect. The following techniques can be used to determine the root cause.

- *Stair-stepping*: the facilitator asks: (i) what is the problem, (ii) are we 100 percent sure this is so, (iii) is that the root cause. After going five times through this series of questions there is a good chance that the root cause will surface. This is the quickest way to get to the bottom of the problem if the root cause is a relatively simple one.

- *Brainstorming* is the most frequently used technique. Brainstorming can be structured or unstructured. In the latter case, the team starts by agreeing on the major groups of potential causes and each group is shown as a branch on a fishbone diagram – also called an Ishikawa diagram – and the inputs of the team members are systematically put on the appropriate branch. AT&T [82] uses a fishbone diagram with up to eight branches (market focus, management, measurement, manpower, motivation, methods, materials, and machines). We recommend using a fishbone diagram with a branch for each of the 5 <P>. The Ishikawa diagram has the advantage of eliciting a systematic, visually aided brainstorming session. Another form of structured brainstorming – also referred to as silent brainstorming – calls for inputs to be written on Post-it® slips and displayed on the wall. The participants group and regroup the Post-it® slips according to their affinity and evolve an *affinity diagram*. Showing on an *interrelation diagraph* the influences that the different factors exert on the other factors can prioritize the headings of the affinity diagram [26].

- 'TOPS', the acronym for *team oriented problem solving*, is a technique used by Ford Motor Company, which is based on an approach developed by Kepner and Tregoe [44]. This approach features a very detailed description of what the problem is and what the problem is not. The problem is further broken down in terms of what, where, when, and how much. The next step is to identify what is different between what the problem is and what it is not, and then to consider what has changed over time. The possible causes are then fed back into the identification of the problem. This is the 'Reilly Filter', which helps to separate the root cause from the possible causes. TOPS is a fairly sophisticated method that is efficient in mass production where a phenomenon can be traced over a period of time.

6.5.3 Discovering the best solution(s)

A number of solutions may be proposed during the brainstorming and they have to be evaluated against the agreed upon criteria that may include effectiveness, robustness, efficiency, flexibility, time cycles, and synergies. The importance and the difficulties of setting the appropriate criteria should not be underestimated.

As concerns their *feasibility*, the proposed solutions should be introduced on the process map in order to visualize the changes required, their cost, their impact on the parties concerned – mainly the personnel and the suppliers – and on the other business enablers. The following methods can be applied to detect potential problems and to plan preventive or contingency measures:

- force field analysis is a simple graphical technique that lists the anticipated resistance to change and plots the countervailing measures and their potential effects [26];

- potential problem analysis [44];

- process decision program chart [26].

The solutions developed should be submitted to the competent management level for approval.

6.5.4 Deployment of the approved improvements

A detailed improvement plan should be developed to show what has to be done, how it should be done, what resources should be deployed, who is the owner, and how the results should be measured and reported.

A tentative schedule and the pertinent procedures needed to stabilize the improved process should be prepared, presented to the process owner and his team, and their approval must be obtained.

The deployment of the improvements should be documented. If problems arise at a later stage, this will help to trace the cause. If the improvements work well, documentation will help stabilize the process, and facilitate the diffusion of the learning.

6.5.5 Diffusion of the learning

As appropriate, the project team needs to coach and facilitate the process team, i.e. the team that is responsible for the management and operation of the process.

The process team will deploy the improvements, and report the results. Once the improved process has stabilized on the higher level of performance, operative management will calibrate the results obtained by the PIT and by the process team and will institutionalize the improvements. The results will be communicated across the organization and should inspire other process or project teams.

6.6 Summary

Even in the smallest of organizations, processes form an intricate construct. We must understand the hierarchy of processes to better understand their interactions. We have presented a mind-map that shows the different levels and the different purposes of processes.

However, the individual processes all have the same basic components, which feature five levers of management and the five elements of their flow. We use the interactions between the levers and the elements of process flow for a first check of the effectiveness and efficiency of the process. We have mentioned more sophisticated methods to improve process performance.

Finally we have outlined the steps of projects that will lead to the improvement of process performances.

■ CHAPTER SEVEN ■

The product

The Plan

A discussion of features and benefits helps us understand the product economics and some of the critical success factors. We can then explore the five steps that lead to product strategies. Our focus will be on new product development and we will try to highlight some of the relevant concepts.

The Mind-Maps

In order to facilitate the implementation of shared management practices, we present in this chapter the following mind-maps:

- the 'product' as a configuration of five interdependent deliverables;
- the product economics as a delicate balance between the cost of features and the benefit the customer perceives;
- the emphasis is on new product introduction.

Introduction

The product is one of the five business enablers that are entrusted to operative management in the frame of the Policy Implementation and Review. The product is the most visible link between the internal and the external environment. It is the interface between the enterprise and the customer.

Pride in the delivery of a superior product, that customers appreciate and that competitors respect, is possibly one of the strongest motivators for all those who have been involved with the product. People do not only identify with an enterprise, but also with its products.

The product delivers different types of value to the customers. In order to analyze them, we will first break down the 'product' into its components or deliverables and then discuss their interdependencies. This will lead us to discuss the features and benefits that make up the product's competitive superiority and profitability. However, product leadership can be an ephemeral victory unless it is part of a broader business policy. In many sectors, such policy is based on new product introduction as a means of staying ahead of the competition. We will therefore emphasize new product introduction as one of the product strategies.

As mentioned in Chapter Three, it is interesting to note that the European Quality Award (EQA), the Malcolm Baldrige National Quality Award, and the ISO 9001:2000 standards do not feature the 'product' as a separate building block of their respective models. It is possible that they focus on the processes and that the product is merely viewed as an outcome. In our opinion, the product is and should be a focal point of a manager's attention. This is corroborated by the fact that well before the word 'benchmarking' entered the managerial dictionary, substantial efforts had been concentrated on competitive product analysis. However, as we have pointed out when discussing the strategic thrust, product orientation can become excessive and may cause an inward looking approach.

The product

7.1.1 The five deliverables of the 'product'

The 'product' is a bundle of the following five components that we call the *deliverables*.

1. The *primary deliverables* comprise the goods, services, and information that meet a need recognized by the customers and that drive a purchase. Specifications, delivery delays, and price are among the major characteristics of the primary deliverables. Remember that logistics is part of the primary deliverable because the time, the place of the delivery and the condition of the deliverables are part of the specification. From the customers' point of view, the value of the

primary deliverables can be expressed in terms of attributes such as: fit for the intended use, value for money, the right thing in the right place at the right time, versatility, field of application, user friendliness, security, safety, etc.

2. The *augmented deliverables* comprise the goods, services, and information that are not the primary inducement of the purchase but which should be appreciated by the customers. Packaging, software, the instruction manual, installation services, after-sales service, security and safety devices are just a few examples of augmented deliverables. This component of the product generally causes additional costs. Its added value should be recognized by the customers and would then justify a commensurate premium or generate a competitive advantage. The value of the augmented deliverable can be evaluated by the customers with attributes such as: time saving, cost saving, user friendliness, practicality, flexibility, comfort, etc.

3. The *auxiliary deliverables* come with the primary product. Albeit adding costs, they are of marginal value to the customer or are just taken for granted. While the auxiliary deliverables seldom generate a competitive advantage, faults can cause a competitive disadvantage. Examples of auxiliary deliverables include invoices, supporting documents, administrative tasks. The value of auxiliary products can be evaluated with attributes such as: timeliness, accuracy, clarity, accessibility, etc.

4. The *personal attention* component contributes to the pleasure the customers have in dealing with their supplier. In the USA, keen competition has made suppliers particularly aware of the importance of personal customer relations. The staff are trained to relieve the customer as much as possible from any hassle, any hurry, or any problem. Personal attention takes on an ever-increasing importance in our society. Personal attention can be provided in many different ways and via many different media.

5. The *intangible deliverables* enhance the value the customers receive and perceive. The reputation of the supplier, the trademark or brand, the different projections of the product imagery are all designed to add value to the various product components. As Rosbeth Moss Kanter put it '[Product] quality and price differentiation are gone. A distinctive brand image is the major defense against a growing commoditization of products'. Imagery can even substantially raise the value of the product. However, it can also substantially raise customer expectations! Both will be taken into

account in the 'customer-recognized value' or CRV, a notion to be expanded on in the next chapter.

Commercial transactions always involve two or more of the five aforementioned deliverables, packaged in what we call the *product configuration*. To be effective, the product configuration should include all the deliverables that contribute CRV.

Customers may recognize the value of individual deliverables, but their judgment is a more or less subjective conclusion drawn from the value recognized in the whole product configuration. Therefore, marketing should go beyond assessing the CRV for individual deliverables. It should try to determine how the different deliverables interact in the judgment customers make of the product configuration. For example superior augmented deliverables or personal attention may offset some of the competitive weaknesses of the primary deliverables. Conversely, the weakness of the augmented deliverables or of personal attention can invalidate the acknowledged superiority of the primary deliverables. As appropriate, correlation studies, the conjunctive model, conjoint measurements can be used as described by Kotler [85].

The concept of the product configuration is relevant to shared management practices as it emphasizes a systemic approach as well as the need for cross-functional cooperation. We feel it is important to introduce the concept of product configuration because when people talk about 'product' they often only consider the primary deliverables. However, having made the point, for simplicity's sake we will use this narrower definition in the following sub-sections.

7.1.2 Features and benefits

Traditionally the product has been defined from the supplier's point of view and expressed as a set of technical specifications. The product that the supplier may consider as fit for use may not necessarily be fit for the use actually intended by the customer. Competition in recent years has forced suppliers to become much more customer-oriented and to view the product through the eyes of the customer.

The emphasis has shifted from *making and selling* to *sensing and responding*. However, sensing and responding have become increasingly complex and delicate as we have gone from *market segmentation* to *market fragmentation*.

Market segmentation allowed the supplier to classify customer requirements in standardized groups that could be related to psychographic, socioeconomic, and demographic criteria. Customers no longer follow fashion, they make fashion. They no longer fit neatly in one standardized group. They are more sophisticated, more assertive, and eclectically migrate from one group to another thereby exploding the traditional classifications and fragmenting the market.

To better understand market fragmentation, we should distinguish between product 'features' and product 'benefits'.

Features are characteristics of the product, which are often expressed in terms of specifications, timeliness, and price. *Benefits* are the advantages that the customers get or expect to get from operating or from owning the product.

Sometimes, one feature may actually engender several benefits. Occasionally several features are needed to support just one benefit. The affinity diagram, possibly in combination with an interrelation diagraph, is a useful tool to filter the inputs made by the customer and to separate the benefits from the features. These tools also help to classify the features according to their level of detail. For example car safety must be an important benefit for drivers and passengers. Several features support that benefit, including road-holding, brakes, etc. Disk brakes are a feature that supports the safety benefit. Disk brakes on the front and rear wheels of a car is a sub-set or the next level of feature.

Understanding the relative importance and interdependencies of benefits and features is a key to planning and delivering a competitive product to the customer. This marketing process collects and analyzes the following inputs from the targeted customers: (i) a list of the expected benefits; (ii) the rating of each of the benefits; (iii) the interdependencies between the various benefits; (iv) the features the customers recognize as more important or less important to support the benefits that have been mentioned. Summarizing the above data we get a detailed profile of *customer recognized value* or CRV. This profile can be put on a matrix showing on the vertical columns the benefits and on the horizontal lines the features. Icons can help the visualization on the matrix of the degree of impact the different features have on the different benefits. If a more precise evaluation of the impact is required, managers should refer to the Quality Functional Deployment technique mentioned in Section 7.2.3. The purpose of these tools is to visualize the prioritization of the features.

Having collected the above-mentioned information from the customers, we recommend that the customer-contact personnel (the sales force, delivery men, the after-sales service, marketing and merchandisers, etc.) be asked to answer the same questions reflecting their knowledge of customer reactions. Comparing the rating of features and benefits as expressed by the customer with the opinions expressed by customer-contact personnel can be enlightening. It can reveal misconceptions and, whenever appropriate, these data can be used as a lever to change the beliefs and attitudes of the relevant personnel.

Confusion between features and benefits often mars sales transactions. Theodore Levitt illustrates this conceptual dichotomy by stating that customers do not buy a drill for its features but for the holes they can make with it [86].

Of course, the communication problems between customers and suppliers engendered by the distinction between features and benefits depend on the sector as well as on the level of sophistication of the parties. Probably the dichotomy between features and benefits is greatest in the case of consumer-durables; it should be smallest with components sold to original equipment manufacturers that are basically transacted on the basis of features.

Services differ from other sectors in as far as features and benefits tend to be intertwined. Furthermore, customers contribute to the quality of the service, but often do not realize this and hence they will not take responsibility for their contribution to non-quality. Services are intangible, perishable, and heterogeneous. They are often supplied in small units therefore there are no economies of scale. Delivery and consumption of the service are simultaneous. We cannot get into service marketing here. However, the literature is quite extensive and readers are recommended to consult Lovelock [87], Zeithaml *et al.* [88], and Albrecht and Bradford [89].

7.1.3 Product economics

Customers and suppliers see features and benefits from a different point of view. The features impact suppliers' costs while benefits ultimately translate into customer recognized value. The CRV and competitive offers determine the price the targeted customers will be willing to pay. The difference between the total cost of features delivered and the price the customers are prepared to pay for a given product configuration represent the suppliers' profit potential. We refer to this as the *product economics*.

Management should carefully evaluate a balance between, on one side, the cost of the features it can package in the product configuration and, on the other side, the competitive value the customers will be willing to pay for. Neither side of this equation is easy to calculate.

First, customers are not interested in suppliers' cost and, as we have already mentioned, they may not be able to provide accurate data on their rating of benefits, on the interactions between various benefits and between various features.

Secondly, technology is decreasing the cost of adding features. This tempts competitors to embark on a *feature frenzy* just to expand their sales arguments. This causes suppliers to forget the fact that generally *price takes precedence over features*. Thus, we get 'over-quality' that generates extra costs – albeit marginally – without engendering commensurate customer value recognition. Occasionally too many features decrease the ease of use and even decrease the CRV. Furthermore, the more numerous and sophisticated the feature, the more difficult, time-consuming, and costly the product's quality assurance becomes. Finally, the enterprise may offer more features than presently required by customers just to extend and expand its critical competencies and core capabilities. The customer will not pay the additional costs entailed, but the supplier expects that this investment will generate future competitive advantages. We refer to this as 'super-quality', a strategy that, combined with forward pricing, has enabled Japanese corporations to make big inroads into Western markets.

To summarize, the supplier has to be careful not to offer product features beyond the point where the customer recognized value becomes marginal or even decreases. That is easy to say but is in practice a delicate affair. In the case of consumer products, the motivation studies advocated by Dichter can be helpful [90]. In Chapter Eight we will expand on customer recognized value and we would refine the concept by distinguishing between the 'musts' and the 'wants'.

7.2 The five steps of product strategies

The product is one of the six factors of the *marketing mix*, which includes product, placement, promotion, price, persons, and politics [85].

Nicholas Hayek, the charismatic CEO of Swatch, stated in a conference at the University of Geneva in 1997 that his strategies are based on the product, which must have true quality, offer a substantial price advantage, and add something emotional in its sales pitch.

This way Swatch delivered a substantial advantage that customers recognized. It achieved high visibility in the marketplace and a large volume of sales. The good profits generated have in part gone to finance the development of technical as well as commercial competencies. This enabled the company to aggressively pursue new product introduction. It presents two collections every year, previous models are discontinued and some of them have become collectors' items.

Many product strategies can lead to success, Hayek's team found one of them. However, it is simplistic and misleading to present *Product*

Innovation Strategy: Pure and Simple [92] as one book title suggests. After all, the resounding successes are outnumbered by dismal failures.

Product strategies are a sophisticated intellectual and organizational process. Together with customer relation strategies with which they are closely connected, product strategies write the bottom line. If the products are just right, customers will beat a path to the supplier's door; if they are not, the salesmen will wear out their shoes chasing after unimpressed customers.

We have structured product strategies in the following five steps:
1. discovering customer needs and market opportunities;
2. defining the product strategies;
3. designing the product and the supporting activities;
4. developing the product including the engineering, manufacturing, logistics;
5. deploying the product strategies for the various phases of the product lifecycle.

The first two steps focus on *doing the right thing*, the following three steps concentrate on *doing the thing right*. The subject of product strategies is a particularly vast one, and we can only touch on some of the important issues.

7.2.1 Discovering customer needs and market opportunities

We have mentioned the tendency of suppliers to be inward looking and, carried away by their own momentum, they continue to work on a narrow spectrum of features. Senior and operative management have to ensure that a comprehensive and updated marketing database be available and that it be used as a basis for product strategies.

(a) The customer

It is essential that intelligence on the CRV, as it concerns benefits and features, not be limited to the primary products or to the present product configuration and to the present needs because in many if not most sectors novelty if not newness drives the market. Customers' propensity to change and the direction of possible change have to be sensed.

Until the 1960s, customers' preferences went to well-established products. The production methods were unstable, the supply was unreliable and it was risky to venture into something new. The modern management of the macro-process concerning the customer value delivery (CVD) has long changed that. Now, people expect the newest to be the best. As product novelty wears off, so does customer interest. 'If it is not new just rename it or repackage it' is an old marketing gimmick that has been used and abused to the extent that it no longer startles the consumer.

Listening to customers' manifest and latent needs is essential but insufficient. We must be alert to opportunities and threats in the market. There may be new technologies, new regulations, and a new competitive thrust that will impact the product strategies. As already suggested by nineteenth-century French economist Jean Baptiste Say and adopted by Reganomics in the USA, the supply side is a dominant factor of our economy [91]. It is the suppliers who stimulate the demand for all but the most basic needs. The present and future needs of the customers must be interpreted by the supplier. Akio Morita, co-founder and former chairman of Sony, said 'Our plan is to lead the public with new products rather than asking them what they want. The public does not know what is possible, but we do'. Of course customers did not go to Sony's Morita asking for a 'Walkman', nor to Apple Corporation's co-founder Steve Jobs asking for a microcomputer, nor to the CERN asking them to develop the Internet system. Deming pointed out that the *customer is ignorant but learns pretty fast*, and of course the competition is only too happy to help the customer learn [42].

(b) The market

In order to understand the opportunities and threats connected with product strategies, management needs to look *at the market* and *at the product lifecycles*. The market lifecycles were discussed in Chapter Three and illustrated in Figure 3.2. The product lifecycle features the following stages:

- development;
- introduction and market penetration;
- volume growth;
- maturity;
- decline or product extension/improvement or innovation/repositioning.

Suppliers need to be attentive to the competitive aspects of the product lifecycle. Each phase of the product lifecycle presents a mixed bag of opportunities and problems that have to be anticipated in order to be able to offer the right product at the right time and place to the right customer.

The market and the product lifecycles are closely related. Schematically we can say that emerging markets are dominated by new product introductions whereby invention and innovation will prevail and will focus on primary and augmented deliverables. Developing markets feature new product introductions whereby innovation is extended to the other deliverables. Maturing markets can get very tough. Improvements on the cost of primary and augmented deliverables, and innovation or even invention on the other deliverables are required to stay in the game. Declining markets tend to focus suppliers' attention even more sharply on costs. However, necessity is the mother of invention and the more dynamic players look for innovation or even invention to start a new cycle in the life of the market.

The classic categorization of the different phases of the market lifecycle has become blurred and the best-in-class do not wait for the market to slumber and to decline. They launch, one after another, waves of new products that maintain the market dynamics.

It is interesting to observe and to analyze how the major competitors contribute to the market dynamics with their product strategies, because they reveal how their strategic profile drives the timing, the scope, and the method of their new product introduction. Furthermore history shows which critical success factors and critical failure factors they have experienced. Competitors do not publish their Policy Fundamentals and their Policy Dynamics, but they give clear indications with their product strategies.

This intelligence on the market combined with an analysis of customer purchase propensities and the market dynamics and lifecycle, help to define the opportunities and threats that will affect product strategies.

7.2.2 Defining the product strategies

A classic but oversimplified model shown by Wheelen and Hunger [23] states that there are four basic product strategies, namely:

1   new products to new customers;
2   new products to old customers;

3   old products to new customers;
4   old products to old customers.

The question before senior and operative management is not which of the aforementioned product strategies to choose from, but what combination of them would optimize the enterprise's marketing position.

The models of portfolio management such as the ones introduced by The Boston Consulting Group, Arthur D. Little, and GE can be adapted to manage the product portfolio. Every alternative among the four basic product strategies has a particular risk to reward ratio through the market lifecycles. New products can probably be very productive in an emerging market, and old products to old customers is a safe and low cost strategy in a severely declining market. To ensure a balanced distribution of investments, risks, and cash flow over the different time frames, the complete product range should be taken into account.

Old products, whether to new or to old customers, are likened to milking the cow and have the advantage of bringing in cash – albeit with low profit margins – and maintaining market presence. However, appropriate sales strategies have to be deployed to make sure they do not hinder the development of new products. Introducing new products to old customers – as we will discuss in the next chapter – can prove beneficial by taking advantage of the favorable disposition of loyal customers.

(a) New product introduction

In many if not most sectors the emphasis of these strategies is on new products. The following observations can help to clarify a complex subject.

- Managers often focus on *new product development* where the emphasis is on technical competencies and capabilities, although substantial marketing efforts should have preceded the project. New product development costs money, it does not create income. It is just a part of a larger project that brings in cash when successful, namely *new product introduction* or NPI. From the time a new product leaves the lab until it is introduced in the market many critical steps have to be taken, and the outcome is not guaranteed. Senior and operative management should focus on NPI, which clearly puts the emphasis on marketing and P+L ownership on the whole project.

THE PRODUCT   169

- *Many a false step has been taken by standing still*. The stronger the competition, the greater the need for change. The pace of change has accelerated to the point that, in sectors like portable PCs, software, the Internet, etc., products become obsolete in as little as three to nine months. On one side the cost of developing new products is rising, and the time cycle is getting longer. On the other side, product lifecycles are shrinking, as brand loyalty has become fickle due to customers becoming 'zappers'. This leaves management confronted by the following dilemma. The frequency of new product introduction is an important factor in retaining customer attention, but new products have little time to return the investments made.

- New needs spur new products, and new products can spur new demand. If human needs are unlimited as the economists say, then there should be unlimited opportunities for new product introduction. Strategies should optimize a combination of opportunities that the enterprise can derive from NPI, namely:
    - attracting new customers;
    - creating new 'wants' that eventually may become 'musts' as exemplified by the ABS braking system in cars and trucks;
    - introducing new applications to existing customers;
    - pre-empting the competition;
    - by being the first entrant there may be the opportunity to blanket the market;
    - motivate the sales force and the distributors;
    - generating new volume and enabling economies of scale, scope, and systems;
    - strengthening the brand image and the image of the enterprise;
    - drawing on the fact that success breeds success and successful NPI encourages NPI;
    - developing competencies and capabilities, and building up a learning curve for NPI.

- Focusing on the primary product alone, or just on the primary product and the augmented product and neglecting the other aspects of the value delivery, can only sub-optimize the opportunities and increase the risk of being overtaken by competitors who will rush to fill the empty spaces left by the first entrant. New product introduction should be visualized on a matrix that shows on five vertical columns, one for each of the deliverables of the product configuration, and on three horizontal lines respectively for improvement, innovation, and invention. Estimates can be given for all relevant opportunities on each square of the matrix so as to justify priorities and resources for the NPI. As mentioned in Chapter Five, no enterprise can afford to confine its efforts to innovation, few can sustain competitiveness with improvements alone. These three levels of novelty or newness call for different levels of competencies. They also have different characteristics in terms of their timeline, costs, risk–reward ratios, which must be put in the frame of their application to one or several of the product deliverables. Each of the columns can show the expected investment, the expected customer recognized value and the competitive advantage for a period that seems reasonable for the sector and for the market segment.

- *Product improvements* should be a constant stream with appropriate promotions. Investment in real improvements are not only necessary to stay in the game but can be well worthwhile. Product updates and brand extensions can be introduced in a short time, and they generate cash to fund innovation or even invention. Cosmetic or novelty improvements limit the improvement to appearances only and should not be over used.

- *Product innovation* takes time and testing. It should anticipate demand-pull rather than focusing on marketing push. Procter & Gamble is a diligent student of consumer needs and purchase patterns as illustrated by the fact that it conducts over 2 million customer interviews per year.

- *Product invention* takes a considerable investment in a combination of performers. It may produce a big bang, but history shows that inventions take on average 20 years to become commercially viable. For example fiber optics were invented in 1955.

- As progress tends to shorten the time cycles, the competition increases the frequency of product upgrades, and it is likely that the time gap between the three enablers of NPI – namely improvement, innovation, and invention – will continue to shrink. Thus, the interaction and interdependence among them deserve attention. As Dr Gail Smith used to say *all generalizations are wrong, including this one*. Let us nonetheless suggest that invention is generally reserved for the primary product, but improvement and innovations can be effectively applied to all other elements of the product.

- As we have shown in Figure 6.1, the macro-process concerning the customer value delivery features five sub-processes, namely marketing, development, production, logistics, and sales and customer service. There has to be a balance between the contribution made by these links of the value delivery chain to the NPI. The most critical success and failure factors can probably be pegged to each of these links.

- Product strategies, in particular NPI because of the risk–reward, must be aligned with the strategic profile of the enterprise as well as with the other strategies for business breakthrough and continuous business improvement. The directives and guidelines of the Policy Fundamentals can encourage NPI as part of the strategic ambitions, and with the RAE and RER. Conversely, a narrow mission statement, the narrow scope of the strategic thrust, the depth and breadth of competencies and capabilities as applied to the links of the value-chain can be restrictive. Since NPI relies heavily on human capital, it is important to understand how the drivers of organizational behavior condition the organizational capital. Finally, the product strategies and in particular the NPI projects integrate the four steps of the Policy Dynamics so that they will be deployed with the appropriate priorities, resources, and empowerment to the Policy Implementation and Review.

The advantages of NPI have launched a new competitive race. This means first come first served at the table of opportunities. Delaying or deleting plans concerning NPI allow competitors *to get to the future first.*

Often, the major limitation to new product introduction is the money available to the customer and the creativity of the supplier. In order to liberate creativity, Robert [92] attacks many myths that surround new product introduction. Let us just mention the following.

- Market saturation and product stagnation are self-taught illusions. Brand extension, product rejuvenation, new applications, new materials or new technologies are among the many levers available to reverse stagnation and saturation.

- Low-cost or differentiation strategies can be combined and recombined to offer almost endless opportunities for successful NPI. The introduction of new technologies enables costs to be lowered.

- Protecting the 'cash cow' optimizes the reward–risk ratio but only for a while. It gets diminishing returns, it lulls personnel into unjustified comfort, and allows the enterprise to sink ever deeper into its own rut. But, most of all, it encourages competitors to come in and steal the show. In order to keep his organization on the toes, Lew Platt, CEO of Hewlett-Packard, let it be known that *'the best defense is preemptive self-destruction and renewal'*.

- Success breeds success should hold true, but many companies have gone to sleep after hitting on one highly successful product.

- As we said earlier, limited resources can be an excuse for lacking entrepreneurship. It is true that NPI consumes considerable resources. However, increasingly, what is required are intellectual resources, which even a small team can provide, as demonstrated by many stunningly successful start-ups on the NASDAQ (National Association Securities Dealers Automated Quotes). Information technology and management tools such as Design of Experiment [93] can be of considerable help. Tangible resources can be obtained if the opportunity can be forcefully communicated to potential suppliers of financial and other capabilities. Companies can no longer afford to throw more resources at the same old thing, at the same old product. This leads to stagnation and demise. Instead management should heed to Drucker's advice and allocate resources to new opportunities rather than to old problems [66].

- By starting to identify problems that are looking for a solution, the enterprise can effectively deploy a critical mass of the required critical competencies and core capabilities to come up with the desired product in the right length of time. Sometimes, building on a cluster of critical competencies or of core capabilities, management may come up with solutions looking for a problem to solve. A combination of these two approaches to NPI can prove effective, but looking for problems to solve definitely has a better pay-off period.

- NPI is in itself a critical competence that builds on a synergistic cluster of competencies and capabilities. The 3M company has been successful in deploying a bundle of some 85 technologies to offer over 50 000 products. NPI builds on previous experiences and, as demonstrated by companies like 3M, we can speak of an NPI learning curve. Organizations that master the NPI process can outthink and outplay the rest of the pack and, by becoming the market maker, they can generate an intellectual and financial momentum that will keep them ahead.

(b) Assessing new product introduction

NPI is like agriculture. Considerable efforts are made at the beginning in order to eventually reap the fruits. The investment and the risks with NPI tend to be greatest in the first two phases of the product lifecycle and progressively diminish. The profitability generally peaks at the phase of volume growth, however, sometimes the maturity stage prunes the competition, and profitability rises for the ones that weathered the price purge.

The success with NPI is inherently unpredictable. Putting the odds in one's favor is justifiable prudence but playing the percentages does not promote daring innovation. Finding a good balance between prudence and profit maximization is a never-ending dilemma.

Companies that use a systemic, stimulating, simple, swift, and systematic approach to NPI can achieve remarkable hit rates. Success with NPI can be measured in terms of the percentage of orders accounted for by products introduced in the last two years. In the high-tech field, Hewlett-Packard reports their ratio as two out of three, and in the mid-tech field Du Pont reports theirs as one out of two. However, there are great differences in the average success achieved through NPI. This emphasizes the importance of analyzing the cause of NPI failures. In France, research conducted in 1997 showed that 70 percent of new product introductions failed, and that 75 percent of the failures were due to marketing deficiencies.

Undoubtedly the risks are great not only in terms of financial dilapidation and employee frustration, but also in terms of loss of goodwill in the marketplace. However, risk can and should be managed and should not deter entrepreneurial action. As they put it at Johnson & Johnson 'if you are not making mistakes, you are not making decisions'. Innovation should not be a gamble but an entrepreneurial decision. Donald Trump, the well-known real estate promoter, made the point with the following poignant statement 'a gambler plays the slot machines, an entrepreneur owns the slot machines'.

In order to assess the effectiveness and efficiency of NPI, the following criteria can be used:

- consistency with the strategic thrust and strategic goals set out in the Policy Fundamentals;
- risk–reward ratios and the realm of possibilities to manage risks;
- alignment with the availability of competencies and capabilities;

- alignment with the window of opportunity. Processes need time to be adjusted, and people need time to assimilate the new procedures, and, if appropriate, customers may need time to accept the changes in imagery;

- the costs and the competitive handicap that could result from missed opportunities.

Management needs to define and assess the potential impact of the critical success factors (CSF) and the critical failure factors (CFF). Robert [92] suggests the following approach.

- Best case and worst case scenarios should be developed for the identified CSF and CFF. The process decision programming chart (PDPC) is a useful tool to devise preventive and contingency plans for the worst case scenario [28]. Promoting actions should be evolved for the best case scenario.

- A reward–risk rating on scale +5 to −5 should be agreed upon in the frame of the advocacy method or nominal group technique. As concerns the rating scale, the following values are suggested by Robert [92]:

+5 landmark opportunity	−5 disaster
+4 major opportunity	−4 highly visible failure
+3 significant gain	−3 significant setback
+2 impact	−2 impact
+1 modest	−1 modest

NPI is normally assessed in terms of financial results. There are, however, intangible results, which, albeit difficult to estimate, can be significant such as:

- the innovation learning curve to which we referred earlier, and opportunities for derivative products (for example toys, games, souvenirs and other items that can be launched with popular movies) and for future brand extensions;

- the motivation of the people who like to identify with a dynamic, innovative organization;

- the goodwill in the marketplace (see 'Marketing capital' in Chapter Eight).

7.2.3 Designing the product and the supporting activities

Thomas Edison, commenting on his remarkable experience as an inventor and as an entrepreneur, reportedly said, 'genius is one percent inspiration and 99 percent perspiration'. It is interesting to note that different local cultures have shifted the focus of activities. Robert [92] provides the following estimates:

Innovation as % of the R&D	Product	Process
USA	70	30
Japan	30	70
Germany	50	50

The Japanese have prided themselves on concentrating on innovating the processes, an approach that has led them to achieve substantial cost savings with *kaizen*-type product improvements. However, as soon as innovation and invention become a dominant factor in successful NPI, the emphasis will probably shift from the process to the product. Looking at the estimates above, Germany appears to have the most balanced approach but the USA is the country that commands leadership in many high-tech sectors.

Juran [97] reminded managers 'You do not make a product better by inspecting, but by planning'. Advanced quality planning as required by the standard of the American automobile industry, QS 9000, is structured as follows.

- *Phase 1*: planning and defining the program and how to determine customer needs and expectations.
- *Phase 2*: product design and development, features and characteristics should be developed to near the final form.
- *Phase 3*: process design and development so that the processes will yield the product-specifications, the quantities, the costs, and the delays, ensuring that the requirements of the customer will be met.
- *Phase 4*: product packaging and process validation through trial runs.
- *Phase 5*: feedback assessment, corrective actions, statistical process control, measurement system analysis, and failure mode evaluation and analysis.

Different local cultures have also evolved different approaches to designing the product. In the USA and in Europe the various activities including market research, product specifications, design, engineering, manufacturing, and cost calculation have traditionally been done in a sequence. The teamwork culture has led Japanese corporations to plan and to review *concurrently* and cross-functionally such activities as market research, product specifications, setting cost targets, design/engineering/supplier pricing, and manufacturing.

This approach has several advantages. First, there is better planning and better review as the points of view of all the different functions involved are considered from the start. Often enough the product designers have insufficient knowledge of manufacturing, the production people have insufficient knowledge of maintenance. Lacking systemic knowledge, the product will be sub-optimized or prove unpractical. Secondly, it saves time and costs as the different functions involved do not have to wait until the preceding function has finished to start their work. Thirdly, the cross-functional cooperation is motivating and fosters the learning organization.

This approach is optimized by a method developed by Japanese academics Akao [94] and Fukuda and known as Quality Functional Deployment or QFD. We cannot go into the details of this approach but can provide a brief overview. QFD uses the management principles we advocate as follows.

- It is a systemic method, which puts the voice of the customer and the voice of the enterprise foremost and manages their interfaces. It also combines commercial and technical arguments.

- It is systematic as it uses the P-D-C-A principle throughout the customer value delivery process and it gathers all the necessary data.

- It is stimulating as it brings together different functional competencies and fosters their cooperative interaction. The cross-functional teams that work on a QFD project are involved in all the steps of the P-D-C-A. Different functions work concurrently through this project and can serve as a basis for concurrent engineering. A number of graphical tools are used to facilitate teamwork.

The American Suppliers Institute [95] has simplified the 40 matrices of the model developed by the Japanese to one master chart and four deployment charts. The master chart, called the 'House of Quality' because of its graphical presentation, merges the following information:

- the voice of the customer;

- the competitive situation and the company's quality plan;
- the relation between customer's 'musts' and 'wants' and the features of the product;
- the interdependencies among the different product features;
- the conclusions leading to action plans.

The results of the master plan are deployed on four matrices. The first one concerns product planning and aligns the customer requirements to the design requirements. The second matrix concerns parts deployment and aligns design requirements and parts characteristics. The third matrix concerns process planning and aligns parts characteristics and manufacturing operations. The fourth and last matrix concerns production planning and aligns manufacturing operations and production requirements.

The Kobe Shipyard of Mitsubishi Heavy Industries in Japan introduced QFD in 1969 and was among the first companies to use this method. The majority of Japanese companies that have received the prestigious Deming Prize use QFD. In the USA, Ford and Xerox have been the first Western companies to introduce QFD starting in the mid-1980s. Several American engineering companies are now using QFD. For quite some time QFD has remained confined to engineering type projects. However, quite recently the American hotel-chain Ritz Carlton has introduced QFD in its 30 hotels worldwide.

Although QFD is well described by Western literature [96], in Europe and in the USA this method has not found wide acceptance. In certain cases senior management fail to support a tool that looks complicated, in other cases it is because QFD requires a cross-functional approach that the organization was not ready to implement. Now that the sectorial standards TCS 16949, VDA 6.1 and AS 9000 require suppliers to use QFD, this method should gain a broader acceptance.

7.2.4 Developing the product including engineering, manufacturing, and logistics

Product development includes engineering, establishing standards of technical quality, manufacturing, and logistics all the way to customer delivery. According to the American Society for Quality, 46 percent of new product development costs are due to failures because measurements are not monitored, and the effective corrective measures are not planned.

But costs are not the only terrain on which the competitive battle is fought. Time-to-market is another critical success factor.

Managing the new product project is critical and the approach should be systemic, stimulating, as simple as possible, swift, and systematic as we advocated in the Process of Management.

Highly competitive and mass produced products may require lean manufacturing methods that favor short vs. long runs, production versatility vs. efficiency, thereby pushing customization towards the end of the supply chain.

7.2.5 Deploying the product strategies from introduction through disposal or trade-in

Management's planning process should cover the critical success and the critical failure factors in all the phases of the product lifecycle. Let us not forget that the specification of the product can be assured through process management, but excellence is the result of the competence and of the motivation of the personnel.

7.3 Summary

Unlike the EQA, the MBNQA, and the ISO 9001:2000, our mind-map features the 'product' as one of the five interactive business enablers which are managed in the Policy Implementation and Review. Together with the customer relation strategies, product strategies contribute to writing the bottom line. To understand product strategies and their economics, we distinguish between the five deliverables that make up the product configuration. We then discussed features and benefits.

Product strategies feature five major steps and we set forth a number of mind-maps that can be useful in these steps. Our focus has been on new product development, which in many sectors is a major contributor to competitiveness if not already a must.

In the next chapter we will discuss the fifth and last of our business enablers, namely the customer as a partner.

■ CHAPTER EIGHT ■

The key partner: the customer

The Plan

The partners are the fifth and last of the business enablers that we call the 5 <P>. The action plans deploy the strategic resources and the processes that enable the enterprise with the collaboration of the supplier-partner to deliver products that satisfy the key-partner, the customer.

We discuss the factors that contribute to customer recognized value, and that enable the enterprise to build up customer capital. Among these factors, customer relation strategies play a key role and we address some of these issues in this chapter.

The Mind-Maps

In order to facilitate the implementation of shared management practices in the frame of the Process of Management, we present in this chapter the following mind-maps with the view of establishing preferential partner relations with the key partner, namely the customer.

- Partnering with the customer.
- Customer recognized value and market recognized value.
- Building customer capital.

Introduction

No customers, no business. To strengthen the business it is necessary to strengthen the relationship with key customers by using advisedly the business policy, the techniques, and behaviors proper to partnering. Partnering will optimize the value delivered to customers and, more importantly, the value recognized by them as well as by the market. The customer satisfaction index is a measure of that value.

Building mutually beneficial relations with customers will build what we refer to as 'customer capital', a key component of 'marketing capital' a concept we developed in Chapter Five. As mentioned in Chapter Two, we also consider critical suppliers and strategic allies as partners. However, because of space limitations we focus here on the key customer.

8.1 Partnering with the customer

The enterprise entertains special relationships with some of its stakeholders. We refer to these preferential relations as partnering. Such relations are built with key customers, critical suppliers and strategic allies. We do not consider the personnel and the shareholders as partners. They are part of the enterprise, they are 'us' while the partners are 'they'.

The purpose of partnering with key customers is to optimize the 'customer capital', the intangible asset which is the livelihood of the enterprise.

Key customers should be as important to the enterprise as the enterprise is important to them. If there is a great discrepancy in the level of importance that the parties involved attach to the partnership, the relationship will be a weak and ephemeral one.

The complexity of the business environment is such that effective cooperation with the partners can be a major asset and an essential competitive advantage. The partners share part of their intellectual capital such as intelligence, opinions, knowledge, competencies, and capabilities. The importance of partnering can be assessed on the basis of the volume, the value, and the frequency of the interchanges and in particular those that concern intellectual capital.

Partnering, i.e. engaging in a purposeful and mutually beneficial partnership, can be a complex relational and organizational construct which requires (i) a commonality of vision; (ii) an agreement on the *modus operandi*; (iii) proximity through physical or virtual presence so as to facilitate continuous contact; (iv) an adequate value and volume of interactions; eventually leading to (v) intimacy.

Customer intimacy refers to a privileged relationship between the partners whereby both parties are prepared to contribute a meaningful amount of their human and organizational capital within the agreed-upon scope of their cooperation. Customers can be led to offer intimacy, they cannot be forced to do so. Intimacy is the result of a long process, which builds mutual understanding and deep trust. Thus, the partners feel comfortable to play with open cards and to allow the other party to penetrate a part of their own sphere.

Of course, the process leading to intimacy requires an investment of the appropriate configuration of performers. The intimacy process will not be adequately funded unless all the parties concerned see very clearly the importance of the project and their particular interest in it. Rational and also emotional and relational considerations determine the willingness to engage in this process as well as the depth of intimacy allowed.

Establishing mutually beneficial relations with key customers raises the following questions:

- who are the key customers?
- what do customers want?
- how do customers evaluate the product delivered?
- how important are they to the enterprise?

We will try to answer these questions in the following sub-sections.

8.2 Customers' decision making

Customers are not equal and they rightfully insist on being treated individually, or as the expression goes 'one on one'. For this purpose several criteria can be used.

First, the *nature of the customer* enables us to distinguish between the private consumer, the reseller, the industrial consumer, the industrial user or converter, and the public organization. As shown by Vice President Gore [99], public or state controlled enterprises are increasingly operating like private industry, but the remaining differences cannot be overlooked. The above mentioned groups of customers have distinctive characteristics that show up in their decision making as well as in their purchasing habits.

Secondly, the *role played* by different persons or groups in the customers' decision making enables us to differentiate between the informer, the influencer, the user, the buyer, the decision maker, and the payer. The supplier also participates in the whole process as an informer and as an influencer. We refer to this group as the *decision-making unit* or DMU. The distribution of the roles within the group and the group dynamics can determine how the decision will be taken. The proximity, the interactions and the intimacy can become delicate as the different participants in the decision-making process – including the supplier – may have a different perspective, different interests or hidden agendas.

Purchases are driven by the timeliness of satisfying a need or by the opportunity to satisfy a need under particularly favorable conditions. Depending on the nature of the purchase, its importance and its frequency, the decision making can be complex.

The customers should envisage: (i) the configuration of the product; (ii) how, where, and when the purchase is made; (iii) how the purchased product will be used; (iv) how often and how long the product will be used for; (v) how the product will be maintained; (vi) how the product will be disposed of; and, last but not least, (vii) the financial and other efforts the customers are willing to make.

The above illustrates the fact that the DMU does not have an easy task. First, its members may not have a clear and comprehensive view of their real needs. Some needs may be manifest while other remain latent. Secondly, at the time of purchase the DMU may not be sufficiently aware of all the aspects of the lifecycle of the product. Thirdly, the parties involved in the decision making or in the supply chain may confuse or distort the issues. As a result, alternative offerings may not be given due consideration. Finally, the DMU may not have an understanding of how to judge the value obtained from the consumption/use or from the ownership of the product.

Therefore, the supplier should provide appropriate assistance because, if customers are not happy with the purchase, the vendor will get the blame and may lose the business.

The third criterion, but by no means the least important, which leads us to treat our customers as individuals is *by the differentiation of their needs*. In order to understand customers' needs we should look into how these needs are determined and related to a product configuration.

8.3 The attributes

Marketing refers to product characteristics as *attributes*. In the previous chapter we distinguished between the five components of the product configuration, which we call deliverables. It is therefore essential that the attributes be aligned with the pertinent deliverables of the product configuration. Zeithaml [88] proposes a standard list of attributes that includes reliability, accessibility, and responsiveness, the quality of communications (clear, concise, convivial, etc.), credibility, security, competence of the personnel, courtesy, and the appearance of the personnel. Such a list is pointless because attributes cannot be generalized. They should be determined by customers on a case by case basis as every customer is a special case. Actually, the particular conditions that lead to the purchase are among the many variables that dismiss a 'one size fits all' type of approach.

Once the customer and the situation have been identified, a master list of attributes can be obtained in the frame of focus groups or customer surveys. Furthermore the importance or *weight* attached by different customers to different attributes will also vary. The weight rating can be determined using the Likert scale, or pair weight rating or the nominal group technique. The Likert scale discussed under 'the customer satisfaction index' later in this chapter enables the translation of qualitative into quantitative inputs. Customers who have the same weight rating for the same shortlist of attributes are deemed to form an affinity group or a *customer segment*.

It is interesting to compare the opinion voiced by customers with the one expressed by customer-contact personnel as concerns the weight given to the attributes and their degree of competitiveness using the same Likert scale. The discrepancies between the two sources should be recorded and carefully analyzed. Customer-contact personnel can get carried away by their own initiatives and values, and lose sight of what the customers really care for. Customer-contact personnel then pass biased inputs upstream in the value delivery chain. As a result, companies become inward looking or focus on competitors rather than on customers. Should this be the case, there will narcissistic talk about the value delivered to the customers rather than the *customer recognized value* (CRV).

In order to get a better grasp on the attributes and on the CRV they engender, we have distinguished in the previous chapter between features and benefits. We can now refine that definition with the 'must' and the 'want'.

Features describe the technical properties or performances of the deliverable. *Benefits* are the value the customers expect to get out of a deliverable or out of the whole product configuration. Anecdotally, we can observe that the customary expression 'features and benefits' starts at the wrong end. It is product rather than customer focused.

In spite of abundant literature on the subject, the term 'quality' remains stubbornly associated with the features and then only with the ones concerning the primary deliverables. Such a limited view can be explained from the supplier's point of view by the fact that (i) the features are the most visible part of the product; (ii) the supplier focuses on the primary deliverables because this is where most of the investments are made; (iii) the salespersons emphasize the features of the primary deliverables because they are easy to document. The customers may find it easier to communicate their expectations to the vendor in terms of features rather than in terms of benefits. Features can be specific; benefits are general and conceptual. Furthermore customers may not be prepared to discuss benefits because in doing so they reveal part of their own interests and operations.

In order to better understand customers' expectations, and in order to be able to measure the CRV, we refer to Kepner and Tregoe's distinction between the 'must' and the 'want' [44].

The 'musts' are non-negotiable or absolute requirements concerning one or several deliverables of the product configuration. Either they are met or the product will not be purchased or repurchased. Logically the 'must' should refer to benefits. However, customers may associate a feature so closely with a benefit that the feature becomes a 'must'. Disk brakes – a feature – are so closely associated with car safety – a benefit – that they have become a 'must'.

The satisfaction obtained on the 'must' is measured in a binary mode; it is either yes or no. Consequently, 'musts' act as a filter that eliminates from further consideration products that do not satisfy the 'must'. However, the 'musts' do not provide a competitive advantage. By definition only products that meet all the 'musts' are in the competitive race, all others are eliminated in the first screening. The 'musts' are not subject to frequent changes, but when changes occur they tend to have a great impact.

The *'wants'* normally focus on 'nice-to-have' features or low priority benefits. They are negotiable and customers should be able to rate them. Competitive advantages are primarily found by combining and recombining the 'want' and this is why they are subject to frequent changes, albeit not necessarily major ones. Sometimes the 'want' simply qualifies a 'must' (for example the 'must' is that a given purchase costs more than $10 000, the 'want' is that it costs as little as possible). It is interesting to note that while the 'musts' tend to concentrate on the primary deliverables, the 'wants' often focus on the augmented, auxiliary, intangible, and personal deliverables, in other words on the periphery of the product configuration.

Features and benefits can be considered objectively and compared within a given customer segment or group. 'Wants' and 'musts' tend to be highly subjective and therefore more attuned to the needs of individuals or of fragmented customer groups.

Features and benefits, 'musts' and 'wants' are complementary concepts. The benefits provide a good first basis for understanding the intended use of the deliverables. Aligning the features with the benefits – as discussed in Chapter Six – gives a first idea on the product economics. The importance attached by the customer to the features supposed to support a given benefit can be measured. However, to put things into the customers' perspective, the relative customer recognized value of the benefits and features must be measured in terms of 'must' and 'want'.

As we mentioned earlier, the 'musts' and the 'wants' enable a much more accurate determination of the value expected as well as of the value recognized by the customers than features and benefits. The 'musts' are evaluated on a binary mode 1 or 0, while the 'wants' are rated on a 10–1 scale. Pair weight rating or the nominal group technique can be used.

We therefore recommend using a combination of the two aforementioned concepts. In principle, the benefits should be 'musts' and the features should be 'wants'. Yet, customers occasionally confuse these issues and that kind of finding may lead to additional insights.

8.4 Customer recognized value (CRV)

We have defined 'quality' as 'the degree of satisfaction of the expectations that have been negotiated with the customer' [13]. This definition covers several important points.

- Customer satisfaction is important and therefore it must be measured and monitored. Because the competitive advantage tends to be achieved on the 'want' and the satisfaction with the 'want' can be measured, we speak of the *degree of customer satisfaction*. Both the European Quality Award and the Malcolm Baldrige National Quality Award rate customer satisfaction as the most important of the results achieved by the enterprise. The importance of scoring well on 'quality', as we have defined it, is underlined by research reported by the Strategic Planning Institute Boston [56] which shows that strong market leaders – i.e. the enterprises that have a share of market 50 percent larger than their next competitor – score 15 percent higher on quality than their next competitor, while weak market leaders may score only 6–7 percent higher on quality. This illustrates the fact that a small difference in quality scores can make a big difference in terms of market share and profitability.

- Customers judge satisfaction as a function of the expectations that have been met and those that have not been met. It is interesting – and frustrating at times – to note that certain expectations only surface when they have not been met. This judgment has a critical impact on the business. Two criteria help us understand *customer satisfaction*.

  First, we should distinguish between the quality that customers perceive and talk about, and the value customers recognize and act on. Customer perceived value may result in compliments and favorable survey results whereas *customer recognized value* or CRV brings in cash and results in repeat orders. Brad Gale [100] suggests that customers will recommend the product and the supplier they really appreciate. One of the divisions of Hewlett-Packard, following this suggestion, asks survey respondents to state from whom they would consider repurchasing and which supplier they are recommending.

  Secondly, Brad Gale adds an important distinction between CRV and *market recognized value* or MRV. Customers tend to see what they are looking for. In other words, customers recognize the value of the deliverables based on what they expect, and their expectations are often only based on what they have been used to getting.

  For quite some time the buzzword has been 'customer focus'. So, companies gave customers what customers asked for. This led to focusing on customers' past experiences because this is essentially all customers know. However, customers will eventually find out what's new and what the marketplace recognizes as the best buy in town. This will push them to look for MRV. The distinction is important. CRV is a reflection of past sales, while MRV provides a more accurate picture of the competitive potential. Indolence and ignorance may keep customers buying from a supplier that is no longer competitive. However, in today's Information Age, ignorance dissipates quite rapidly. Admittedly, when the supply chain is relatively long and traditions entrenched, the communication noise and the hidden agendas of intermediaries may distort the situation. However, transparency eventually prevails and constantly updates the MRV.

- Customers expectations are a mixture of objective and subjective elements, which should be clarified through communication or negotiation between the vendor and the customer, resulting in an appropriate understanding or service-level-agreement (SLA). Unless framed by such an understanding, customer expectations will run wild and leave the supplier chasing figments.

  Whenever the product does not meet the negotiated expectations, we speak of bad or of low quality. Low quality places the supplier at a competitive disadvantage that will result in lost sales. Whenever the negotiated expectations are met we talk about 'conformance quality'. Conformance quality reduces costs by emphasizing *getting it right the first time* (GIRFT). Noriaki Kano – a Japanese quality guru – talks about 'unexpected quality' when the CRV is higher than customers had expected. Customers have a long memory for extraordinary performances, whether they are exceptionally good or exceptionally bad. Ordinary performances are just taken for granted. Inventing unexpected quality involves a variety of analytical and creative tasks whereby, as John Brook pointed out, 'talking to customers tends to counteract the most self-destructing habit of personnel, that of talking to themselves'.

Of course, satisfying the customers is becoming increasingly difficult. First, we are moving from selling simple products to selling complete systems. Second, customers like to touch and feel the product, to try things out. Hewlett-Packard Europe has a staff of some 800 people in Holland just to provide the customers with information often found in the instruction manuals provided with the product. Being de-personalized, electronic commerce could actually aggravate these types of problems. Thirdly, global competition has increased customers' alertness to the MRV and, as a result, customers have become increasingly demanding. An executive of a well-known producer of electronics equipment told us: 'in the 1970s customers came back when the product did not work; in the 1980s they complained because the product did not do what they wanted to do with it; in the 1990s they are complaining if the product does not do what they thought it might do'. The EC is now pushing for legislation that would extend customer protection to the point where the product may be returned 'no questions asked' even after an extended time since purchase. In the USA retailers are already very accommodating and customers may return the purchased product 'no questions asked'.

The fact that customers are increasingly difficult to satisfy just throws into relief the importance of monitoring customer satisfaction and, more importantly, the motivation of customer satisfaction.

8.5 The customer satisfaction index (CSI)

What we define as 'the degree of satisfaction of customers' justified expectations' is commonly referred to as the *customer satisfaction index* or CSI.

The assessment of the CSI can be as complex as it is important. Actually, the process of measuring customer satisfaction is more important than getting a figure. It should enable the supplier to gain a deeper understanding of customers' expectations as well as of customers' evaluation of competitive offers, and therefore point to areas for improvement.

We will now describe the two steps of this process, namely (i) a definition of what is to be measured; and (ii) how it should be measured, and what actions should be taken.

8.5.1 Defining what is to be measured

The first step of this process should define what is to be measured. As a result, the data collection strategy is established. For this purpose, we need to understand the main attributes (features and benefits) and their respective weight or rating ('wants' and 'musts').

Individual sessions with key individual customers and focus groups can describe the situation and provide valuable guidance on how to structure more detailed research.

One of the dangers of personal interviews is hearing what one wants to hear. This is why professionals are brought in to facilitate these sessions. It should also be borne in mind that focus groups and individual interviews are not necessarily representative of the whole customer population because the number of participants is small and the selection criteria are likely to be slanted.

Some companies limit this part of the research to identifying a short list of attributes and their weights. However, a deeper understanding of all the factors influencing the CRV and MRV and of their interdependencies is generally preferable. Unless a sharply focused segmentation is possible, it is likely that the needs of the customer population will disperse over a larger number of attributes.

The subject and scope, the format, the media, and the timing of in-depth research have to be defined. We can highlight some of the points to be investigated.

First, the *whole product lifecycle* should be considered. The 'moments of truth', in other words the pregnant moments when the customers come into contact with the product and the supplier, should be determined. These are the moments that have the greatest impact on the CSI. They occur at various phases of the product lifecycle, starting with the customer's first exposure to the product and ending with the sale or disposal of the product. However, not all the contact customers have with the product or the supplier is critical. Typically, moments of truth occur when a difficult decision must be taken, or when customers need help to solve a problem. Identifying the moments of truth is a relatively simple matter: customers will tell. Surveys and focus groups can help to determine how customers feel about the experience of doing business with the supplier vs. its competitors.

Secondly, the moments of truth should be related to the relevant deliverables of the product configuration. Whenever appropriate, consideration should be given to the emotional state of the customers at the time and place of the moment of truth.

The degree of satisfaction recognized by the customers tends to be a somewhat arbitrary conclusion drawn from the different elements that enter this decision process. As previously mentioned, it may be interesting to gain an understanding on the interactions between the moments of truth as they may show up in reinforcing loops, balancing loops, or delays.

Thirdly, questions may also be included to probe the degree of customer loyalty.

8.5.2 How to measure the CSI

The strategy concerning data collection and analysis should be carefully thought out in order to obtain the planned results. The quantitative intelligence provided by surveys should be complemented with the qualitative intelligence that can be obtained by focus groups and in-depth interviews with a representative selection of customers.

Whenever the list of attributes is fairly long, it is advisable to use the hierarchy of attributes that the focus group can define. Care should be taken not to lump together attributes that, although apparently similar, trigger different purchase drivers or different satisfiers.

Surveys can be used to determine the degree of satisfaction with the major attributes. The value expected as well as the CRV for each attribute should be recorded and compared with the value that management believes that the enterprise has delivered. Surveys should also provide valuable intelligence on how the major competitors are found to perform on key attributes. We would advocate that surveys cover the relevant deliverables of the product configuration.

The survey should be done on a random sample of customers as well as *non-customers*. The breakdown between customers and non-customers can reflect the share of market of the supplier. For example a supplier that has a 40 percent share of market could include in their surveyed sample 40 percent of customers and 60 percent of non-customers.

Often the questions asked are too broad and therefore mislead by providing generalizations that, while statistically accurate, are perfectly useless. Pre-purchase surveys should be supplemented with post-purchase and, whenever applicable, post-installation surveys. The value of post-purchase surveys seems to be severely underestimated. Customers should be encouraged to provide comments for each item as well as spontaneous comments. Obviously terms should be carefully chosen so that the targeted respondents unequivocally understand the questions. It should be borne in mind that customers may have difficulty expressing their needs and that they assume there are limits to supplier's possibilities.

Surveys can only provide tenuous indications of *customer loyalty*. First, surveys are an instantaneous picture of a moving object, namely the market. Secondly, customer loyalty goes first and foremost to themselves, then possibly to suppliers, finally to products. *Market observation*, the flow of intelligence that should be provided on an ongoing basis by the customer-contact personnel, is the necessary complement to periodic customer research. Additional intelligence on the competition is obtained by using consultants and literature searches.

Focus groups and customer surveys are farmed out to independent companies who will not identify the name of the supplier to ensure objectivity. Of course, management decides the intelligence needed and the resources to be invested. Management and the specialized consultant should work out the targeting of the survey taking into account the market segmentation or fragmentation applicable. The design and the implementation of a survey require the particular competencies of specialists. A well-designed and well-implemented survey can get a higher rate of response, and gathers more accurate data. The survey should help respondents to think through the particular subject and yet enjoy doing it.

From the outset, the organization of the data should be established in order to facilitate retrieval. The periodicity of the survey is also important. Hewlett-Packard carries out semi-annual or annual surveys concerning customer satisfaction with its product, with its services, and with its personnel. It is advisable to keep the survey model unchanged in order to draw trends over time.

The data should be organized and presented to permit scanning using different criteria. At Hewlett-Packard the data are analyzed cross-functionally to see what each part of the organization can do to improve customer satisfaction. Hewlett-Packard has also developed proprietary software that can be used in certain businesses to simulate the results of certain actions.

Should more detail be required, for each of the major attributes, the supplier can design a table which shows – for each of the five deliverables of the product configuration and for each of the moments of truth – the value expected by the customer, the planned quality, and the CRV. The gaps that will show up point to areas for improvement.

The system to measure the CSI needs to be determined. We recommend using a Likert scale of four grades, as used by AT&T and other companies, in order to avoid ambiguous middle of the road responses. We use the following wording for the grades on the scale: very important or extremely happy, rated 4; useful or satisfied, rated 3; not important or barely satisfied, rated 2; useless or very unhappy, rated 1. When collecting information on customer satisfaction, it makes sense to start with internal sources before going to external sources, the differences in the results between internal and external evaluations of customers' satisfaction on the various attributes should be analyzed and should trigger appropriate actions.

Surveys provide mainly quantitative information on CSI as well as on the direction and the pace of change in customers' needs and in their system of evaluation. Surveys also point at areas for improvement.

The CSI and the research approach need to be validated with data such as those supplied by the complaint and repurchase records.

As pointed out earlier, the CSI is not as simple an indicator as may be assumed. If poorly used, survey results can be misleading. An independent study found that no matter how much trouble their supplier is in, on average 70 percent of the respondents indicate that they are satisfied – unhappy customers not do not even bother to reply. Therefore, before planning actions, survey results should be analyzed carefully because the following factors can lead to misleading conclusions.

- Some of the models proposed in the copious literature on this subject simplify CSI to a relation of price vs. quality. Customers understand prices but not necessarily the value. The price is generally related only to the primary deliverables. Quality is a composite whose elements and their interdependencies are not necessarily obvious to the customer.
- The vendors differentiate their product bundles deliberately to mask price comparisons.

- As mentioned earlier, many surveys target existing customers or even focus on loyal customers. By omitting to poll non-customers, the tool is biased from the very start. Furthermore, potential customers are not considered.

- Asking the customers to quantify their satisfaction is often limited to certain aspects of the product, and generally concerns the present situation rather than their experience over time.

- Often dissatisfaction does not directly describe what customers are dissatisfied about.

- Communication can be a problem. One of the dangers in questionnaire design, as well as in personal interviews, is to ask for what one wants to hear.

- As mentioned earlier, some surveys focus on the company's products and neglect asking for a competitive rating.

- The last of the moments of truth is likely to be mentioned first and will probably be overstated.

8.6 Customer capital

Given the considerable efforts deployed to add value to the customer, it makes sense to ask *what value does the customer add to the enterprise*? The notion of goodwill is not new, but additional insights have been contributed by authors like Brad Gale [100] and Peppers and Rogers [101].

The value of the customers to the enterprise is called *customer capital*. It is one of the intangible assets, not shown in the traditional accounting, that reflects not only past business, but also the potential of the customer to the enterprise. As we will see, that potential is defined in broader terms than just sales. Customer capital is one of the essential elements of the *marketing capital*, one of the performers discussed in Chapter Five.

Of course, the assessment of customer capital is not as straightforward as subtracting liabilities from the assets on the balance sheet. This intangible asset consists of the various, interrelated elements whose value for the enterprise can – admittedly with some difficulty – be estimated. Different business units of an enterprise may serve the same customer, however, the customer recognized value will either amalgamate the value delivered by the different units or be biased as a result of a bad experience with just one of them. The goodwill or customer capital will be extended by the customer to the whole enterprise without much distinction between the different business units. This observation is heavy with consequences. First, senior management must ensure that shared management practices establish a high standard of performance for all the nodes of the organization – as is well known, a chain is only as strong as its weakest link. Furthermore, senior management cannot allow units that are considered less important to be neglected, because their sloppiness may erode the customer capital of the whole enterprise.

Customer capital consists of the following factors.

- *Loyalty* is a key factor of customer capital. Past sales and past margins are not a guarantee for the future of the company, however customer loyalty can be. While it is difficult to foresee the *customer lifecycle* – the period of time during which the customer will continue buying – the benefits of customer loyalty to the enterprise are quite tangible.
    - First, if the shipments are quite regular, and the sales forecasts reasonably accurate, it should have a favorable impact on the delivery economics of the supplier. The value of the customers to the enterprise can be calculated over the anticipated customer lifecycle in terms of resulting savings and a stream of future net profits to be realized. While valid in principle, this type of calculation is unreliable because market shifts will alter the customer's lifecycle as well as the volume and the margin of transactions.
    - Secondly, various research findings conclude that it costs five times more to acquire new customers than to maintain the existing ones. Servicing new customers means that the delivery systems have to be aligned between customer and supplier. Furthermore new customers may require special attention and training.
    - Thirdly, loyal customers are better payers. This is one of the signs that the customer appreciates the value received from the supplier.
    - Fourthly, research has shown that loyal customers who tend to be very satisfied customers (rated four out of four on our Likert scale) are five times more susceptible to trying new products from their supplier than satisfied customers (rated three out of four). At a time when new product introduction plays such an important role in the product strategies, the ability to rely on a loyal customer base to be early adopters of new products can be a critical success factor.

- Fifthly, generalizing, we can say that enterprises with the highest customer retention tend to be the most profitable provided they retain valuable customers.

  The opposite of loyalty is *customer defection* that – according to Peppers and Rogers [101] – could amount to losing as much as one third of the customer base every three years. Defecting customers not only disrupt the cash flow, but they can also bring valuable competitive intelligence to their new supplier. Furthermore, defecting customers are very hard to get back. Customer retention programs are expensive. The discounts offered tend to retain only the bargain hunters, and alienate loyal customers. Therefore, the defection of formerly loyal customers is one of the most serious warning signals management can get. If the appropriate actions are not taken very quickly the enterprise may be losing most of its customer capital.

- *Partnering*. Customer intimacy, partnering, and customer loyalty are mutually reinforcing. The value to the enterprise of accessing the customer's knowledge and competencies may be hard to quantify in figures, but it can be an appreciable contributor to the enterprise's intellectual capital. Contribution to the human capital can go as far as participating in the design of a new product, while contribution to the organizational capital can be made in the frame of aligning the business systems.

  Working together with the customers and benefiting from an open exchange of information should enable the supplier to get smarter with every contact, with every transaction. The supplier can learn from the proximity, from the interactions, and from the intimacy with the customers not only on how to improve the delivered quality, but also on how to deliver better value to other customers with similar needs. The old saying *the more you know, the more you learn* also applies to the interactions with the customer and drives the *customer relation learning curve*. The enterprise that is more advanced in its learning with loyal and important customers, in other words who is more advanced on the customer learning curve, should be able to draw a competitive advantage from the information it is privy to.

- *Referrals*. A happy customer will refer other people to his supplier, and in turn research shows that referred customers tend to be more loyal than customers acquired by the supplier because of the trust they put in the referring party.

As holds true of any intangible asset, the valuation of customer capital is difficult, it requires a fair amount of data collection, and the results are approximate at the best. Summarizing the points made above, we can suggest the following be used as indicators of customer capital.

- The level of customer intimacy and the frequency of interactions can be rated, the trends can be analyzed.
- The loyal customer's contribution to the enterprise's human and organizational capital can be evaluated and the trends can be analyzed.
- Early adoption of new products by customers considered loyal can be assessed and its traction on followers can be estimated.
- Referrals by loyal customers should be recorded first of all to appraise the value of these contributions, and secondly to give credit to the referrer.
- Activity Based Costing enables the supplier to calculate the net margin by customer. Combined with other indicators, such as share of the customer's business, the net margin by customer could show the difference between loyal, regular, and occasional customers. Regular customers may be frequent buyers, but many of above mentioned traits of the loyal customer do not apply to the regular ones. Occasional customers come and go and generally leave the smallest of track records.

The supplier can influence customer loyalty and the customer lifecycle in several ways.

- Having identified the customers who offer high value to the enterprise, the supplier should be prepared to provide top-notch quality. AT&T's Kordupleski stated that only stellar performance counts for customer loyalty [102].
- The supplier should optimize differentiation strategies by offering customized products.
- The most valued customers should receive highly personalized attention in order to foster intimacy, and knowledge interchange [103].
- Partnering and business system alignment should be optimized so as to better service the customer.

- The supplier can increase customer loyalty by taking appropriate means which will make loyalty more economical and practical for the customers than switching supplier. Coase [104] has studied what he calls *transactional cost*, namely the cost of changing supplier. This cost can be substantial whenever the customer and the supplier share their information technology or some of the systems concerning the management of the value chain or some of the components that go into the final product. Letting the customer participate in the production of the product reduces the costs to both parties and ties the customer to the supplier. Inertia tends to offset weak efforts of changing supplier. The supplier can take advantage of this fact by making the customer interactions with the supplier particularly easy and comfortable.

Far from being exhaustive, customer relation strategies as mentioned above should result in an *ascending spiral of loyalty*. The more a customer interacts and shares information with the supplier, the more loyal the customers will become. Conversely, the less interactive the relationship, the less the supplier will be able to follow the changing 'wants' of the customer, and the more volatile the customers will become. Operative management should be particularly attentive to the evolution of the chosen indicators of customer loyalty. Following the evolution of sales is indispensable, but it is only a lagging indicator. Customer relation indicators as established in the customer relations strategies are a key – they are a leading indicator.

Adequate customer relation strategies can produce handsome results. However, a number of factors beyond the control of the supplier may affect customer loyalty and increase the likelihood of customer defection; for example:

- the impact of technological innovations and new technical standards on the product lifecycle;
- shifts in the marketplace resulting from changes in the economic–financial, socio-cultural, and regulatory environment;
- shifts in the industry structure, in the competitive rules of the game;
- customer policies concerning the number of their suppliers and the relationship with them.

Operative management should recognize the factors that may lead to customer defection and whatever prevention and contingency measures are deemed necessary should be included in the appropriate scenario.

8.7 Managing customer relations

Customer capital is the life-blood of the enterprise. As has been described in the previous sub-section, its importance is such that appropriate strategies must be developed and deployed to optimize customer relations. The objective is not only continuously to increase customer capital, but also to increase it faster than the competition because it assures that the enterprise will stay ahead of the game in years to come.

Customer relation strategies are among the actionable alternatives considered in the policy deployment process as a means of achieving the strategic objectives. Research provides several pointers that should be considered in the customer relation strategies. While figures differ and some of the findings are dated, here is a list of the information we have retained.

- Development Decisions International found that a 5 percent increase in customer retention increases profitability from 25–85 percent. Among the tips they offer to increase customer retention are:
  - give employees a high degree of training and of empowerment to meet customers needs;
  - encourage customer-contact personnel to offer innovative ideas to increase CRV;
  - organize frequent interchanges between customer-contact personnel and personnel in support functions;
  - arrange for personnel in support functions to meet customers;
  - demonstrate the link between the actions taken by personnel and their impact on customer satisfaction.
- Research Forum Corp. reported that 70 percent of customers changed suppliers for reasons other than dissatisfaction with the primary deliverables; 50 percent of them were unhappy with the service while 50 percent of them were unhappy with the personal attention they received.
- The US Office of Customers Affairs conducted seminal research in 1986 and reported that:
  - customers have a long memory for performances that stand out from the ordinary, i.e. for exceptionally good and exceptionally bad performances;
  - customers are five times more likely to switch vendors because of perceived service problems than because of the price or

non-conformance of the product. And since it costs five times as much to gain a new customer as it does to keep an existing one, it makes good financial sense to improve service processes and to take care of customers when they encounter problems.
- on average, a dissatisfied customer will tell 8 to 16 people about their experience but over 10 percent of them tell it to more than 20 people;
- on average, for every customer who bothers to complain there are 26 others who remain silent;
- 91 percent of unhappy customers will never purchase goods or services from that supplier again. However, if the supplier makes an effort to remedy the customer's complaint, 82–95 percent of them will not change. The importance of complaints handling is therefore thrown into relief. Suppliers are well advised to organize the collection of complaints from all sources. Some companies use a form to record the subject data, and to monitor the whole process of complaint handling as well as the results obtained.

- A more recent study provides complementary and occasionally different findings about customers complaints:
   - customers whose complaints are satisfactorily resolved are three times more likely to repurchase than customers whose complaints are not resolved, and they are six times more likely to repurchase than dissatisfied customers who do not complain;
   - even if complaints are not satisfactorily resolved, customers who complain are twice as likely to repurchase than dissatisfied customers who do not complain;
   - customers who complain tend to be the more loyal ones, taking care of the complaint keeps them loyal;
   - complaints need to be solicited via toll-free hot lines where they are collected by contact personnel; response cards should be included in product packaging. Efficient programs to solicit, to collect, and to process customers' complaints can pay off handsomely. It was found that the cost of handling complaints can earn a 15–400 percent return on investment.

We cannot discuss in detail here the strategies that shape the relations between supplier and customer. However, we can distinguish between two different strategies, namely:

1. the traditional market segmentation;
2. market fragmentation: dealing 'one-on-one' with valued customers.

8.7.1 The traditional market segmentation

The traditional marketing approach looks to fit customers into a relatively small number of predetermined categories – or *market segments* – in order to supply them with standardized products. Demographic, psychographic, and socioeconomic criteria are used to rationalize the affinity in customer needs and purchase habits.

Once the profile of needs within the market segments has been established, marketing decides the targeting of the segments and the products that should be offered. One of the objectives is to sell the same product to as many customers as possible so as to optimize economies of scale. The salesforce goes after the targeted market segment offering the products marketing has aimed at that market segment.

The traditional approach continues to prevail partly because many companies have invested more on products and in internal capabilities than in customer relations. It should come as no surprise that, having focused on the internal environment, they try to schematize and to simplify the external environment.

Market segmentation can be successful when the needs of the customers have no differentiation potential or as long as the supplier can count on a fairly unique value proposition.

8.7.2 Market fragmentation: dealing 'one-on-one' with valued customers

Market segments are too rigid a frame of reference for today's fickle customers. The centripetal forces that cause the convergence of the masses have created by reaction centrifugal forces that push the individual to assert his/her difference. As a result we can take a cue from Matsushita's prediction that 'eventually there will be a market of one', and market segmentation will be replaced by 'market fragmentation'. This is where the enterprise deals 'one-on-one' with the individual customer.

Smart suppliers thrive on addressing the differentiated needs or wishes of every customer. The differentiation aims at the 'wants' because by definition the 'musts' have to be satisfied. However, differentiation strategies can reconfigure the weight given by the customer to features and even to the benefits. As a result, the rating of the 'wants' are modified and, more importantly, the whole configuration of the features and benefits changes.

Rather than focusing on share-of-market or share of segment, marketing one-on-one focuses on *share of the customer's* business and on selling more customized products to the same customer. It aims to contribute to the customer's success and/or pleasure by customizing the deliverables in a cost-efficient manner.

8.7.3 One-on-one strategies

Dealing one-on-one with the customers is based on the following practices.

- Identify all the customers who have differentiated needs or wishes be they manifest or latent. Customers that have no potential for differentiation are in the realm of customer segmentation. Fortunately they are a minority.

- Estimate the added-value the customers would recognize if the supplier addressed their differentiated needs; establish priorities among the differentiated customers' needs.

- Assess the present competitive situation and the probable competitive responses.

- Estimate the potential customer capital that could be developed by addressing the customers' differentiated needs, and rank the customers according to the potential customer capital offered.

- Plan and deploy the appropriate customer relation strategies.

(a) Identifying customers' differentiated needs

Peppers and Rogers rightly observed that customers have a variety of needs and wishes, some of which are manifest while others remain dormant or latent [101]. The 'must' and the most important 'want' are generally manifest. Perspicacity and a holistic view of the needs across the product configuration can bring out the *'latent wants'*, and creativity can discover new needs and wishes that (i) customers may not even been aware of; (ii) just did not care to voice; or (iii) simply assumed could not be filled in a practical and economical way by the supplier.

In order to find out the value that would be added by differentiating customers' needs, the supplier needs to *listen to the customers with a strategic ear*. The obvious way to find out what customers think and what customers do, is by asking some of the right questions. However, the customers will only disclose their problems and opportunities if the supplier has achieved a privileged status by establishing a relation of *proximity*, *interactivity*, and *intimacy*, which may lead to partnering. The supplier will then – but only then – be given an opportunity to discover how things really look from the customers' perspective.

This type of relationship will also benefit key customers. By working together, the supplier and the customer share a mutually beneficial learning experience.

(b) Estimate the CRV resulting from differentiation

Peppers and Rogers [101] relate what we call customer capital to the potential of differentiation of customers' needs and wishes. They illustrate this concept with a matrix whereby high–medium–low valuation of customer capital is plotted against high–medium–low potential of differentiation of customers' 'musts' and 'wants'.

Differentiation is a valid and well-known strategy that Porter advocated in the 1980s [52]. However, assuming that highly differentiated needs correspond to a high potential for customer capital can prove to be an over-simplification.

The differentiation potential should be assessed using criteria such as the following.

- We should not assume that the more potentially differentiated the customer needs, the more valuable the customized product configuration will be to the customer. The needs are infinite according to the classic economist, but they only convert into purchases after price and priorities have been considered. As mentioned in the previous chapter, today price takes precedence over features.

- *Inertia* is a force that should be reckoned with. When the offered differentiation entails changes or transactional costs, the customers may not be willing to go along.

- The customer's policy may limit the share of the business that each supplier is allowed to have.

Having uncovered the potential for differentiation, the supplier can define the *customized product configuration* that should satisfy the enhanced set of customer 'musts' and 'wants'. The customer's reactions to the offer of the customized product configuration can be tested in terms of their impact on achieving some of the supplier's goals, such as the following.

- The differentiation should attract loyal customers rather than bargain hunters. The supplier will therefore be able to count on extending the customer lifecycle.

- Customized products should be unique to a sufficient degree so as not to compete head-on with standard products.

- To the extent that customization adds CRV, a premium can sometimes be charged.

- Riding the learning curve together with the customer, the supplier can adapt customization as a function of the evolution of the customer's differentiated 'musts' and 'wants', thereby increasing customer loyalty.

- Loyal and satisfied customers provide recognition that motivates personnel at least as much, if not more than, recognition by their own superior.

(c) Assessing the competitive situation and competitive responses

Customizing the product configuration may require a substantial investment in resources be they competencies, capabilities, or time. It makes sense to consider *competitive maneuverability* and response time. Fair pricing or forward pricing can be used to discourage competitors.

(d) Estimation of potential customer capital as a function of differentiation

In the previous chapter we talked about 'product economics'. At this juncture management can compare the value of customer capital against the additional cost of attending the customer's differentiated needs. 'Activity based costing' can provide useful information on what it costs to serve individual customers. The primary purpose here is to be able to rank customers in terms of their value to the enterprise, and to plan accordingly the strategies and the resources to be deployed.

(e) Plan and deploy the appropriate customer-relation strategies

Theoretically there is an almost unlimited potential for differentiation. In order to increase customer capital, Peppers and Rogers are strong proponents of *migration strategies* whereby the supplier tries to move customers from a low differentiation of needs and wishes to a high differentiation [101].

Undeniably, customers are becoming more sophisticated, and their needs are becoming more differentiated. To take advantage of this trend, the supplier needs to fine-tune the customization of the product configuration and add value on the five big categories of benefits, namely economics, practicality (ease of use), good relations (ease of contact), emotional (pleasure in dealing with the product and with the supplier), and intellectual (knowledge interchange, learning curve).

The enablers of customization and of migration strategies include: interactivity, flexibility, and the client database.

- *Interactivity* – Customization cannot be a one shot deal because it may require an investment of resources on the side of the supplier, and because customer needs continue to evolve. The relationship between supplier and customers must be a frequent and an interactive one, both parties contributing to each others success, making the product-configuration more valuable.

    Interactivity involves adequate physical or virtual proximity to facilitate the information flow. It should result in intimacy allowing for sufficient depth and breadth of interchange. This is important because customization requires that the customer and supplier jointly determine the best way to serve the differentiated needs and wishes. The customer may have to disclose the relevant part of its policies, processes, and performers. The supplier contributes, as appropriate, his intellectual capital and capabilities to optimize the value of customization throughout the product lifecycle.

    The dialogue with the customers should be a sequence of interactions. The more involved the key persons on the customer's side are in working with the supplier, the more they will take an interest in and claim ownership of the interactive process. Of course interactivity cannot become an imposition. In the business of original equipment manufacturer, interactivity can provide advance notice of projects and timely information on the specifications for a forthcoming job.

    Establishing a personal relationship with the key persons on the side of the supplier and the decision-making unit on the customer's side is very important. Trust, availability, and responsiveness must be carefully nursed because they are a prerequisite to intimacy. The parties are also entitled to get pleasure out of their relationship. Addressing the customers by name, inviting the personnel of the customers to participate in focus groups or in mixed task forces, and showing appreciation by extending special treatment to important visitors are among the many ways the relationship can be made closer and more personal.

Remembering customer's requirements on frequent purchases is convenient and gratifying for the customer, it is also cost-efficient for the supplier.

Interactivity raises two issues, namely *the vehicle and the content of the communication*. As the breadth and frequency of communication increases, customers' attention spans may decrease. Furthermore, long channels and the noise factor may distort the message. When the supplier is separated from the customer by several distribution layers, direct dialogue can be invited through questionnaires attached to the warranty (return typically 20 percent), and post-sale follow up. The Internet has proven to be a very efficient media for direct customer–supplier dialogue. Amazon.com is a good example of effective and cost-efficient tracking and interacting with customers.

Partnering raises the level of interactivity when both customer and the supplier contribute a substantial part of the value of the product-configuration.

- *Flexibility* – Peppers and Rogers [101] emphasize the importance of *flexibility in the delivery system* throughout the product lifecycle as well as *flexibility in the communications* with the customer. As concerns the flexibility of the delivery system, several management methods – such as lean manufacturing, concurrent engineering, total preventive maintenance, and logistics – enable cost-efficient customization. As concerns the flexibility of communication, technology offers an array of tools to facilitate efficient virtual proximity such as Extranet, video conferencing, and Groupware.

  Sophisticated systems and technology are of limited effectiveness unless matched by appropriate individual and organizational behavior. A smile cannot be commanded, but the attitude leading to a smile can be developed if a conducive environment has been created. Management must be particularly vigilant in order to ensure that the 5 <S> that drive organizational behavior already discussed in Chapter Five do not restrict behavior and hamper the organization from being focused, fluid, and fast.

  Among the many potential problems, the following can be mentioned. Filtering through the ranks, the strategy can become ambiguous and the focus become blurred. Management systems, and in particular the review–evaluation–reward system, can cause actions to deviate from the strategy. Vertical structures can hamper responsiveness. Divisional and functional structures with their respective systems and procedures tend to fragment customer intimacy and they can impair flexibility by departmental impermeability. Most companies talk to the customers, but only a few listen with a strategic ear. This may be due to the fact that customer-contact personnel do not have sufficient exposure to the company's strategies, or that the company culture is one of self-satisfaction, or that the customers feedback system is inefficient.

Flexibility should also allow for *cross-selling*. As mentioned earlier, the one-on-one enterprise is focusing on share-of-customers before looking at the share-of-market. Whenever appropriate, share-of-customers should be optimized by cross-selling, in other words selling products from different business units. In order to facilitate the interactions, the customer should be able to interface with one account executive responsible for the various units that deliver products.

The various self-managed units of the enterprise should be *focused*, *fluid*, *and fast* as they group in networks as appropriate to deal with the customer one-on-one.

- *The client database* – The database allows the supplier to tell the customers apart and to remember them individually. The *customer value map* tracks all the interactions with the customers starting with the first contact the customers have with the product and the vendor. It shows how the information and the deliverables are transferred from one interaction to the next. The tangible and intangible experiences the customers make on each step are identified. The client database should show the frequency of the transactions, the volume and value of the purchase, the type of purchase, and, whenever appropriate, the time, place, and event of the purchase. The database should also feature, at least for major transactions, adequate feedback on customer satisfaction and, whenever appropriate, competitive performance. Monitoring the customer value map can serve as an early warning system to pick up and correct problems before they start eroding customer loyalty. The client database needs to be updated regularly by customer-contact personnel, and analyzed by operative management.

    For the purpose of monitoring performances, the supplier can run side by side the customer value map and the *delivery value map*. The delivery value map shows all the processes, the departments/

functions, and people that contribute the added-value planned for each of the transactions with the customer, the resources invested, and – whenever appropriate – the actual performance as opposed to plan. The customer value map and the delivery value map show two sides of the same story. They help to identify the areas for improvement.

The total cost of the transactions with customers can be monitored in order to determine those customers that bring little but cost a lot in terms of service requirements.

8.8 Summary

If there are no customers, there is no enterprise. Satisfying the needs of the customers and at the same time satisfying the needs of the enterprise is the main challenge of any organization.

The needs of the organization have been established in the Policy Dynamics and deployed in the business plan. The needs of the customers are often more difficult to determine because of market fragmentation.

In order to feel the needs of the customer, we have refined the concepts of features and benefits presented in the previous chapter by introducing the concepts of 'musts' and 'wants'. We have borrowed from Brad Gale the notion of customer recognized value and of market recognized value. 'All efforts that are not recognized by the customers are wasteful!'.

Customer capital is an essential component for marketing capital, a concept we introduced in Chapter Five. In order to optimize the customer capital, we have explored various customer relation strategies including dealing 'one-on-one' with the customer.

With the customer as the key partner we have covered the last of the five business enablers that are managed in the Policy Implementation and Review. In the next chapter we will discuss the last of the four sub-processes of the Process of Management, namely the Policy Assessment and Audit.

CHAPTER NINE

The Policy Assessment and Audit

The Plan

We discuss here the Policy Assessment and Audit, which is the fourth and last of the sub-processes of the Process of Management.

We have chosen to start with the quarterly review because, while being part of the preceding sub-process, it is closely connected with the policy assessment. Then, we explain our approach concerning the policy assessment and the assessment criteria, which enable operative management to check whether the organization has been doing the right thing in managing the business enablers.

Complementary to the assessment, the management audit allows senior management to estimate the value added by the enterprise during the planning period. We introduce the concept that we call the 'business value', which is an original approach to estimating the worth of the enterprise.

Finally, if in spite of good management in the operations, the business value has not been increased according to the strategic goals, both the Policy Fundamentals and the Policy Dynamics will have to be reviewed.

The data and the insights gathered by the senior and operative management of the SBU during their Policy Assessment and Audit can also serve as presentations to corporate management or to the Board of Directors.

The Mind-Maps

In order to facilitate the implementation of shared management practices in the frame of the Process of Management or POM, we present in this chapter the following mind-maps:

- The quarterly review.
- The policy assessment.
- The 'business value'.

Several of the mind-maps presented here outline ongoing research conducted by the author, who will return in his next work to the implementation of the methods. Nonetheless, the reader may find food for thought.

Introduction

The first two sub-processes of the POM dealt with business policy because unless it manages *to do the right thing* the enterprise will struggle and sink. In the third sub-process we discussed certain aspects of *doing the thing right* that we consider important to establish a basis for shared management practices in day-to-day management. In the fourth and last sub-process of the POM, we explore original approaches to enable management to check whether the enterprise has been *doing the right thing right*, and whether it is well positioned to sustain success.

Assessments and audits are learning trips that management takes periodically in order to understand complex situations more fully, and subsequently to program the necessary improvement. The Policy Assessment and Audit pursue the following purposes: (i) conduct an in-depth analysis of the business performance during the previous planning cycle in order to detect the areas in need of improvement; (ii) search for possible improvements in the methodology so as to ensure a dynamic evolution of shared management practices; and (iii) make the appropriate inputs to the next planning cycle.

There are many models concerning the evaluation of business performance. A majority of them focus on reporting financial results and forecasts. Some, however, take a broader approach and consider enablers of business performance as well as the results. We place in the latter group the models published by the organizers of quality prizes such as the European Quality Award (EQA) and the Malcolm Baldrige National Quality Award. Models developed by academics and consultants such as *The Balanced Scorecard* [105] and *Vital Signs* [106] follow some of the principles of the quality prizes but tend to be somewhat more limited in scope.

In spite of all the models available, Peter Drucker [107] wrote in the *Wall Street Journal Europe* 'We need new measurements – call them business audit – to give us effective business control'. Indeed, the subject deserves management's attention and some original thought.

Senior management is primarily concerned with the medium- to long-term implications of doing the right thing. Operative management is responsible for doing the thing right and focuses on short- to medium-term actions. Yet, *doing the right thing and doing it right* must be aligned.

In order to connect effectively these two perspectives, we advocate that senior and operative management start by conducting different tasks. The former audits the value added by the business, the latter assesses the management of the business enablers in the day-to-day operations. The two levels of management then get together to evolve conclusions.

The Policy Fundamentals set the strategic ambitions and strategic goals concerning the value of the enterprise. They also provide the directives and guidelines in the review–evaluation–recognition process concerning the quarterly reviews and the annual policy assessment and audit.

We will start by discussing the quarterly review because it serves as a major input for the policy assessment. Then we will review the mind-map we use for the assessment and the assessment steps. Finally, we will introduce the concept of the 'business value'.

9.1 The quarterly review

The quarterly review is conducted by operative management with the participation of the personnel involved in the management of the business breakthrough (BBT) and of the continuous business improvement (CBI). The performance achieved in the previous one to two quarters is compared with the strategic objectives set in the Policy Dynamics and deployed in the action plans. In addition to checking the lagging indicators, the leading indicators concerning the management of the five business enablers are taken into account.

The strengths and weaknesses in dealing with opportunities and threats during the period under consideration are reviewed. The progress made on the action plans that had been laid down in the previous quarterly review is examined and new action plans are discussed and deployed. As a result, the quarterly review evolves a forecast for the next one to two quarters. Whenever the business environment is subject to brisk fluctuation, we advocate a policy of flexible plans and budgets that, if necessary, allow the necessary modification of the annual plan, subject to approval by to senior management.

The directives and guidelines for the quarterly review are outlined in the Policy Fundamental's review–evaluation–recognition process. The quarterly review affords an opportunity to formally commend those who have over-performed and to encourage those who need support.

The quarterly review has a relatively short time-horizon that does not allow for an in-depth study of the business environment. Senior management's alert system (second step in the outer ring of the Policy Dynamics) continues to gather intelligence and, as appropriate, it can make inputs to the quarterly review.

A synthesis of the learning acquired in the quarter is discussed, and as appropriate this knowledge is documented and communicated throughout the organization.

9.2 The assessment model

9.2.1 The principles of the policy assessment

Everything that is worth doing, is worth assessing. The assessment is a joint effort between the assessors and the assessed, designed to find ways to improve – and to keep improving faster than competition. The role of the assessors is to lead this annual project in accordance with the directives and guidelines set in the Policy Fundamentals.

As applies to all managerial activities, the assessment involves communication. It affords the opportunity for the assessed to speak up and to be heard. In order to facilitate this interchange, we suggest that the assessors chosen from among the operative management assess a different group or unit than the one they are responsible for. Managers form the tutorial and shared services management group, knowledge managers, quality managers, and controllers can be good assessors in as far as they bring a different perspective.

The assessors should prepare a checklist as a guide, but not as blinkers, as they conduct their investigations partly on the basis of desk research and partly on the basis of field research. We offer guidance on the method and on the evaluation criteria, but we do not present a prefabricated questionnaire. Managers should know what is important for their business and they should be able to compose their checklist putting it in their own way, in their own words. Beyond avoiding the 'not invented here syndrome', the profound knowledge gained from preparing the assessment can be enriching and will facilitate the implementation of the processes. 'Sometimes the trip is more important than the destination'. Best-in-class companies like Hewlett-Packard have developed their own assessment model and train their own people to conduct the interviews.

The checklist is circulated to enable the managers to be assessed to prepare for their meeting with the assessor. It is advisable that the assessed prepare a document including both an evaluation of performances over the past planning period and the business forecasts for the next planning period. Supporting data including copies of the quarterly reports of the past four quarters should be enclosed. This document should be sent to the assessor in anticipation of the scheduled assessment meeting in order to permit due preparation.

The key is that (i) management can identify with the chosen criteria and principles; (ii) their assessment system be consistent with other elements of the Process of Management; (iii) there be a reasonable stability over time so as to facilitate comparison; (iv) the assessment be sufficiently simple and swift to elicit the full cooperation of the assessed and cause minimal disruption to daily work; and (v) the assessment system be a powerful driver of sustained superior performance.

The ISO 9001:2000 international standard, and the corollary guidelines ISO 9004:2000 facilitate the work of the assessors thanks to the documentation of the various steps of progress achieved in the operations.

Both the Policy Assessment and Audit and the quality prizes are designed to help the enterprise sustain superior performances. However, while the assessors' checklist that we advocate is a customized internal communication tool, questionnaires such as the ones of the EQA and the Baldrige are standardized in order to provide an egalitarian basis for picking a winner from the applicants. Yet, they can be valuable for comparison after management has developed its own assessment system, but should not be used as a replacement for this important thinking process. Once management maturity has been achieved following whichever route is the best suited to the enterprise, the pursuit of quality awards can crown the efforts made.

The policy assessment covers the performance of the management of the five *business enablers* in order to achieve strategic objectives deployed by the Policy Dynamics for both BBT and CBI. As mentioned in Chapter Two, our mind-map concerning the enablers is quite similar to the model of the EQA and of the ISO 9001:2000. However, we have included the product as one of the business enablers. Furthermore, we emphasize the connectivity and interactions among the business enablers.

9.2.2 The criteria of the policy assessment

The check–alert–planning–deploy model used by senior management in the outer ring of the Policy Dynamics has been expanded as follows to provide assessment criteria: check of effectiveness–alert and knowledge–planning for innovation–deployment and efficiencies. In Chapter Four we discussed the advantages we see in this model vs. the approach–deployment–scope–results advocated by the EQA.

These criteria are applied to each of the five business enablers, to assess the performance achieved in the past planning period or business cycle. The data and insights thus gathered enable operative management to analyze whether the proposed plans for the next planning period are realistic and sufficiently ambitious. The purpose of this analysis is not to evolve a studious report, but rather to serve as a basis for discussion with the empowered personnel so as to come to an agreement on the proposed plans or on whatever modifications may be advisable.

Let us briefly explain the use of this mind-map.

- The *check of the effectiveness step* compares the results achieved with the pertinent strategic objectives set in the policy deployment process. The analysis of how the performances have been achieved should throw into relief the interactions between the enablers or the 5 <P>. Improvements achieved in the degree of effectiveness should be highlighted. This step gathers internal intelligence and knowledge, before engaging in benchmarking and collecting external intelligence. The proposed performance plans for the next planning period are discussed in the light of the impact and feasibility of the improvements necessary.

- The *alert and knowledge step* explores the effectiveness and efficiency of management alertness to passive and to positive changes and the related processes such as the early warning system. Learning curves, and the diffusion of the learning from pregnant experiences throughout the organization should be examined. This step is very important. It seeks to ensure that the acquisition, storage, distribution, and use of knowledge and know-how endow the business units with a competitive level of critical competencies pertaining to the relevant business enablers. It is most useful to probe whether the alert and the knowledge plans are consistent with the performance plans for the next planning cycle.

- The *planning for innovation step* aims to ensure the effectiveness and efficiency of the managerial activities concerning action plans, and reviews. Strategic coherence and consistency among the various units needs to be reviewed. The key issue here is to ascertain that innovation is planned as appropriate at all levels. Operative management should also examine how the planned improvements, innovations, and inventions have contributed and will continue to contribute to staying ahead of the competition. Unlike the proposed model of the EQA: 2000, we advocate that innovation be assessed for each of the 5 <P> before drawing a consolidated picture. As we pointed out in Chapter Five, a good balance of improvement and innovation among these five management levers is more important than achieving a peak performance in one of them.

- The *deployment and efficiencies* step focuses on the efficiencies in the deployment of the action plans. While effectiveness is concerned with achieving the strategic objectives, efficiencies are concerned with the resources consumed in the process. Costs are a big issue of course but intangible costs like internal frictions and dissatisfaction among the personnel also have to be assessed. Progress made should be highlighted as well as residual or potential problems.

We should emphasize again that the assessment of what has happened over the past planning period is not about crying over spilled milk or about a pat on the shoulder. Learning from the past serves as a jumping board to plan the next planning period. The assessment criteria are a mind-map to guide the discussions between the assessor and the assessed on how to achieve superior performances in the next planning or business cycle.

In addition to the above mentioned assessment criteria, the assessors can additionally use the principles we suggested as a guide concerning the approach taken on the management of the 5 <P>. They can examine if the approach taken by the empowered managers is systemic, stimulating, simple, swift, systematic. However, for simplicity's sake we have selected two of the five principles for each of the 5 <P> as shown in Figure 9.1.

9.3 The policy assessment process

The policy assessment process features the following steps:
- updating the knowledge base with the quarterly reviews and other inputs;

FIGURE 9.1 The assessment model

BUSINESS ENABLERS	CRITERIA	CHECK EFFECTIVENESS	ALERT KNOWLEDGE	PLANNING INNOVATION	DEPLOY EFFICIENCIES
PLANS	SYSTEMIC				
	STIMULATING				
PERFORMERS	STIMULATING				
	SIMPLE				
PROCESSES	SIMPLE				
	SWIFT				
PRODUCTS	SWIFT				
	SYSTEMATIC				
PARTNERS	SYSTEMATIC				
	SYSTEMIC				

- establishing the assessment checklist;
- identifying and rating areas for improvement and areas for investment;
- inputs for the next planning cycle.

The policy assessment can be as comprehensive and detailed as required. We can only outline hereafter the steps of this process.

9.3.1 Updating the knowledge base

Operative management analyzes the quarterly reviews of the past four quarters. Trends are drawn on the performances of the business enablers. Critical success stories and critical failure stories of the enterprise as well as of its competitors should be the object of an in-depth study.

The quarterly reviews concerning the past three to four quarters are focused on short-term opportunities and threats while the Policy Assessment has a medium-term perspective. Therefore, the assessment needs a broader base of knowledge on the business environment. For this purpose an appropriate intelligence gathering strategy must be evolved and implemented. Among the types of intelligence that will be sought are:

- the evolution of the customer satisfaction index;
- the evolution of the satisfaction of the critical suppliers, and strategic allies;
- the evolution of personnel satisfaction;
- internal and external benchmarking on the performances of the business enablers in critical areas;
- the evolution of the competitive position by product line and by market segment.

The assessment needs to provide forecasts to serve as input for the next planning period. Operative management has to look ahead to the next four to twelve quarters. Senior management prepares forecasts as part of its tasks in the check step of the outer ring of the Policy Dynamics. This intelligence should be used in the assessment.

9.3.2 Establishing the assessment checklist

Check/effectiveness and deploy/efficiencies focus on quantitative data. Alert/knowledge and planning/innovation throw into relief qualitative data, and may require in-depth study. Because of time limitations and their action orientation, the quarterly reviews tend to be more informative on quantitative than on qualitative intelligence. Therefore the assessors need to plan for adequate desk and field research.

The managers who will carry out the assessment agree on the checklist and on the presentation of the findings. Information should be available to and coaching provided for the assessed personnel concerning the method of the assessment as necessary. Figure 9.1 can be formatted and used as a summary.

9.3.3 Identifying and rating areas for improvement and areas for investment

The assessment should evaluate the organization's strengths and weaknesses in their interactions with the opportunities and threats of the past year. It serves as an indicator of the improvement measures that have been implemented in order to achieve the plans for the next business cycle.

As a result of the assessment, the areas for improvement as well as additional investments should be agreed upon between the assessor and the assessed. These areas should be prioritized using a rating system based on a 4-point Likert scale. Some companies use icons and colors to enable a quick focus on the key issues. The team of assessors then gathers to review the findings, to discuss the interactions between the various areas of the organization that have been assessed, and to draw their conclusions.

9.3.4 Inputs for the next planning cycle

The desk and field research by the assessors affords an opportunity to make recommendations on ways and means to further strengthen the organization in the light of the future opportunities and threats that can be anticipated. The group of operative managers that have conducted the assessment prepares a report that is discussed with senior management and that will serve as input in the next planning cycle.

9.4 The policy audit

9.4.1 The business value

As mentioned in Chapter Two, we accept Taylor's principle of separating tasks according to competencies. We recognize the fact that senior and operative management have different but complementary perspectives and roles. Operative management is responsible for the effectiveness and efficiencies of the operations, in other words for *doing the thing right*. Thus, its day-to-day management of the business enablers adds value to the customer and ultimately to the enterprise. Senior management sets the direction and the pace of the enterprise and makes sure that it is *doing the right thing*. It takes overall responsibility for the value of the enterprise and it is accountable to the shareholders and, on their behalf, to the Board of Directors.

The duality and complementarity of these responsibilities suggest that senior management conducts an audit of the value added by the enterprise during the past business cycle, and that operative management carries out an assessment of the effectiveness and efficiencies in the operations.

If the operations have done the thing right and the business policy has directed the organization to do the right thing, then the value of the enterprise should have increased according to the strategic ambitions and the strategic goals established in the Policy Fundamentals. Should this not be the case, than the enterprise is not doing the right thing. Failure to do the right thing must be caught in time or the survival of the enterprise is endangered. Thus, it is essential that the balance of doing the thing right and doing the right thing be periodically examined. Assessing the effectiveness and efficiencies of the operations is clearly insufficient.

Admittedly the difficulty lies in the valuation of the enterprise, and a number of approaches are available. The *book value*, an appraisal of the present value of the tangible assets of the organization, is inadequate at a time when the intangible assets are the key to the future of the enterprise. Current models of *shareholder value* are essentially based on the valuation of assets that can be expressed and extrapolated in financial terms, and therefore are mostly tangible assets. The *market value* of publicly traded companies is the result of speculations on what the stock might be worth in the next hour, in the next day, or in the next month. The volatility of the market value is an indication of the psychological drivers at play that can be only loosely correlated to the projected value of the enterprise. Finally, the *merger and acquisition value* of a company is highly tainted by the powerplay among its various suitors.

All of the above approaches contribute valuable but partial answers to an important issue. We suppose that this led Drucker to call for new measures in order to develop what he called a 'business audit'. This prompted us to revisit the subject and to think in terms of *business value*, in other words what a business is really worth and what should be envisaged to increase its future worth and to ensure a sustainable competitive advantage. We now present the mind-map we developed for our ongoing research.

A classic model shows the difference between the net value of the assets at the beginning and at the end of the business cycle as the value-added. As shown in Figure 9.2, we have translated that model using the strategic resources as the 'business value'.

The strategic resources or 'performers' are the combination of tangible and intangible assets that determine the competitiveness and profitability of the enterprise. The performers are deployed on to the business enablers and show up as value-added at the end of the business cycle. We are now looking at the performers in the frame of the worth of the enterprise, a notion that is complementary to the day-to-day management of the business enablers.

The financial assets (core capabilities) together with the interactions between organizational capital, human capital, and time cycles (critical competencies) generate marketing capital (often a combination of

FIGURE 9.2 The business cycle

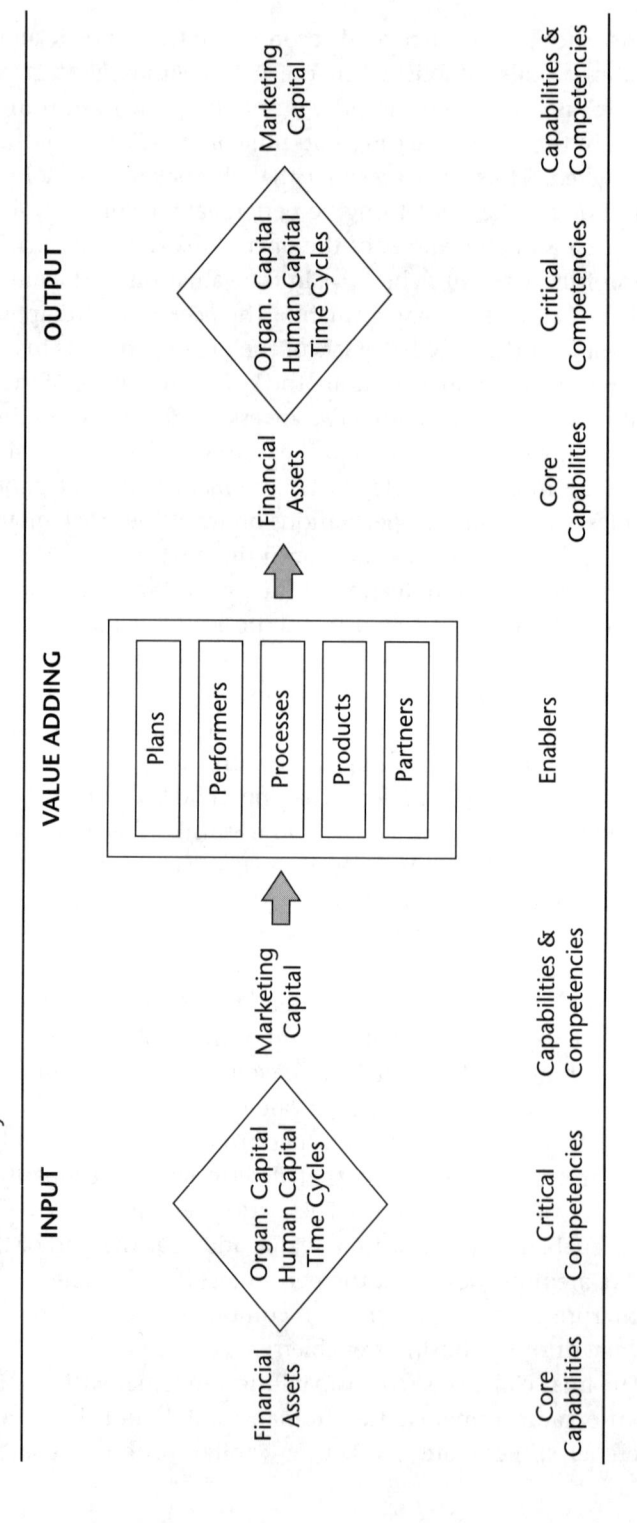

INPUT	VALUE ADDING	OUTPUT
Financial Assets		
Organ. Capital / Human Capital / Time Cycles (diamond)	Plans / Performers / Processes / Products / Partners	Organ. Capital / Human Capital / Time Cycles (diamond)
Marketing Capital	→	Financial Assets →
		Marketing Capital

| Core Capabilities | Critical Competencies | Capabilities & Competencies | Enablers | Core Capabilities | Critical Competencies | Capabilities & Competencies |

competencies and capabilities). The inputted performers add value in different ways. They are (i) recycled for economies of scope, in other words reused in different applications; (ii) leveraged for economies of scale, in other words used on a larger scale; and (iii) developed to a higher level of sophistication through the learning curve.

We are tempted to say that the bottom line of the business value is the marketing capital because this is the basis on which the enterprise will build its future. It will ensure the cash flow indispensable for the business cycle to continue. Of course the situation is more interactive and complex. On one hand the financial and the critical competencies push to generate new marketing capital, on the other hand the generated marketing capital pulls the financial and critical competencies.

9.4.2 The valuation of the performers

Admittedly the valuation of intangible assets is approximate at the best. Several factors can help management in this endeavor.

First, increasingly the organization is managed on a project by project basis. The Policy Dynamics establish clear priorities, strategic objectives, and empowerment for the projects and in particular for the business breakthrough, for the major continuous business improvement, and for the long range projects. Management can select the projects that justify valuating the performers and can establish the desired measurement system. Over a reasonable period of time trends will appear that will allow analysis as well as an evaluation of future potential.

Secondly, the mind-map of the 5 <P> is useful to pinpoint the areas where performers are adding value, to show the spillover effect on other business enablers, and the evolution of the value-added.

Finally, the shared management practices as facilitated by the knowledge-manager and by the tutorial and shared services management enable the spill-over of performers from one business unit to the other to be followed.

We are working on methods that will enable the valuation of intangibles but we will offer here one idea on the direction of our research. We use the following guiding criteria to value the performers:

- The present and potential *value* of each of the five performers. Insufficient value generation of the performers will quickly put the enterprise at a competitive disadvantage.

- The *volume* of the five performers that has been and that probably will be generated. The critical mass is a factor that should be taken into account. If the volume of the performer generated is too low, it will be difficult and costly to step up efforts. Furthermore, there is what the Battelle consultants call the 'sparkle factor', which stimulates emulation and creative one-upmanship.

- The *time cycle* of the generation of the performer. If it takes too long to generate the required performers, major opportunities will be missed.
- The *synergies* between the performers.
- The company *internal* or *external factors* that could affect any of the above mentioned points.

We are preparing a matrix that will show valuation criteria for each of the five performers. Of course additional research will be required to fine-tune the application of this mind-map. As concerns the 'customer capital', the main component of marketing capital, we would refer readers to Chapter Eight.

9.5 The output of the Policy Assessment and Audit

Operative management contributes an assessment of the performance in the operations, its strengths and weaknesses, identification of the areas for improvement, and forecasts concerning opportunities and threats. Senior management provides estimates on the value added to the 'business value' that should shed a different light on the organizational performance.

It is possible that the enterprise is managing the business enablers well but that the added value is falling behind comparable competitors or simply behind expectations. This would mean that, while the Policy Implementation and Review is operating according to plan, the Policy Dynamics and possibly also the Policy Fundamentals are not or are no longer adequate. Senior management with the participation of members of the operative management should then review the Policy Dynamics and the Policy Fundamentals.

Even it the enterprise seems to be doing the right thing right, it is important that with the appropriate periodicity, the Policy Fundamentals and the Policy Dynamics be reviewed because in a world of constant change nothing can remain immobile. By completing the review from the last sub-process to the first sub-process of the POM, management ensures that the enterprise is well positioned to sustain success in a foreseeable future. The Policy Assessment and Audit conclude with inputs for the planning step of the next business cycle.

9.6 Summary

Having gone top-down from the long range directives and guidelines to the day-to-day management, the Process of Management reverses its direction and goes back to check the performances and to seek to improve first the management of the business enablers in the Policy Implementation and Review, then, as called for, the methodology and in particular the Policy Fundamentals and the Policy Dynamics where the business policy is set and strategic objectives are deployed.

For the assessment of doing the right thing in the management of the business enablers, the Policy Fundamentals provide the directives and guidelines to the quarterly review and the policy assessment that are carried out by the operative management. Both apply the same evaluation criteria to the 5 <P>. This mind-map enables operative management to evolve their own checklist and to plan the assessment.

The policy audit conducted by senior management annually or biannually complements the assessment by looking at the big picture and considering the value added by the enterprise during the business cycle. For this purpose, we introduce the concept of the 'business value', which is based on the valuation of the strategic resources or the performers. If the business value has not been increased in accordance with the strategic ambitions and with the strategic goals set in the Policy Fundamentals, the enterprise may be doing the thing right but not doing the right thing. This situation would call for senior and operative management to review the Policy Fundamentals and the Policy Dynamics. This way the loop of the four sub-processes of the POM will have been completed.

■ CHAPTER TEN ■

The conclusions

Best management practices are methods that can increase the efficiency of a particular activity, but, to increase the effectiveness of the whole enterprise *shared management practices* are needed because they help to establish a common basis for mental, behavioral, and action processes.

Shared management practices ensure that all the nodes of the organization are interdependently connected and that they are capable of interacting dynamically within a shifting business environment. As markets and the organizations that serve them have become increasingly complex, it has become increasingly important to provide a compatible way of working that facilitates communications, commitment, cooperation, and collective creativity.

Shared management practices require a comprehensive and integrative framework. The best-in-class have developed their own system of shared management practices, but even some of the most prestigious names struggle with a patchwork of methods and measures of performance.

In order to help management introduce and support the appropriate shared management practices, the author presents the *Process of Management*, an interactive and integrative framework of management, which ensures transparency and understanding from mission statement to measures of performance. The Process of Management, or POM, features four interactive sub-processes:

- The *Policy Fundamentals* set corporate guidelines for direction and behavior.

- The *Policy Dynamics* harmonize the activities of senior and operative management as they evolve separate strategies for *business breakthroughs* and for *continuous business improvement*, and then deploy them through empowered action plans.

THE CONCLUSIONS   223

- The *Policy Implementation and Review* ensures effective day-to-day management of the action plans, the strategic resources, the processes, the products, and with the partners (customers and suppliers). The interdependencies among the five aforementioned business enablers are emphasized and it is these interdependencies which set the basis for cross-functional cooperation;

- The *Policy Assessment and Audit* features operative management's assessment of the effectiveness of day-to-day management, and senior management's valuation of the strategic resources that constitute the *business value* of the enterprise. In addition to tangible assets the strategic resources include intangible assets, such as human and organizational capital, time cycles, and marketing capital.

Connected provides a comprehensive itinerary that managers can follow to introduce shared management practices or they can use it to improve the management system already in place. This map is illustrated in Figure 2.1.

The mind-maps presented, including some original ones, have been designed to anchor shared management practices around the implementation of key concepts. The mind-maps comprise several interactive building blocks. The following briefly summarizes the key mind-maps discussed in this book.

- The 'glob-local' organization (Figure 1.1) features three interactive layers that facilitate the combination of global thinking and local acting. The directives and the guidelines evolved by the Policy Fundamentals provide for purposeful connectivity throughout the enterprise. Then the Policy Dynamics take over and develop and deploy the strategies focusing the enterprise on doing the right thing. Together, these two sub-processes of the POM set the basis for shared management practices.

- The Policy Fundamentals integrate five building blocks (Figure 3.1), namely the mission, the strategic thrust, the strategic goals, leadership, and the resource–allocation–empowerment and the review–evaluation–recognition processes. The interplay among them helps to clarify the strategic profile of the enterprise and thereby ensures consistency of purpose. This mind-map also aids understanding of the strategic profile of competitors, their strategic maneuverability, and can therefore contribute to designing more effective competitive strategies.

- The 'strategic thrust', one of the building blocks of the Policy Fundamentals, is one of the cardinal points of the business strategy. We have shown how it interacts on one side with competencies and capabilities and on the other with the market cycles (Figure 3.2).

- Leadership, another of the building blocks of the Policy Fundamentals, has been the subject of a vast literature. We emphasize the importance of building a comprehensive and cohesive 'leadership network'.

- The Policy Dynamics is a highly participative process that fosters commitment, cooperation, and collective creativity. In order to optimize this sub-process of the POM, the mind-map of the 'Two Rings' (Figure 4.1) helps to harmonize the activities of senior and operative management as they develop and deploy the strategic objectives.

- The day-to-day management of the five business enablers in the frame of the Policy Implementation and Review ensures that the organization is doing the right thing. This mind-map (Figure 2.6) helps to emphasize the interactions between the business enablers or 5 <P> as we call them, which include the plans, performers, processes, products and partners.

- We call the five strategic resources 'performers' because of their critical contribution to the performance of the enterprise. This mind-map, (Figure 5.1), stresses the interactivity between these resources, which include financial assets, time cycles, organizational capital, human capital, and marketing capital. We emphasize the intangible assets among the performers as they pave the way to a promising future.

- We have identified the drivers of organizational behavior (Figure 5.3), and describe the role they play in the frame of organizational capital to support human capital.

- We have presented the hierarchy of processes (Figure 6.1) whose architecture enables senior management to ensure the purposeful connectivity of the management systems.

- The product is defined as a configuration of deliverables. This mind-map helps to clarify the balance of features and benefits as seen from the customers' point of view and enables an analysis of the product economics.

- The customer capital, the main component of marketing capital, one of our performers, consists of intangibles that produce tangible results, namely loyalty, partnering, and referrals. Ways to build up customer capital are discussed and ideas concerning its valuation are presented.

- We have discussed a mind-map (Figure 9.1) that helps to assess the performance of the day-to-day management of the business enablers using the following criteria: check of effectiveness, alert and knowledge, planning for innovation, deployment and efficiencies.

- We have presented schematically the way an enterprise adds value during the business cycle. The added value is at the basis of the concept of 'business value' (Figure 9.2).

A high-impact television advertisement suggested that companies cannot perform unless they perform together. We would add that companies cannot perform together unless they are connected by shared management practices.

The interactive and integrative framework that we call the *Process of Management* presented in this book has been designed to be systemic for effectiveness, stimulating for creativity, and systematic for efficiencies. The author hopes it will assist management to optimize shared management practices and welcomes comments and questions from the readers on sulandwa@iprolink.ch

Bibliography

1. Finger, M. 'Moderniser la gestion publique', *ATAG* February 1998.
2. Senge, P.M. *The Fifth Discipline*, Doubleday 1990.
3. Gleick, J. *Chaos*, Cardinal 1987.
4. Osborne, D. and Gaebler, T. *Reinventing Government* Plume 1993.
5. Drucker, P. *The Age of Discontinuity* Harper & Row 1968.
6. Drucker, P. *Managing in Turbulent Times* Penguin 1980.
7. Wheatley, M.J. *Leadership and the New Science* Berrett-Koehler 1992.
8. Davis, S. and Meyer, C. *Blur* Addison Wesley 1998.
9. Scott-Morgan, P. *The Unwritten Rules of the Game* McGraw-Hill 1994.
10. Maslow, A. *Personality and Motivation* Harper Row 1954.
11. Jantsch, E. *The Self-Organizing Universe* Pergamon Press 1980.
12. Strategic Leadership Forum *Management Tools and Techniques – An Executive Guide* 1996.
13. Sussland, W.A. 'Le manager, la qualité et les normes', ISO, *PPUR* 1996.
14. Bangemann, M. 'The European Way to Excellence', DG III EC 1998.
15. European Commission DG III 'Working Document on a European Quality Promotion Policy' 1995.
16. Imai, M. *Kaizen* Random House 1986.
17. Juran, J. M. *Jurans Quality Control Handbook* McGraw-Hill 1988.
18. Crosby, P.B. *Quality is Free* McGraw-Hill 1979.
19. Oakland, J.S. *Total Quality Management* Butterworth-Heinemann 1993.
20. Shiba, S., Graham A. and Walden, D. 'A New American TQM, *Productivity* 1993.
21. Sussland W.A. 'Communication et confiance', paper presented at Association Romande Qualité 1992.
22. Peters, G. *Price Waterhouse Study for the World Bank* 1995.
23. Wheelen, T.L. and Hunger, D.J. *Strategic Management* Addison Wesley 1996.
24. Soin, Sarv Singh *Total Quality Control Essentials* McGraw-Hill 1992.
25. Sussland, W.A. 'Les 5 <P> de la performance totale', *Schweizerische Gesellschaft fur Personalmanagement* March 1993.
26. Brassard, M. *The Memory Jogger Plus* 1989.
27. Conti, T. 'Organizational Self-Assessment' Chapman Hall 1997.
28. Schwartz, P. *The Art of the Long View* Doubleday Currency 1991.
29. Reichheld, F. *The Loyalty Effect* Harvard Business School Press 1996.
30. Drucker, P. *The Practice of Management* Butterworth-Heinemann 1964.
31. Sun Tzu *The Art of War* Oxford University Press 1963.

32 Moss Kanter, R. *Frontiers of Management* Harvard Business School Press 1997.
33 Harris, T.A. *Im ok You're ok* Avon Press 1973.
34 Stevenson Gumpert 'Vision', *Harvard Business Review* March 1985.
35 Sussland, W.A. La qualité dans les resources humaines *SGP* May 1993.
36 Sussland, W.A. 'The Intrapreneur' conference February 1990.
37 De Bono, E. *Lateral Thinking* Ward Lock Education 1970.
38 De Bono, E. *The Six Thinking Hats* Key Porter Books 1985.
39 De Bono, E. *The Masterthinkers Handbook* Penguin 1985.
40 Ritter, D. and Brassard M. 'The Creative Tools' Goal/QPC 1998.
41 King, R., Domb, E. and Tate, K. *TRIZ An Approach to Systematic Innovation*.
42 Deming, W.E. *Out of Crisis* MIT Press 1986.
43 Deming, W.E. *The New Economics* MIT Press 1993.
44 Kepner, C.H. and Tregoe, B.B. *The New Rational Manager* Princeton Research Press 1981.
45 The Caux Round Table Principles, Switzerland, July 1994.
46 Chandler, A. *Strategy and Structure* MIT Press 1962.
47 Monello, B. and Kunan, D. Harvard Business School study 1991.
48 Tregoe, B. and Zimmerman J. *Top Management Strategy* Simon and Schuster 1980.
49 Galbraith, J.R. and Kazanjian, R.K. *Strategy Implementation* West Publishing 1986.
50 Robert, M. *Strategy Pure and Simple* McGraw-Hill 1993.
51 Lele, M.M. *Creating Strategic Leverage* John Wiley & Sons 1992.
52 Porter, M.E. *Competitive Strategies* The Free Press 1980.
53 Hamel, G. and Prahalad, C.K. *Competing for the Future* Harvard Business School Press 1994.
54 Campbell, A. and Sommers-Luchs, K. *Core Competencies Based Strategy* International Thomson Press 1997.
55 Orion International *Envisioning* Orion International 1988.
56 Strategic Planning Institute Boston *Profit Impact from Marketing Strategies*.
57 Akao, Y. *Hoshin Kanri* Japanese Standards Association 1988.
58 Akao, Y. *Hoshin Kanri, Policy Deployment for Successful TQM* Productivity Press 1991.
59 Brunetti, W.H. *Achieving Total Quality* Quality Resources 1993.
60 Johnston, C.G. and Daniel, M.J. *Setting the Direction: Management by Planning* Conference Board of Canada 1993.
61 Merli, G. *Managing by Priority* John Wiley & Son 1996.
62 Sussland, W.A. 'Enquête sur la qualité', *Bulletin de l'Association Romande Qualité* 1992.
63 Camp, R.C. *Business Process Benchmarking* ASQC Press 1995.
64 Combs, R.E. and Moorhead J.D *The Competitive Intelligence Handbook* The Scarecrow Press 1992.
65 de Geus, A. *The Living Company* Harvard Business School Press 1997.
66 Drucker, P. *Innovation and Entrepreneurship* Harper Business 1985.
67 Emery, M. and Purser, R.E. *The Search Conference* Jossey Bass 1996.
68 De Gaulle, C. *Le fil de lépée* Berger Levrault 1944.
69 Ostrenga, M.R. *The E&Y Guide to Total Cost Management* John Wiley & Sons 1992.
70 Wiersema, W.H. *Activity Based Management* Amacom 1995.
71 Griego, P.L. and Pilachowski, M. *Activity Based Costing* PT 1995.
72 Stewart, G.B. *The Quest for Value* Harper Collins 1991.
73 Thomas, P.R. *Getting Competitive* McGraw-Hill 1991.
74 Thomas, P.R. *Competitiveness Through Total Cycle Time* McGraw-Hill 1990.

75 Servan Screiber J.- L. 'L'art du temps' Fayard 1983'.
76 Stewart, T.A. *Intellectual Capital* Nicholas Brealey 1997.
77 Edvinsson, L. *Intellectual Capital* Harper Business 1997.
78 Belbin, Dr M. *Management Teams* Heinemann 1990.
79 Margerison, C. and McCann, R. *Team Management* Mercury 1990.
80 Winslow, W. *Strategic Business Transformation* McGraw-Hill 1996.
81 Sussland, W.A. 'Transforming the Organization' postgraduate seminar EPFL/ESST May 1996.
82 AT&T *Quality Managers Handbook* AT&T 1990.
83 Kume, H. *Business Management and Quality Cost: The Japanese Way* Quality.
84 Hammer, M. and Champy, J. *Reenigneering the Corporation* Harper 1993.
85 Kotler, P. *Marketing Management* Prentice-Hall 1984.
86 Levitt, T. *The Marketing Mode* McGraw-Hill 1969.
87 Lovelock, C.H. *Service Marketing* Prentice-Hall 1991.
88 Zeithaml, V., Parasuraman, A. and Berry, L. *Delivering Quality Service* Free Press 1990.
89 Albrecht, K. and Bradford, L. *The Service Advantage* R. Irwin 1990.
90 Dichter, E. *La strategia del desiderio* Garzanti 1963.
91 Gilder, G. *Wealth and Poverty* Basic Books 1981.
92 Robert, M. *Product Innovation Strategy Pure and Simple* McGraw-Hill 1995.
93 Juran, J.M. *Juran on Quality by Design* The Juran Institute 1992.
94 Akao, Y. *QFD* Productivity Press 1990.
95 Eureka, W.E. and Ryan, N.E. *The Customer Driven Company* American Suppliers Institute Press 1988.
96 Marsh, S., Moran, J.W., Nakui, S. and Hoffherr, G. *Quality Functional Deployment* Goal/QPC 1991.
97 Juran, J.M. *Juran on Planning for Quality* The Free Press 1988.
98 Hughes, J. Ralf, M. and Michels, W. 'Transform your Supply Chain' International Thomson Press 1998.
99 Gore, F.A. *Creating a Government that Works Better and Costs Less* Plume 1993.
100 Gale, B.T. *Managing Customer Value* The Free Press 1994.
101 Peppers, D. and Rogers, M. *Enterprise One-To-One* Piatkus 1997.
102 AT&T Quality Steering Committee *Achieving Customer Satisfaction* AT&T 1990.
103 Burchill, G. and Hepner Brodie, C. *Voices into Choices* Joiner 1997.
104 Coase, R.H. 'La nature de la firme', *Revue Economique* 1987.
105 Kaplan, R. and Norton, D. *The Balanced Scorecard* Harvard Business School Press 1996.
106 Hronec, S.M. *Vital Signs* Amacom 1993.
107 Drucker, P. quoted by Cambridge Strategy Publications Ltd..

Index

action plans 103
Akao, Y. 176
Albrecht, K. and Bradford, L. 163
alert 88, 212
   drivers of change 88-9
   macrotrends 89–91
   megatrends 89, 90–1
   passive change 88
   proactive change 88

Bangemann, Martin 18
Belbin, M. 120
Berne, Eric 38
Blanchard, K. 40
Brassard, M. 42
business breakthrough (BBT) 93–4, 104
business maintenance (BM) 93
business value 216–19, 225
   book 217
   market 217
   mergers/acquisitions 217
   shareholder 217

Campbell, A. and Sommers-Luchs, K. 67
catchball procedure 103, 107
Caux Round Table principles 61
Chandler, A. 62
change *see* drivers of change
chaos theory 4–5
checks 85–6, 212
   inputs/outputs 87
   medium-term 86–7
   quantitative/qualitative 86
   short-term 86

Conti, Tito 48
continuous business improvement (CBI) 93, 94, 104
core capabilities 67–8
critical competencies 67
Crosby, P.B. 146
customer 180
   attributes 183–5
   decision making 181–2
   one-on-one dealing 199–200
   partnering 180–1
customer capital 192–3, 225
   customer relation strategies 196
   indicators 195
   loyalty 193–4
   partnering 194
   referrals 194
   suppliers 195–6
customer recognized value (CRV) 183, 185–7
customer relations
   managing 197–206
   strategies 196
customer satisfaction index (CSI) 188
   defining what is to be measured 188–9
   how to measure 189–2
customer value delivery (CVD) 135, 137, 138–40
customization/migration strategies
   client database 205–6
   flexibility 204–5
   interactivity 203–4

De Bono, E. 127
decision-making unit (DMU) 182
Delphi technique 70–1
Deming, W.E. 79, 80, 166
Deming Wheel 42–3
drivers of change 88–91, 224
Drucker, Peter 3, 35, 80, 126, 127, 172

economy of proximity, vs global economy 1–4
Edison, Thomas 175
Edvinsson, L. 130
European Quality Award (EQA) 44, 48, 81, 185

feedback loops 105–6
financial assets 113–14
Finger, Matthias 2
flowcharts
  ANSI 146
  block 146
  time cycle 146, 147

Galbraith, J.K. 116
Galbraith, J.R. and Kazanjian, R.K. 64
Gale, B.T. 186, 192
Galvin, Bob 88
Gleick, J. 2
glob-local organization 8–9, 222
  corporate management 9–10
  self-managed units 11–12
  tutorial/shared services management 10–11
global economy, vs economy of proximity 1–4
global environment, managing in 4–8
global/local harmonization 36–7
Goldratt, Eli 130
Gore, F.A. 181
Gumpert, Stevenson 39

Hamel, G. and Prahalad, C.K. 67
Hammer, M. and Champy, J. 152
Henkoff, R. 154
Hofstede, G. 40
hoshin planning 80–1
human capital 116–18
  communities of practice 121–3
  creativity 126–7

flow 125–6
individuals/teams 118–21
management 123–5
process 123–7

Imai, M. 150
intellectual capital 115–16
internal/external environment 7, 114–15

Juran, J.M. 146, 175

kaizen 19–20, 150–1
Kano, N. 187
Kanter, R.M. 38
Kennedy, John F. 68
Kepner, C.H. and Tregoe, B.B. 59, 142, 155, 184
King, Martin Luther 68
Kotler, P. 161
Kotter, J. 40
Kume, H. 147

Lao Tzu 15
leadership network 73–5, 76, 224
Lele, M.M. 66, 75
Levitt, T. 163
Lovelock, C.H. 163

macro-processes 135–7
  customer value delivery 135
  resource allocation and empowerment 135
  review-evaluation-reward 135
  social 135
  strategic 135
  support 135
Malcolm Baldrige National Quality Award 18, 45, 81, 185
management approach
  simple/swift 51
  stimulating 51
  systematic 51
  systemic 49–50
management by objectives (MBO) 78
  criticism of 79–80
  financial year-end results 79
  individual performances 78–9
  results 79

management by policy (MBP) 80
  business breakthrough 80–1
  continuous business improvement 80–1
  SWOT 80
management of human capital
  architecture 124–5
  empowerment 124
  indicators/targets 125
  objectives 123
  performance asessment 125
management methodology 13–15
  introduction of 21–4
  loose terminology/quality jargon 17
  narrow scope of tools/techniques 16–17
  turnover of tools/techniques 15–16
management of process 140–2
  architecture 143
  empowerment 143
  indicators/targets 143–4
  objectives 142–3
  performance measurement 144–5
Margerison, C. and McCann, R. 120
market fragmentation 161–2, 199–200
market recognized value (MRV) 186, 187
market segmentation 161–2, 199
marketing capital 131–2
  brand 131
  customer 131
Maucher, Helmut 2
micro-processes 137
migration strategies *see* customization/migration strategies
mission statement 59–60, 153–4
  corporate values/code of conduct 60–1
  strategic biases 61–2
Morito, Akio 166

new product introduction (NPI) 168–2
  assessment 173–4

one-on-one strategies 199–200
  assessing competitive situation/responses 202
  customization/migration 203–6
  estimate CRV resulting from differentiation 201–2
  estimation of potential customer capital 202
  identifying customers' differentiated needs 200–1
  plan/deploy appropriate customer-relations 202–3
organizational capital (OC) 127–8
  competencies 130
  motivation 130
  strategies 129
  structures 129, 130–1
  style 129, 130
  synergies 129
  systems 129
  vision 130
outer ring
  alert 88–92, 212
  check 85–7, 212
  deployment 96–100, 213
  planning 92–6, 212–13

Peppers, D. and Rogers, M. 192, 194, 200, 204
performance indicators 94–5
performance measurement 144–5
  STEPS 144
performers 112–13, 224
  financial assets 113–14
  human capital 116–27
  intellectual capital 115–16
  marketing capital 131–2
  organizational capital 127–31
  time cycles/timing 114–15
  valuation 219–20
plan-do-check-act (P-D-C-A) model 37, 42–3, 81, 84, 176
planning 92–6, 212–13, 216
policy assessment 47–9, 82, 208–9
  criteria 212–13
  establishing cheklist 215
  identifying/rating areas for improvement/investment 215–16
  inputs for next planning cycle 216
  output 220–1
  principles 210–11
  process 213–16
  updating knowledge base 214–15

policy audit 47–9, 82
  business value 216–19
  output 220–1
  valuation of performers 219–20
policy deployment
  actionable alternatives 100–1
  bottom-up negotiations 103
  continuous business improvement 104
  go-ahead 104
  middle management 100–2
  RAE and RER 103–4
  selection of strategies 101–2
  senior to middle management 100
  supervisory management 103
  visual based management 104
policy dynamics 37–8, 77–8, 81–3, 224
  building commitment 38–40
  cooperation 40
  creativity 40–1
  implementing 106–9
  inner ring 104–6, 109
  management by objectives 78–80
  management by policy 80–1
  outer ring 85–104, 109
  two rings 83–5
policy fundamentals 30–1, 55
  aligning strategy/operations 34–6
  building blocks 57–8
  doing the right thing 55–7
  harmonizing global vs local considerations 36–7
  leadership network 73–5
  mission 59–62
  optimizing stakeholder satisfaction 31–4
  resource allocation and empowerment process 72–3
  review, evaluation and recognition process 72–3
  strategic ambitions 68–72
  strategic profile 75–6
  strategic thrust 62–8
policy implementation/review 41–2
  action plans 47
  Deming Wheel/P-D-C-A Model 42–3
  enablers 44–7

problem-analysis
  brainstorming 155
  stair-stepping 155
  TOPS 155–6
process efficiencies/effectiveness
  checking 148–9
  costs 146–8
process flow 145–6
Process of Management (POM) 24, 25, 27, 222–3
  business enablers 52
  policy assessment/audit 29, 47–9, 223
  policy dynamics 29, 37–41, 222
  policy fundamentals 29, 30–7, 222
  policy implementation/review 29, 41–7, 223
  principles 49–51
  as a road map 27–30
process performance improvement 149
  architecture innovation 152–3
  continuous improvement 150–1
  correction of sporadic dysfunctions 149–50
  correction of systematic dysfunctions 150
  simplification 151
process simplification 151
  bureaucracy 151
  improvement of time cycles 151
  optimization of use of resources 151
  partnership 151
  rationalizaion 151
processes 133–4
  customer value delivery 138–40
  hierarchy 134–8
  performance improvement 149–53
  project by project improvement 153–7
  structure and management 140–9
product 158–9, 224
  designing/supporting activities 175–7
  developing 177–8
  economics 163–4
  features/benefits 161–3, 162
  improvements 170
  innovation 170
  introduction of new 168–9

INDEX

product deliverables
  augmented 160
  auxiliary 160
  intangible 160–1
  personal attention 160
  primary 159–60
product strategies 164–5
  customer needs 165–6
  defining 167–74
  deploying 178
  market opportunities 166–7
project by project improvement 153
  definition of project/mission 153–4
  deployment of approved improvements 156–7
  diagnosis of opportunities 153–6
  diagnosis of problems 153–6
  diffusion of learning 157
  discovering best solution 156

Quality Functional Deployment (QFD) 176–7
quality management 17–18
  ISO 9000 registration 18–19
  kaizen and 9000 Pro 19–20
  TQM 20–1
quarterly review 209–10

Reimann, Bernard 18
resource allocation and empowerment (RAE) process 72–3, 76, 103, 135
review, evaluation and recognition (RER) process 72–3, 76, 103, 135
Robert, M. 75, 171, 174, 175
Rummler, and Brache 90

Say, Jean Baptiste 166
scenario management 90
Scott-Morgan, Peter 10, 72, 73
self-managed units
  responsibilities without control 13
  SBU 11–12
  systemic thinking 12
  trust 12–13
Senge, Peter 7, 22
shared management practice 10–11, 222
Shewhart, Walter 42
Shiba, S. 42

Soin, Sarv Singh 20, 47, 106
stakeholders
  glob-local 7
  optimizing satisfaction 31–4
Stern, Stefan 15
strategic ambitions 68–71
  goals and the road map 71–2
strategic business units (SBUs)
  in glob-local organization 8
  self-managed 11–12, 25
strategic decision-making unit (DMU) 61–2, 70
strategic thrust 62–4
  critical competencies/core capabilities 67–8
  implications of 64–6
  value-chain 66–7
strategy
  alignment with operations 34–6
  cross-functional deployment 102
  selection 101–2
SWOT (strengths-weaknesses-opportunities-threats) model 69

Taylor, Frederick 22, 84
teamwork 41
time cycles/timing 114
  external environment 114
  individuals/teams 115
  internal environment 114–15
Total Quality Management (TQM) 20–1, 23–4, 41, 80, 81
Tregoe, B.B. and Zimmerman, J. 63, 64, 75
trend testing 89–91
two rings 83–5
  inner ring 1046
  outer ring 85–104

value-chain 66–7
vision 39–40, 130

Wheatley, Margaret J. 5, 12
Wheelen, T.L. and Hunger, D.J. 22, 70, 83, 167
Whitehead, Alfred North 30

Zeithaml, V. *et al* 163